EUROPEAN HANDB

BENEL
RAILWAYS
LOCOMOTIVES & COACHING STOCK

FOURTH EDITION

The complete guide to all Locomotives and Coaching Stock of the Railways of Belgium, the Netherlands and Luxembourg

Brian Garvin, David Haydock and Peter Fox

PLATFORM 5

Published by Platform 5 Publishing Ltd., Wyvern House, Sark Road, Sheffield, S2 4HG, England.
Printed in England by Hubbard Print, Dronfield, Sheffield, S18 2XQ.
ISBN 1 902336 08 9

Former Belgian Class 62 diesel loco, now ACTS Class 67 No. 6703, is seen near Rotterdam on 10/07/1999 hauling the Leeuwarden to Maasvlakte container service between Kijfhoek yard and Maasvlakte. At the rear of the train is loco 6702. **Quintus Vosman**

CONTENTS

INTRODUCTION

This book contains full details of all locomotives, multiple units and coaching stock of the railways of the 'Benelux' countries, i.e. Belgium, the Netherlands and Luxembourg. Information is updated to May 2000.

The word 'Benelux' is cobbled together from the first two or three letters of the three countries concerned, Belgium, the Netherlands and Luxembourg. These three countries had a free trade area with no customs inspection at borders before the European Community was formed.

In the Netherlands the language spoken is, of course, Dutch or *Nederlands* to give it is proper name. In Belgium two main languages are spoken. The north of the country, Flanders (*Vlaanderen*) is Dutch speaking with the population referred to in English as Flemings whilst the south, Wallonia (*Wallonie*) is French speaking with the population referred to in English as Walloons. The Flemish people refer to their language as *Vlaams* (Flemish), but it is actually the same as Dutch. Indeed, the *Nederlandse Taal Unie* (Dutch language union) is actually based in Belgium. Brussels is an exception being the only official dual-language area. Brussels, the capital of Belgium is officially a dual-language city and is named Brussel in Dutch and Bruxelles in French. In addition there is a part of Belgium around Eupen where the population's first language is German. In Luxembourg two languages are in common use. These are French and a low dialect of German known as *Letzeburgisch*. Standard German is also spoken.

English is understood by a large proportion of the population of the Netherlands and a lesser proportion of Dutch-speaking Belgians. It is difficult to know what language to speak in Luxembourg. One of the authors once went to Macdonald's there and found the menu behind the counter in a mixture of English and German with an assistant who only spoke French!

Common terms used in French and Dutch are detailed in Appendix 4 on page 175.

LAYOUT OF INFORMATION

For each class of vehicle general data and dimensions in metric units are provided. Vehicle lengths are lengths over couplers. The following standard abbreviations are used:

km/h	kilometres per hour	m	metres
kN	kilonewtons	mm	millimetres
kW	kilowatts	TE	tractive effort

Builder codes see Appendix 1 on page 172. For explanation of codes used for accommodation in hauled coaching stock and multiple units see Appendix 2. on page 173.

For each vehicle the number is given in the first column. Where a vehicle has been renumbered the former number is generally shown in parentheses after the current number. Further columns show, respectively, the livery (in bold condensed type), any detail differences, the owning company in serif type (Dutch locos only), the depot allocation and name where appropriate. Depot and livery codes are shown seperately for each railway in the appropriate section.

For an explanation of the UIC hauled stock numbering system see Appendix 3 on pages 173 and 174.

ABBREVIATIONS

Standard abbreviations used in this book are:

CFL	Chemins de Fer Luxembourgois (Luxembourg Railways)
CS	Centraal Station (Central Station)
DB	Deutsche Bundesbahn (former German Federal Railway) or Deutsche Bahn AG (German Railway)
DR	Deutsche Reichsbahn (former East German State Railway)
EU	Eurostar (UK) Ltd.
NS	Nederlandse Spoorwegen (Netherlands Railways)
NMBS	Nationale Maatschappij der Belgische Spoorwegen (Belgian Railways – *Dutch language*)
PKP	Polskie Koleje Panstwowe (Polish State Railways)
SBB	Schweizerische Bundesbahnen (Swiss Federal Railways)
SJ	Statens Järnvägar (Swedish State Railways)
SNCB	Société Nationale des Chemins de Fer Belges (Belgian Railways – *French language*)
SNCF	Société Nationale des Chemins de Fer Français (French Railways)

GETTING THERE FROM GREAT BRITAIN

By Rail

Around 11 Eurostar services run daily from London Waterloo to Brussels Midi taking around 2³/₄ hours. There are onward connections to Amsterdam either by Thalys or by the hourly "Benelux push-pull" service. These services also call at Antwerpen, Roosendaal, Dordrecht, Rotterdam CS, Den Haag HS and Schiphol.

By Sea

Stena Line offer a Harwich–Hoek van Holland HSS fast ferry service which takes around 3³/₄ hours but is timed rather awkwardly for UK passengers. North Sea Ferries operate Hull–Zeebrugge/ Rotterdam (12½/14½ hrs). DFDS Seaways run daily from Newcastle International Ferry Terminal at North Shields to IJmuiden taking 15–16 hrs. The fastest sea crossing is by Hoverspeed "Seacat" catarmaran from Dover to Oostende (2 hrs).

By Air

There are flights from all London airports and many regional airports direct to Amsterdam and Brussels. Amsterdam airport (Schiphol) and Brussels airport are both rail-connected, as are the London airports of Gatwick, Heathrow, Luton and Stansted and the British regional airports at Birmingham and Manchester. Newcastle Airport is served by the Tyne & Wear Metro. Flights also operate from the UK to Rotterdam and Eindhoven.

ROVER TICKETS

Railway enthusiasts will find railrover tickets very useful. At the time of writing the following were available:

The Benelux Tourrail Card offers unlimited travel in Belgium (SNCB/NMBS), Luxembourg (CFL) and the Netherlands (NS). Prices: 5 days in a month – under 26 year olds BEF 3100 (£58, over 26s BEF 4400 (£82) 2nd, BEF 6600 (£122) 1st. Obtainable from major Belgian and Luxembourg stations (not Netherlands) and from Holland Rail in the UK.

Belgium

The 'B Tourrail' is valid for any 5 days in a month. Price – BEF 2200 2nd, BEF 3390 1st. The Eurodomino 3 day ticket is £35 (2nd) £53 (1st) and £26 (under-26 2nd), Extra days cost £4/£6/£3 respectively.

Luxembourg

A day ticket is available (valid until 08.00 next day). It allows unlimited travel on all public transport (CFL plus AVL/TICE/RGTR buses) in the Grand Duchy. Can be used in First Class accommodation. The user must validate the ticket at a machine before use. The price is LUF 160. A carnet of 5 tickets is available for the price of 4. The Eurodomino 3 day ticket is £12 (2nd) £17 (1st) and £9 (under 26 2nd), Extra days cost £2/£2/£1 respectively.

The Netherlands

The Eurodomino 3 day ticket is £32 (2nd) £48 (1st) and £24 (under-26 2nd), Extra days cost £10/ £15/£8 respectively. The Holland Rail pass can be obtained in Britain from Holland Rail or Trains Europe for three or five days travel within a month. A second person travels at half price. Prices (1st/2nd): 3 days – £55/36 (adult), £44/29 (senior/under-26); 5 days – £82/55 (adult), £66/44 (senior/under-26). Children are half-price. The 'Zomertoer' pass (valid from 1st July– 4th September) gives unlimited second class rail travel for 3 days out of 10 for 1 person – NLG 98 or 2 persons – NLG 129. Supplements are payable on EC trains. The 'Zomertoer Plus' pass also includes all trams, buses and metros. 1 person – NLG 118 or 2 people – NLG 157. Also there is a 'Dagkaart' (Day Ticket) for NLG 75.50 (2nd) or NLG 117 (1st), and for an additional NLG 8.50 bus, tram and metro is added.

For details of all European Rover tickets, see the annual feature in 'Today's Railways'.

ACKNOWLEDGEMENTS

We would like to thank all who have helped with the writing of this book, especially Messrs. Marcel Barthel, Tery Lea (STARS), Michel Van Ussel, Quintus Vosman and G. Verhoeven (Département de Matériel SNCB/NMBS) also the Groupement Belge pour le Promotion et l'Exploitation Touristique du Transport Ferroviare (GTF), Liège and Philippe de Gieter of Patrimoine Ferroviare Touristique (PFT).

KEY TO MAPS:

Electrification of Lines:

———	Non-electrified
———	Electrified 3000 V d.c. overhead
———	Electrified 1500 V d.c. overhead
———	Electrified 25 kV a.c. 50 Hz overhead
———	Electrified 15 kV a.c. 16²/₃ Hz overhead
———	High Speed 25 kV a.c. 50 Hz overhead

Types of Lines:

———	Passenger or Passenger and Freight
- - - - -	Freight Only
··········	Planned or Under Construction
———	Tramway or Metro
·—·—·—	Country Borders

Other Symbols:

Tilburg	Hoogovens	*Kijfhoek*	AZ
Station	Freight Terminal	Marshalling Yard	Depot or Works

NORTH SEA

Harlingen

Sneek

Stavoren

Den Helder

Medemblik

SHM

Enkhuizen

Heerhugowaard

Alkmaar

Hoorn

Lelystad

Uitgeest

Hoogovens
Ijmuiden

Zaandam

Haarlem

Amsterdam

Zandvoort aan Zee

Haarlem Works

Schiphol

Hilversum

Baarn

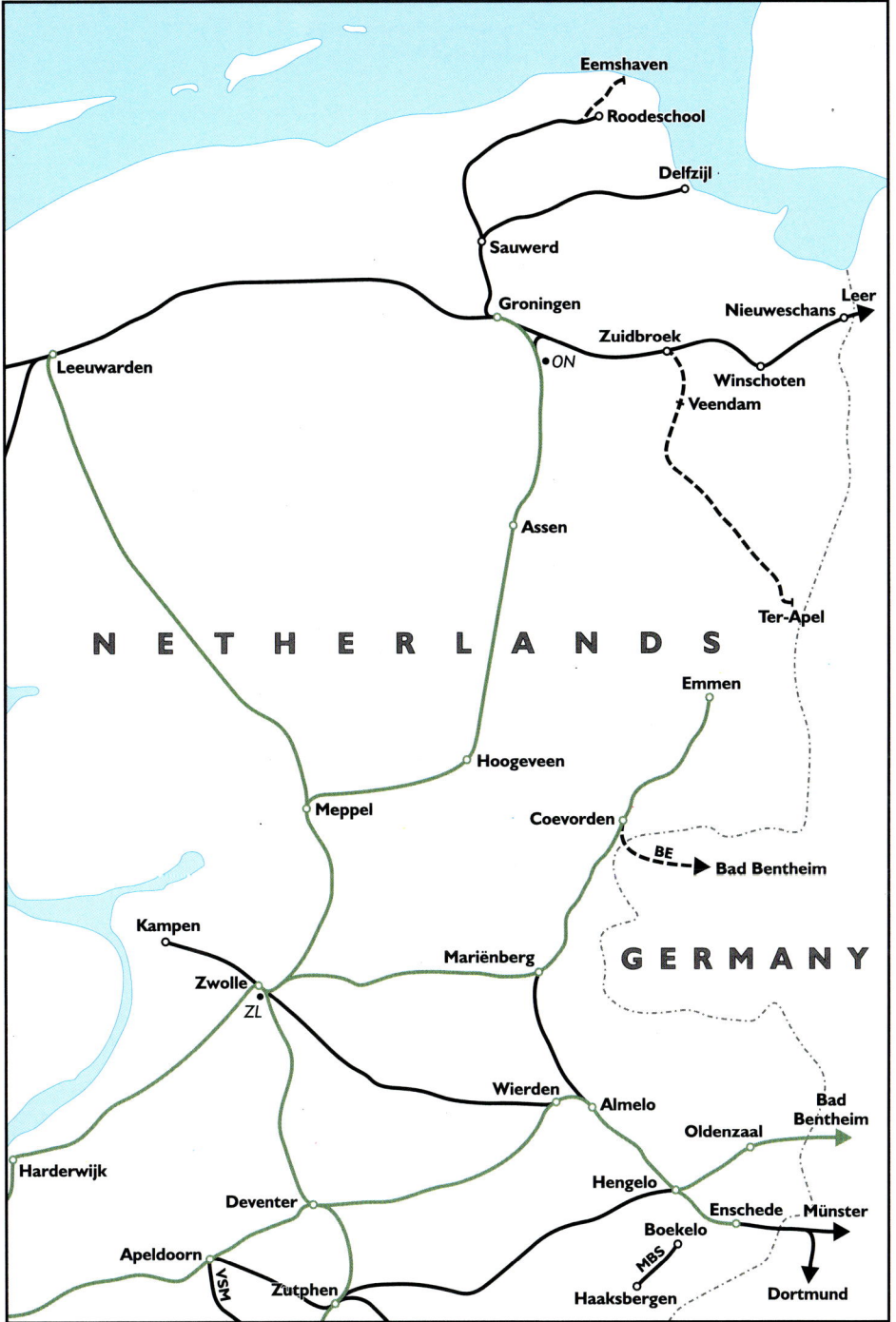

Eemshaven
Roodeschool
Delfzijl
Sauwerd
Groningen
ON
Zuidbroek
Nieuweschans
Leer
Winschoten
Veendam
Leeuwarden
Assen
Ter-Apel
N E T H E R L A N D S
Emmen
Hoogeveen
Meppel
Coevorden
BE
Bad Bentheim
Kampen
Mariënberg
G E R M A N Y
Zwolle
ZL
Harderwijk
Wierden
Almelo
Bad Bentheim
Oldenzaal
Deventer
Hengelo
Enschede
Münster
Apeldoorn
Boekelo
VSM
MBS
Zutphen
Haaksbergen
Dortmund

AMSTERDAM

Metro/Sneltram lines are shown in grey

Koog Bloemwijk
Zaandam-Kogerveld
Zaandam
Westhaven
• AZ
Sloterdijk
Isolatorweg
Amsterdam Centraal
Lelylaan
Muiderpoort
• WG
RAI
Amstel
Diemen
Zuid WTC
2
Schiphol
1
Bijlmer
Gaasperplas
Weesp
Poortwachter
Gein

1 Duivendrecht
2 Diemen Zuid

NORTH SEA

IJMEER

Middelburg
Goes
Vlissingen
SGB
Oudelande

NETHERLANDS

Terneuzen

Zeebrugge
Knokke
Blankenberge

Tramway

Oostende
• FSD
Maldegem
SCM
Moerbeke
De Lijn
Brugge
Eeklo
Lokeren

De Panne
BELGIUM
Gent Zeehaven
Dunkerque
Gent
• FKR
Lichterfelde
Deinze
De-Pinte
Burst
Ieper
Zottegem
Poperinge
Kortrijk
Oudenaarde

Leiden

Alphen aan
den Rijn

Amersfoort

Den Haag

LD

Woerden

Utrecht

Delft

Gouda

Veenendaal

Rhenen

Hoek Van
Holland

Rotterdam

FO

Maasvlakte

Freight Route
Under Construction

Geldermalsen

Tiel

Kijfhoek

Gorinchem

Under Electrification
25 kV a.c. 50 Hz

Dordrecht

Oss

N E T H E R L A N D S

's-Hertogenbosch

Lage Zwaluwe

Breda

Boxtel

TB

Tilburg

Roosendaal

Eindhoven

Essen

Opening 2005

Turnhout

Projected

Neerpelt

Antwerpen Nord

Mol

FNDM

Herentals

Antwerpen
Centraal

Sint
Niklaas

Lier

B E L G I U M

Puurs

Waterschei

SDP

Diest

Genk

Dendermonde

FM

Mechelen

Aarschot

FHS

Hasselt

Aalst

Brussels
National
Aeroport

Denderleeuw

Leuven

Brussels

VSM

Ede-Wageningen

Dieren

NETHERLANDS

Arnhem

Doetinchem

Winterswijk

Zevenaar

Nijmegen

Emmerich

Oberhausen

oou

Kleve

Krefeld

GERMANY

Helmond

Venlo

Kaldenkirchen

Mönchengladbach

Weert

Roermond

oou

Dalheim

Mönchengladbach

BELGIUM

As   LSV

Eisden

Sittard

Mönchengladbach

Schijn op
Geul

Herzogenrath

MT

Maastricht

ZLSM   ZLSM

Kerkrade

Simpelveld

Köln

Aachen

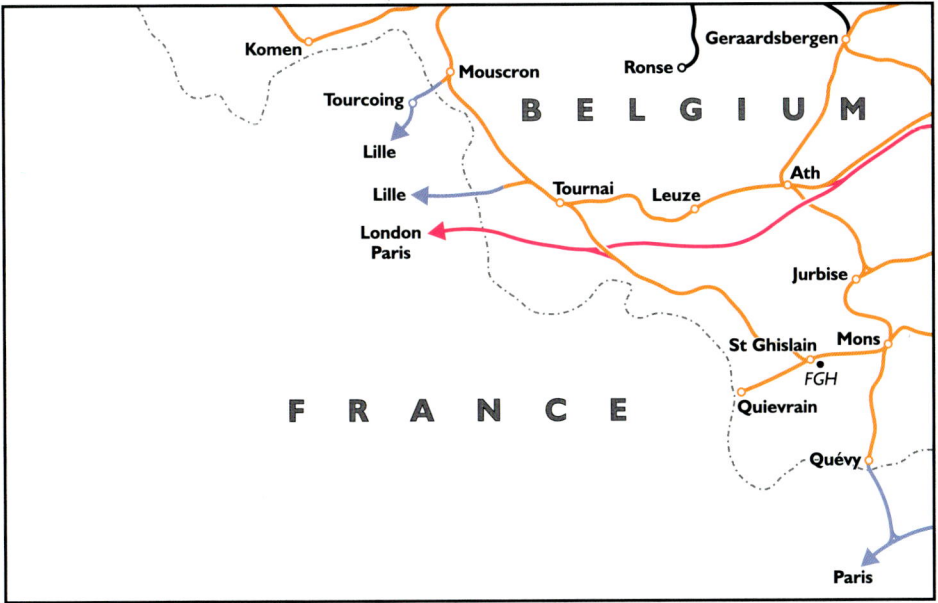

Komen
Mouscron
Ronse
Geraardsbergen
Tourcoing
Lille
B E L G I U M
Lille
Tournai
Leuze
Ath
London
Paris
Jurbise
St Ghislain
Mons
FGH
F R A N C E
Quievrain
Quévy
Paris

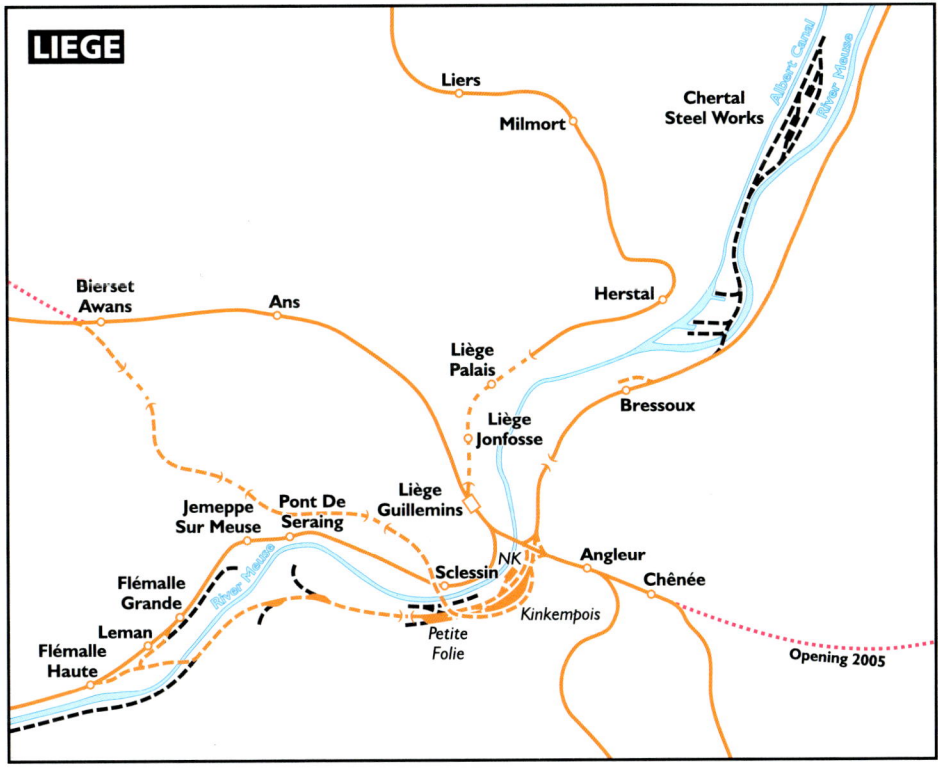

LIEGE

Liers
Milmort
Chertal
Steel Works
Albert Canal
River Meuse

Bierset
Awans
Ans
Herstal

Liège
Palais
Bressoux

Liège
Jonfosse

Liège
Guillemins

Jemeppe
Sur Meuse
Pont De
Seraing
NK
Angleur
Chênée

Flémalle
Grande
River Meuse
Sclessin

Leman
Kinkempois
Opening 2005

Flémalle
Haute
Petite
Folie

Enghien

Halle

Braine-le-Comte

Manage

Luttre

La Louvière Sud

Binche

Ottignies

Louvain-la-Neuve

Gembloux

Landen

Opening 2003

Huy

Namur

Ronet

FAZ

Tamines

Monceau LNC

GCR

Châtelet

Charleroi Sud

B E L G I U M

Ciney

Jeumont

Walcourt

Dinant

CFV3V

Marloie

Jemelle

Beauraing

Mariembourg

CFV3V

Treignes

Givet

Couvin

CFV3V

Valenciennes

Chimay

Charleville-Mézières

Anor

Libramont

Charleville-Mézièrs

Bertrix

F R A N C E

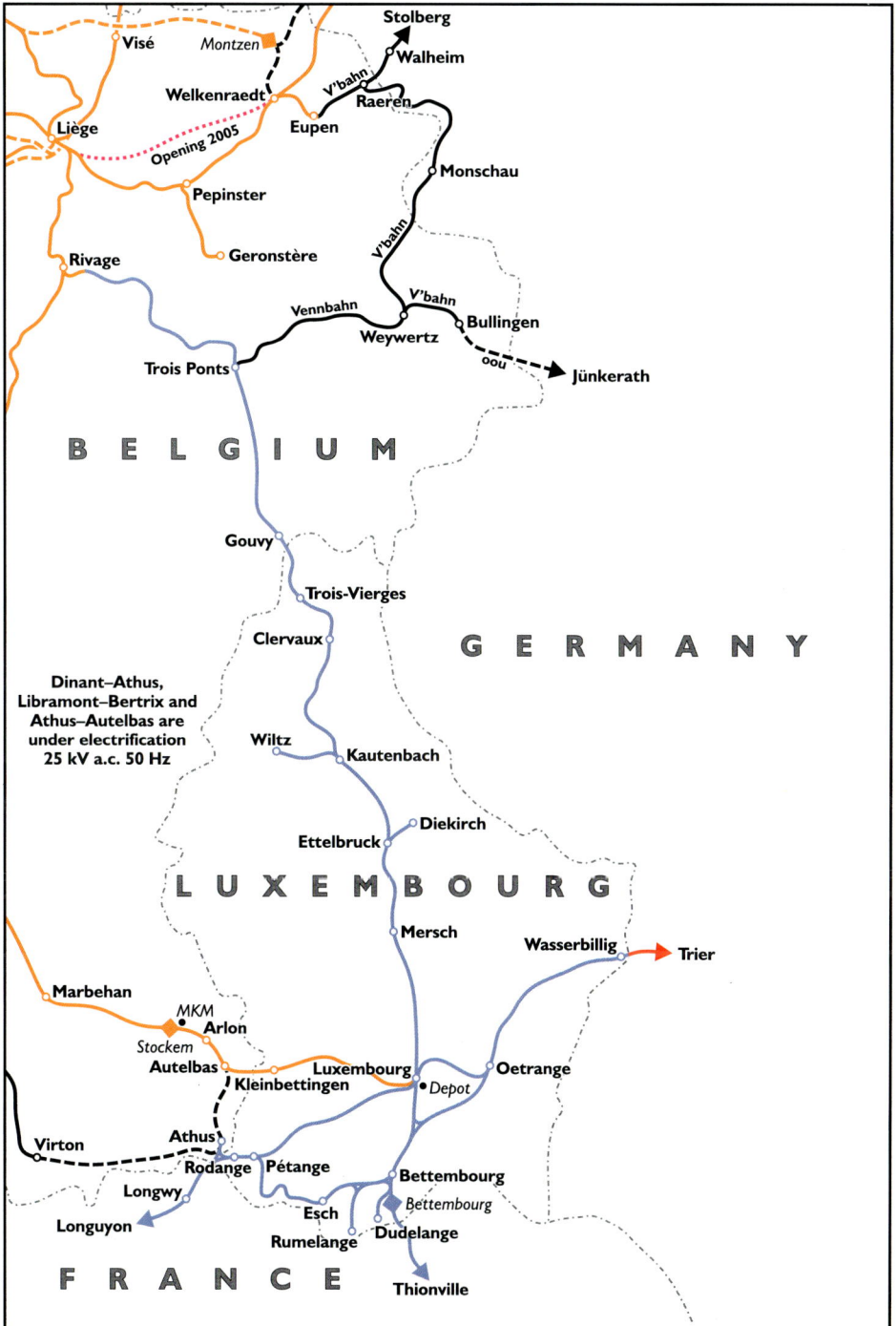

Stolberg

Visé
Montzen
Walheim
Welkenraedt
V'bahn
Raeren
Liège
Eupen
Opening 2005
Monschau
Pepinster
Rivage
Geronstère
V'bahn
Vennbahn
V'bahn
Bullingen
Weywertz
Trois Ponts
oou
Jünkerath

B E L G I U M

Gouvy

Trois-Vierges

Clervaux

G E R M A N Y

Dinant–Athus,
Libramont–Bertrix and
Athus–Autelbas are
under electrification
25 kV a.c. 50 Hz

Wiltz
Kautenbach

Diekirch

Ettelbruck

L U X E M B O U R G

Mersch

Wasserbillig
Trier

Marbehan
MKM
Arlon
Stockem
Autelbas
Luxembourg
Oetrange
Kleinbettingen
Depot

Virton
Athus
Rodange
Pétange
Bettembourg
Longwy
Bettembourg
Longuyon
Esch
Rumelange
Dudelange

F R A N C E
Thionville

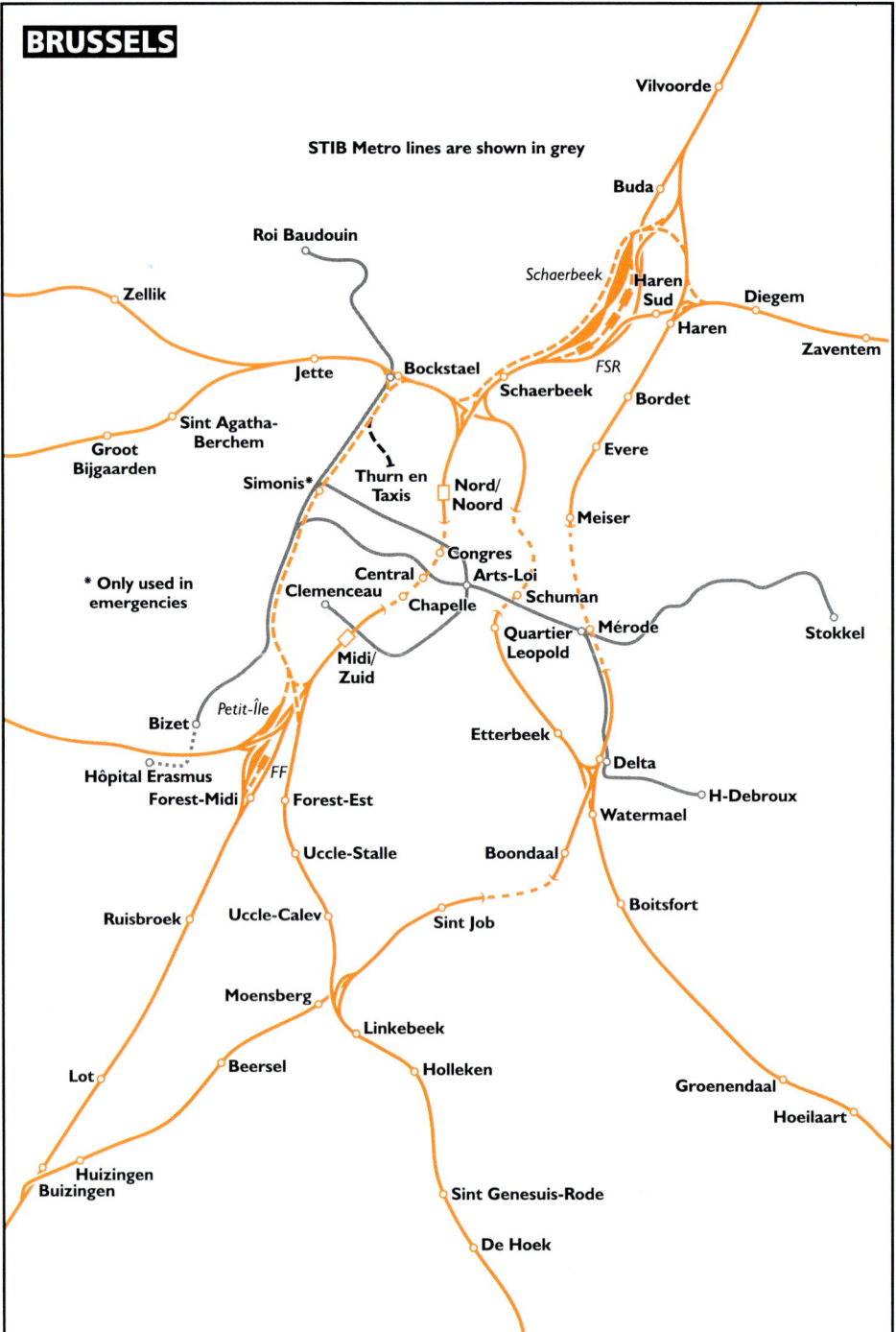

BRUSSELS

STIB Metro lines are shown in grey

Vilvoorde

Buda

Roi Baudouin

Schaerbeek

Haren
Sud

Diegem

Zellik

Haren

Zaventem

Bockstael

Jette

FSR

Schaerbeek

Bordet

Sint Agatha-
Berchem

Groot
Bijgaarden

Simonis*

Thurn en
Taxis

Nord/
Noord

Evere

Meiser

Congres
Arts-Loi

Central

Clemenceau

Chapelle

Schuman

Mérode

Stokkel

* Only used in
emergencies

Quartier
Leopold

Midi/
Zuid

Bizet

Petit-Île

Etterbeek

Delta

H-Debroux

Hôpital Erasmus

FF

Forest-Midi

Forest-Est

Watermael

Uccle-Stalle

Boondaal

Ruisbroek

Uccle-Calev

Sint Job

Boitsfort

Moensberg

Linkebeek

Lot

Beersel

Holleken

Groenendaal

Hoeilaart

Huizingen
Buizingen

Sint Genesuis-Rode

De Hoek

▲ Syntus has two ex-NS "DE2" DMUs plus a spare which it uses on the Marienberg–Almelo line. No. 180 is seen at Marienberg on 22/03/2000 forming the 15.04 to Almelo. **Peter Fox**

▼ Strukton's ex-NS Class 2200 diesel electric loco No. 302282 'Anneke' in plain yellow livery stabled at Watergraafsmeer. **Brian Garvin**

Along Different Lines

For European Rail Tours

Acknowledged (even by the Belgians !) as the leading provider of Belgian rail tours, ADL also offers occasional tours to the Netherlands and to Luxembourg.

ADL tours are designed to suit many tastes and interests. 'Number Crunchers', Branch Line Enthusiasts, Steam Enthusiasts, and those that just like to travel friendly railways in pleasant company, and enjoy good food and drink, are all well-catered for. Occasionally we even have Belgian ale specially brewed and bottled for us !

ADL tours are noted for charter trains which employ unusual 'haulage' (often freight and shunting locos), and go down 'rare' lines. ADL is also famous for its 'Grand Belgian Depot Tours', during which well in excess of 400 locos are usually seen in a single day.

ADL publishes an extensively illustrated monthly News Letter, giving updates on tour development and other items of interest. To find out more about ADL Benelux tours, and tours in many other parts of Europe (and occasionally beyond), please contact ADL at the address below, or visit our Web site. You will be glad that you did !

(all pictures are of ADL charters in Benelux countries)

Along Different Lines

16, Willesley Gardens
Ashby de la Zouch
Leicestershire
LE65 2QF
England

Tel.: (+44) 01530 413121
Fax: (+44) 01530 415405
e.mail: adl.tours@virgin.net

http://homepage.virgin.net/adl.tours/

along
ifferent
ines

Ⓑ

1. BELGIAN NATIONAL RAILWAYS (NMBS/SNCB)

Because of the language situation, Belgian National Railways use their logo rather than initials as these differ according to the language used! In Dutch the railway company is NMBS (Nationale Maatschappij der Belgische Spoorwegen) whilst in French it is SNCB (Société Nationale des Chemins de Fer Belges).

The opening of the high speed line from the French border to Brussels and the introduction of Eurostar and Thalys trains together with recast timetables including through services to a new Brussels Airport station have brought big changes to the Belgian network. Further changes are to take place in the early years of the 21st Century with a high speed line north to the Dutch border involving major works in Antwerpen including a new underground station, also a high speed line from Brussels to the German border, works for both of which are well underway. Orders for new diesel and electric locomotives as well as DMUs will transform the traction scene with most of the first generation locomotives being replaced. The alterations in Antwerpen will see the existing locomotive depot moved to a new site nearer the main freight yards whilst in the south of the country there is to be a new depot in Charleroi which will replace both Monceau and St. Ghislain.

PLACE NAMES

Listed below are some of the Belgian towns and cities with their alternative rendering. Lille in France is included since Dutch speaking Belgians refer to it as such and it is a frequent destination for through trains. At Gent the departure sheet referred to it as Lille, but the announcer called it Rijssel! NL. Dutch, F. French.

Usual Name	Alternative	Usual Name	Alternative
Aalst	Alost (F)	Kortrijk	Courtrai (F)
Arlon	Aarlen (NL)	Leuven	Louvain (F)
Antwerpen	Anvers (F)	Lille	Rijssel (NL)
Ath	Aat (NL)	Liège	Luik (NL)
Brugge	Bruges (F)	Mechelen	Malines (F)
Dendermonde	Termonde (F)	Mons	Bergen (NL)
Gent	Gand (F)	Namur	Namen (NL)
Geraardsbergen	Grammont (F)	Oudenarde	Audenarde (F)
Ieper	Yprès (F)	Tournai	Doornik (NL)

PASSENGER TRAIN SERVICES

Belgian Railways are mostly electrified and operate regular interval services over most routes. The principal express services are Intercity (IC) and Inter Regio (IR) which call at principal centres. Local trains (L) serve the other routes and stations. Other types of trains are

EC	Eurocity
INT	International train
P	Peak hour
T	Tourist train
Thalys	High speed TGV with special tariff

INTER CITY SERVICES

The network has route letters in upper case. Details of the routes and usual traction:

A	Oostende–Brussels–Eupen/Köln	Class 13 and I11 stock to Eupen
		Class 16 and I11 stock to Köln
B	Brussels–Amsterdam	Class 11 and Benelux push-pull stock
C	Oostende–Kortrijk–Lille;	AM96
	Antwerpen–Gent–Kortrijk–Lille	AM96
D	Herstal–Liege–Namur–Mons–Lille	AM96
E	Knokke/Blankenberge–Brussels–Hasselt	AM96
F	Quievrain–Mons–Brussels–Liege–Verviers	Class 21 and M4 push-pull

G	Oostende–Gent–Antwerpen	Class 13 and I11 stock
H	Mouscron–Tournai–Halle–Brussels N	Class 21 and M4 push-pull
I	Charleroi–Nivelles–Brussels–Antwerpen	AM96
J	Brussels–Luxembourg	AM96
K	Genk–Landen–Brussels–Aalst–Gent	AM80
L	Poperinge–Denderleeuw–Brussels–St. Niklaas	AM80
M	Liers–Liège–Namur (Dinant)–Brussels	AM80
N	Antwerpen–Brussels	Class 27 and M5 stock

INTER REGIO SERVICES

This network is identified by a route letter in lower case. Details of routes and usual traction :

a	Antwerpen–Mechelen–Leuven	AM86
b	Antwerpen–Brussels–Nivelles	AM75
c	Berchem–Hasselt–Liège–Maastricht	AM66/70 etc.
d	Geraardsbergen–Halle–Brussels	AM66/70 etc.
e	Berchem–Neerpelt	Class 62 and M2 push-pull
f	Kortrijk–Gent–Mechelen–Leuven	Class 21 and M4
g	Manage–Brussels–Mechelen–Turnhout	AM80
h	Gent–Aalst–Brussels–Brussels Airport	AM80
i	De Panne–Gent–Brussels–Brussels Airport	AM80
j	Quevy–Mons–Brussels–Brussels Airport	AM80
k	Tournai–Mons–Charleroi–Chatelet	AM66/70 etc.
l	Binche–La Louviere–Brussels–Louvain La Neuve	AM75
m	Liège–Gouvy–Luxembourg	CFL 3000 and SNCB/NMBS I10 stock
n	Jambes–Namur–Charleroi–Brussels–Essen	AM75
o	Brussels–Brussels Airport	AM86

LOCAL SERVICES

These are normally two-car EMUs but there are still some non-electrified lines served by diesel railcars or diesel-hauled services. The following non-electrified routes are worked by loco-hauled or push-pull services (Class 62): Antwerpen–Neerpelt; Gent–Eeklo; Gent–Ronse; Gent–Geraardsbergen; Hasselt–Mol; Charleroi–Couvin. Other non-electrified lines use the existing DMUs of Classes 44 and 45. Services on these routes will all change to Class 41 DMUs during 2000–2004.

PEAK SERVICES

Examination of the Belgian timetable for the Brussels area will show many peak hour extras. These bring a lot of variety into the scene with all sorts of locos and stock appearing such as Class 22 and 23 as well as Classes 21 and 27 on double-deck sets. Further examination of the timetable will show that "P" trains cover some rare curves and routes!

TOURIST SERVICES

These operate in the summer months to coastal resorts as well as places in the Ardennes. Look out for the Neerpelt–Blankenberge train which has a Class 51 from Hasselt depot and the Namur–Houyet train which then shuttles between Dinant and Houyet and is formed of M2 stock top and tailed by Class 52s.

NUMBERING SYSTEM

The SNCB list is quite straightforward. The present scheme dates from 01/01/71 and is as follows:

0001–1000	Electric multiple units. (Leading '0' not carried).
1001–2000	Electric locomotives. Multi-voltage.
2001–3000	Electric locomotives. 3000 V d.c. only.
3001–4000	Now used for Eurostar sets.
4001–5000	Diesel railcars (43xx series is also used for Thalys and 45xx for TGV Réseau)
5001–6000	Diesel locomotives. Higher power.
6001–7000	Diesel locomotives. Medium power.
7001–8000	Diesel shunting locomotives. Heavy duty.
8001–9000	Diesel shunting locomotives. Medium power.
9001–9999	Diesel shunting locomotives. Low power.

ORGANISATION, DEPOTS & STABLING POINTS

Since the first edition of this book appeared, there have been many reorganisations on Belgian Railways. These have eventually caught up with the traffic and motive power sections which have been reduced from eight areas to five regions. The list of stabling points is far from complete and does not include every station where the odd EMU may be stabled.

Central Region.
Depots: Brussels Midi/Zuid, Schaarbeek Diesel, Schaarbeek Electric.
Departmentals: Forest/Vorst, Schaarbeek.
Stabling points: Brussels Midi/Zuid station, Ottignies.

North East Region.
Depots: Antwerpen Dam, Hasselt.
Departmentals: Antwerpen Oost, Leuven.
Stabling points: Aarschot, Antwerpen Noord, Antwerpen Schijnpoort, Leuven station, Leuven yard, Mechelen, Mol, Turnhout.

North West Region.
Depots: Merelbeke, Oostende.
Departmentals: Brugge.
Stabling points: Aalst, Brugge, Denderleeuw, Dendermonde, De Panne, Gent St. Pieters, Geraardsbergen, Kortrijk, Oudenaarde.

South East Region.
Depots: Kinkempois (Liège), Stockem.
Departmentals: Angleur, Arlon, Jemelle, Kinkempois, Visé.
Stabling points: Arlon, Huy, Jemelle, Liège Guillemins, Liers, Montzen, Namur, Stockem Yard, Virton, Welkenraedt.

South West Region.
Depots: Monceau (Charleroi), St. Ghislain.
Departmentals: Charleroi Sud, Mons.
Stabling points: Ath, Charleroi Sud, Châtelet, Mons, Tournai.

DEPOT CODES

The SNCB has used codes for depots for many years dating back to the days of the telegraphic system. These codes are still in use today as official abbreviations. However on locomotives the allocation is normally stencilled on in full on the mainframe somewhere below the cab. EMUs and diesel railcars do not normally carry their allocations but sometimes the code will be found on them against repair data etc. (S) after the allocation denotes the vehicle is stored whilst (D) means it is in departmental service.

FAZ	Salzinnes Works (Namur)	FR	Brugge
FCR	Charleroi Sud	FSD	Oostende
FEO	Ronet (Namur)	FSR	Schaarbeek Diese
FF	Forest-Vorst	FSRE	Schaarbeek Electric
FGH	St. Ghislain	FTY	Tournai
FGSP	Gent St. Pieters	FVS	Visé
FHS	Hasselt	GCR	Charleroi Sud Quai
FKR	Merelbeke (Gent)	GNS	Antwerpen Oost
FLV	Leuven	LJ	Jemelle
FMS	Mons	LL	Aarlon
FNDM	Antwerpen Dam	LNC	Monceau (Charleroi)
FNND	Antwerpen Noord	MKM	Stockem (Arlon)
FNR	Namur	NK	Kinkempois (Liège)

WORKSHOPS

There are only two workshops for the general overhaul of locomotives and multiple units. However it should be stated that most of the main depots can undertake quite heavy repairs. The main works are:

Mechelen: All EMUs, DMUs and coaching stock.
Salzinnes: All locomotives.

LIVERIES

Electric Locomotives: The standard electric locomotive livery is blue with a yellow band and this livery has now been applied to older electric locos. Class 11 are painted in the Benelux livery which reflects their international use, as the upper half of the body is painted Bordeaux red, the former SNCB Inter-City colour, whilst the lower part is painted yellow, the NS colour. Class 13 is in the new Inter City livery of white to match the new I11 IC stock whilst Class 25.5 retains the old Benelux livery of dark blue with a yellow band.

Diesel Locomotives: The main-line diesel locomotive fleet was being repainted in green with a yellow band, but this then gave way to the current scheme of yellow with a green band. Exceptions are Class 55 fitted with e.t.h. which are blue with a yellow band.

Diesel Railcars: The old livery is yellow and red, but some vehicles have been repainted in blue, white and yellow. Class 41 units are to carry the new white livery.

Electric Multiple Units: Old EMUs and were painted plain green. The "Break" and AM86/89 "Snorkel" EMUs were introduced in Bordeaux red, and all remaining old EMUs have been re-painted in that colour, as have the type AM75/76/77 four-car units, which were originally painted grey and orange. However the "Break" units have now all been repainted in the silver/red/blue "Memling" livery. New EMUs are being delivered in a new standard livery of pale grey with blue bodyside stripes and red doors. The old EMUs numbered from 600 onwards are being refurbished and painted in this new livery.

Loco-hauled Coaches. Coaches for internal Belgian services were painted plain green. M4 and M6 loco-hauled stock were built in Bordeaux red livery and all remaining M2 coaches have been repainted in that colour. Much international stock is painted orange, but certain hauled coaches were repainted in the silver/red/blue "Memling" livery, as have locos 1601 and 1602. New Class I11 coaches have been delivered in a new standard livery of pale grey with blue bodyside stripes and red doors. M4 stock and international stock is now being repainted in this livery.

LIVERY CODES

Unless a code is shown, electric locos are blue with a yellow band, diesel locos are yellow with a green band and loco-hauled coaching stock vehicles are Bordeaux red.

The following livery codes are used in this section. Where two colours are shown, the first colour mentioned is the colour on the lower half of the body.

A   Advertising livery.
B   Benelux push-pull livery (yellow & bordeaux red).
C   SNCB/NMBS couchette livey (dark blue with pink stripe)
D   SNCB/NMBS diesel railcar.livery (red & yellow).
G   Original green livery.
M   "Memling" livery. Silver with red and blue. So called because it was first applied to stock used on the EC "Memling" service.
N   New standard EMU/internal stock livery (white with red and blue lower bodyside stripes and red doors).
O   Orange with white stripe (Eurofima livery).
P   Post office red.
S   Class specific livery (refer to text).
U   Unpainted stainless steel with coloured stripe.
Y   Blue lower bodyside & yellow upper bodyside or departmental yellow.
W   New standard international coach and DMU livery (white with dark grey lower bodyside stripe and window surround).

1.1. ELECTRIC MULTIPLE UNITS

Belgian EMUs operate in fixed formations and therefore only unit numbers are quoted. All classes of EMU may work in multiple with one another except for types AM80/82/83, AM86 and type AM96, which may work with other members of the same type only. "Type" refers to the year in which the batch of units were ordered. Seating is 2+2 in first class and 2+3 in second class, except where stated otherwise. Individual car numbers are normally the unit number with a figure 1, 2, 3 or 4 for the position in the set. Hence the B car of unit 151 is 1511 and the ABD is 1512. Exceptions can occur to this and note that the AM80/82/83 "Break" units had the centre cars inserted randomly and therefore these do not conform to the general scheme. All units except Type AM54P have electro-pneumatic braking and disc brakes.

TYPE AM62/63/65   2-CAR UNITS

These units are in general use on local services over a wide area.

BD + AB (DMBSO–DMCO).

Wheel Arrangement: A1-1A + A1-1A.
Built: 1962–1965. 151–210 are type AM62, 211–250 are type AM63 and 251–270 are type AM65.
Builder–Mech. Parts: BN, Ragheno, BLC, ABR, Germain, CWFM.
Builder–Elec. Parts: ACEC.
Traction Motors: 4 x 155 kW.
Accommodation: –/104 1T + 28/48 1T.
Weight: 52 + 50 tonnes.
Length over Couplers: 23.71 + 23.59 m.
Max. Speed: 130 km/h.

Originally numbered 228.151–270.

153	MKM	183	FKR	213	FKR	242	FGH
154	MKM	184	FKR	214	FKR	243	FGH
155	MKM	185	FKR	215	FKR	244	FGH
156	MKM	186	FKR	216	FKR	245	FGH
157	MKM	187	FKR	217	FKR	246	FGH
158	MKM	188	FKR	218	FKR	247	FGH
159	MKM	189	FKR	219	FKR	248	FGH
160	MKM	190	FKR	220	FKR	249	FGH
161	MKM	191	FKR	221	FKR	250	FGH
162	MKM	192	FKR	222	FKR	251	FGH
163	MKM	193	FKR	223	FKR	252	FGH
164	MKM	194	FKR	224	FKR	253	FGH
165	MKM	195	FKR	225	FGH	254	FGH
166	MKM	196	FKR	226	FGH	255	FGH
167	MKM	197	FKR	227	FGH	256	FGH
168	MKM	198	FKR	228	FGH	257	FGH
169	FKR	199	FKR	229	FGH	258	FGH
170	FKR	200	FKR	230	FGH	259	FGH
171	FKR	201	FKR	231	FGH	260	FGH
172	FKR	202	FKR	232	FGH	261	FGH
173	FKR	203	FKR	233	FGH	262	FGH
174	FKR	204	FKR	234	FGH	263	FGH
175	FKR	205	FKR	235	FGH	264	FGH
176	FKR	206	FKR	236	FGH	265	FGH
177	FKR	207	FKR	237	FGH	266	NK
178	FKR	208	FKR	238	FGH	267	NK
179	FKR	209	FKR	239	FGH	268	NK
180	FKR	210	FKR	240	FGH	269	NK
181	FKR	212	FKR	241	FGH	270	NK
182	FKR						

TYPE AM80/82/83   3-CAR UNITS

These units are the EMU version of the M4 coaches and are thyristor controlled. Built as two-car sets they have all been made up to three-car by the insertion of a trailer with 2+2 second class seating. At the same time units have been repainted into the new silver livery. The trailer numbers are out of sequence as the new trailers were built in number order but inserted into any set that just happened to be in works at the time. (e.g. set 428 is formed 4281, 3752, 4283). The units are used mostly on IR services with some still on IC services until replaced by AM96 sets. Some trailers carry "Brussels Airport Express" markings. Sets 325 and 326 belong to CFL. Some sets have been sold to the USA and leased back (e.g. set 345 is leased from Wilmington Trust Co.).

B + B + ABD (DMSO–TSO–PDTBCO).

Wheel Arrangement: Bo-Bo (+ 2-2) + 2-2.
Built: 1980–85. 301–335 are type AM80, 336–370 are type AM82 and 371–440 are type AM83.
Builder–Mech. Parts: BN.
Builder–Elec. Parts: ACEC.
Traction Motors: 4 x 310 kW.
Accommodation: –/99 1T + –/82 1T + 32/40 1T
Weight: 61 + 43 + 47 tonnes.
Length over Couplers: 25.425 + 24.96 m + 25.425 m.
Max. Speed: 160 km/h.

Regenerative braking.
b Brecknell-Willis pantograph.
325 and 326 are owned by CFL.

301	M	MKM	336	M	FHS	371	M	FKR	406	M	FKR
302	M	MKM	337	M	FHS	372	M	FKR	407	M	FKR
303	M	MKM	338	M	FHS	373	M	FKR	408	M b	FKR
304	M	MKM	339	M	FHS	374	M	FKR	409	M	FKR
305	M	MKM	340	M	FHS	375	M	FKR	410	M	FKR
306	M	MKM	341	M	FHS	376	M	FKR	411	M	FKR
307	M	MKM	342	M	FHS	377	M	FKR	412	M	FKR
308	M	MKM	343	M	FHS	378	M	FKR	413	M	FKR
309	M	MKM	344	M	FHS	379	M	FKR	414	M	FKR
310	M	MKM	345	M	FHS	380	M	FKR	415	M b	FKR
311	M	MKM	346	M	FHS	381	M	FKR	416	M	FKR
312	M	MKM	347	M	FHS	382	M	FKR	417	M	NK
313	M	MKM	348	M	FHS	383	M	FKR	418	M	NK
314	M	MKM	349	M	FHS	384	M	FKR	419	M	NK
315	M	MKM	350	M	FHS	385	M	FKR	420	M b	NK
316	M	MKM	351	M	FHS	386	M	FKR	421	M b	NK
317	M	MKM	352	M	FHS	387	M	FKR	422	M	NK
318	M	MKM	353	M	FHS	388	M	FKR	423	M	NK
319	M	MKM	354	M	FHS	389	M	FKR	424	M b	NK
320	M	MKM	355	M	FHS	390	M	FKR	425	M b	NK
321	M	MKM	356	M	FHS	391	M	FKR	426	M	NK
322	M	FHS	357	M	FHS	392	M	FKR	427	M	NK
323	M	FHS	358	M	FHS	393	M	FKR	428	M	NK
324	M	FHS	359	M	FHS	394	M	FKR	429	M	NK
325	M	MKM	360	M	FKR	395	M	FKR	430	M b	NK
326	M	MKM	361	M	FKR	396	M	FKR	431	M	NK
327	M	FHS	362	M	FKR	397	M	FKR	432	M	NK
328	M	FHS	363	M	FKR	398	M	FKR	433	M	NK
329	M	FHS	364	M	FKR	399	M	FKR	434	M	NK
330	M	FHS	365	M	FKR	400	M	FKR	435	M	NK
331	M	FHS	366	M	FKR	401	M	FKR	436	M	NK
332	M	FHS	367	M	FKR	402	M	FKR	437	M	NK
333	M	FHS	368	M	FKR	403	M	FKR	438	M	NK
334	M	FHS	369	M	FKR	404	M	FKR	439	M b	NK
335	M	FHS	370	M	FKR	405	M	FKR	440	M	NK

TYPE AM96   3-CAR UNITS

These three-car sets are the latest IC units that have brought new standards of comfort to Belgian main line services and are equal to the new I11 carriages. Front end design is based on the successful "rubber nose" of Danish IC3 DMUs. There are two versions with the dual-voltage sets being used on services into France (Antwerpen–Lille, Oostende–Lille and Liège–Lille). The d.c. sets are working IC services from the coast to Hasselt and will filter onto other IC routes as more units become available.

B + B + AD (DMSO–SO–DFSO).

Wheel Arrangement: Bo-Bo + 2-2 +2-2.
Built: 1996–1999.
Systems (441–490): 3000 V d.c., 25 kV a.c. 50 Hz.
Builder–Mech. Parts: Bombardier.
Builder–Elec. Parts: Alstom.
Traction Motors: Four 4EXA3046 asynchronous of 350 kW.
Accommodation: –/79 1T + –/88 1T + 45/– 1T.
Weight: 60 + 50 + 50 tonnes.
Length over Couplers: 26.40 + 26.40 + 26.40 m.
Max. Speed: 160 km/h.

Dual-voltage sets:

441	N	FSD	454	N	FSD	467	N	FSD	479	N	FSD
442	N	FSD	455	N	FSD	468	N	FSD	480	N	FSD
443	N	FSD	456	N	FSD	469	N	FSD	481	N	FSD
444	N	FSD	457	N	FSD	470	N	FSD	482	N	FSD
445	N	FSD	458	N	FSD	471	N	FSD	483	N	FSD
446	N	FSD	459	N	FSD	472	N	FSD	484	N	FSD
447	N	FSD	460	N	FSD	473	N	FSD	485	N	FSD
448	N	FSD	461	N	FSD	474	N	FSD	486	N	FSD
449	N	FSD	462	N	FSD	475	N	FSD	487	N	FSD
450	N	FSD	463	N	FSD	476	N	FSD	488	N	FSD
451	N	FSD	464	N	FSD	477	N	FSD	489	N	FSD
452	N	FSD	465	N	FSD	478	N	FSD	490	N	FSD
453	N	FSD	466	N	FSD						

3000 V d.c. sets:

501	N	FHS	519	N	FHS	537	N	FHS	554	N	FHS
502	N	FHS	520	N	FHS	538	N	FHS	555	N	FHS
503	N	FHS	521	N	FHS	539	N	FHS	556	N	FHS
504	N	FHS	522	N	FHS	540	N	FHS	557	N	FHS
505	N	FHS	523	N	FHS	541	N	FHS	558	N	FHS
506	N	FHS	524	N	FHS	542	N	FHS	559	N	FHS
507	N	FHS	525	N	FHS	543	N	FHS	560	N	FHS
508	N	FHS	526	N	FHS	544	N	FHS	561	N	FHS
509	N	FHS	527	N	FHS	545	N	FHS	562	N	FHS
510	N	FHS	528	N	FHS	546	N	FHS	563	N	FHS
511	N	FHS	529	N	FHS	547	N	FHS	564	N	FHS
512	N	FHS	530	N	FHS	548	N	FHS	565	N	FHS
513	N	FHS	531	N	FHS	549	N	FHS	566	N	
514	N	FHS	532	N	FHS	550	N	FHS	567	N	
515	N	FHS	533	N	FHS	551	N	FHS	568	N	
516	N	FHS	534	N	FHS	552	N	FHS	569	N	
517	N	FHS	535	N	FHS	553	N	FHS	570	N	
518	N	FHS	536	N	FHS						

TYPE AM70A (SABENA)   2-CAR UNITS

These units were built for exclusive use on the Brussels Airport service when this was just a shuttle service. Since the construction of a new station at the airport services from the south of Brussels now run through to the airport and the Sabena units have been put into the general pool of suburban units.

B + ABD (DMSO–DMBCO).
Wheel Arrangement: A1-1A + A1-1A.
Built: 1970–71.
Builder–Mech. Parts: Ragheno.
Builder–Elec. Parts: ACEC.
Traction Motors: 4 x 170 kW.
Accommodation: –/74 1T + 32/12 1T.
Weight: 52 + 52 tonnes.
Length over Couplers: 23.71 + 23.59 m.
Max. Speed: 140 km/h.

595	FSRE	597	FSRE	599	FSRE	600	FSRE
596	FSRE	598	FSRE				

TYPE AM66/70   2-CAR UNITS

Units 601–782 are now starting to be refurbished with around 25 units per year being done at Mechelen works between 1999 and 2006. Changes include new doors and altered seating giving fewer first class seats and smoking accommodation. Used on some IR routes but mostly used for local and peak services.

B + ABD (DMSO–DMBCO).

Wheel Arrangement: A1-1A + A1-1A.
Built: 1966/70–71.
Builder–Mech. Parts: BN, Ragheno, BLC, ABR.
Builder–Elec. Parts: ACEC.
Traction Motors: 4 x 170 kW.
Accommodation: –/104 1T + 28/48 1T (r –/102 1T + 20/58 1T).
Weight: 56 + 52 tonnes.
Length over Couplers: 23.71 + 23.59 m.
Max. Speed: 140 km/h.

* Fitted with Timken roller bearings.
r Refurbished
Originally numbered 228.601–664.

601		FGH	617	N r	FGH	633	N r	FGH	649	FSRE
602		FGH	618		FGH	634		FGH	650	FSRE
603	N r	FGH	619		FGH	635		FGH	651	FSRE
604	N r	FGH	620		FGH	636		FGH	652	FSRE
605		FGH	621		FGH	637		FGH	653	FSRE
606	N r	FGH	622		FGH	638		FGH	654	FSRE
607	N r	FGH	623		FGH	639		FGH	655	FSRE
608	N r	FGH	624	N r	FGH	640		FGH	657	FSRE
609		FGH	625		FGH	641		FGH	658	FSRE
610	N r	FGH	626		FGH	642		FGH	659	FSRE
611	N r	FGH	627		FGH	643		FSRE	660	FSRE
612		FGH	628		FGH	644		FSRE	661	FSRE
613		FGH	629		FGH	645		FSRE	662	FSRE
614		FGH	630	N r	FGH	646		FSRE	663	FSRE
615		FGH	631		FGH	647		FSRE	664	FSRE
616		FGH	632		FGH	648		FSRE		

TYPE AM70TH   2-CAR UNITS

The "TH" in the type classification denotes thyristor control, these being the first Belgian units so fitted. Timken roller bearings. Use as for AM66/70.

B + ABD (DMSO–DMBCO).

Wheel Arrangement: A1-1A + A1-1A.
Built: 1971–72.
Builder–Mech. Parts: CWFM.
Builder–Elec. Parts: ACEC.
Traction Motors: 4 x 170 kW.
Accommodation: –/104 1T + 28/48 1T.

Weight: 56 + 53 tonnes.
Length over Couplers: 23.71 + 23.59 m.
Max. Speed: 140 km/h.

665	NK	668	NK	671	NK	674	NK
666	NK	669	NK	672	NK	675	NK
667	NK	670	NK	673	NK	676	NK

TYPE AM73/74/78/79   2-CAR UNITS

These are the production series of thyristor-controlled units. Use as for AM66/70.

B + ABD (DMSO–DMBCO).

Wheel Arrangement: A1-1A + A1-1A.
Built: 1972–80.
Builder–Mech. Parts: BN (707–730 CFCF).
Builder–Elec. Parts: ACEC.
Traction Motors: 4 x 170 kW.
Accommodation: –/102 1T + 28/48 1T.
Weight: 56 + 52 tonnes.
Length over Couplers: 23.71 + 23.59 m.
Max. Speed: 140 km/h.

677	NK	704	NK	731	FHS	757	FSD
678	NK	705	NK	732	FHS	758	FSD
679	NK	706	NK	733	FHS	759	FSD
680	NK	707	NK	734	FHS	760	FSD
681	NK	708	NK	735	FHS	761	FSD
682	NK	709	NK	736	FHS	762	FSD
683	NK	710	NK	737	FHS	763	FSD
684	NK	711	NK	738	FHS	764	FSD
685	NK	712	NK	739	FHS	765	FSD
686	NK	713	NK	740	FHS	766	FSD
687	NK	714	NK	741	FHS	767	FSD
688	NK	715	NK	742	FHS	768	FSD
689	NK	716	NK	743	FHS	769	FSD
690	NK	717	NK	744	FHS	770	FSD
691	NK	718	NK	745	FHS	771	FSD
692	NK	719	NK	746	FHS	772	FSD
693	NK	720	NK	747	FHS	773	FSD
694	NK	721	NK	748	FHS	774	FSD
695	NK	722	NK	749	FHS	775	FSD
696	NK	723	FHS	750	FHS	776	FSD
697	NK	724	FHS	751	FHS	777	FSD
698	NK	725	FHS	752	FHS	778	FSD
699	NK	726	FHS	753	FHS	779	FSD
700	NK	727	FHS	754	FHS	780	FSD
701	NK	728	FHS	755	FHS	781	FSD
702	NK	729	FHS	756	FSD	782	FSD
703	NK	730	FHS				

TYPE AM75/76/77   4-CAR UNITS

These thyristor-controlled units are gangwayed within the sets only. Pantographs are fitted to only one of the motor coaches. Pressure ventilation. Used on IR services b,l and n.

AD + B + B + B (DTBFO–PMSO–MSO–DTSO).

Wheel Arrangement: 2-2 + Bo-Bo + Bo-Bo + 2-2.
Built: 1975–1979.
Builder–Mech. Parts: BN.
Builder–Elec. Parts: ACEC.
Traction Motors: 8 x 170 kW.
Accommodation: 56/– 1T + –/100 1T + –/106 1T + –/96 1T.
Weight: 51 + 60 + 60 + 49 tonnes.

Length over Couplers: 25.11 + 24.40 + 24.40 + 25.11 m.
Max. Speed: 140 km/h.

Disc and tread brakes.

801	FSRE	812	FSRE	823	FSRE	834	FSRE
802	FSRE	813	FSRE	824	FSRE	835	FSRE
803	FSRE	814	FSRE	825	FSRE	836	FSRE
804	FSRE	815	FSRE	826	FSRE	837	FSRE
805	FSRE	816	FSRE	827	FSRE	838	FSRE
806	FSRE	817	FSRE	828	FSRE	839	FSRE
807	FSRE	818	FSRE	829	FSRE	840	FSRE
808	FSRE	819	FSRE	830	FSRE	841	FSRE
809	FSRE	820	FSRE	831	FSRE	842	FSRE
810	FSRE	821	FSRE	832	FSRE	843	FSRE
811	FSRE	822	FSRE	833	FSRE	844	FSRE

TYPE AM86/89   2-CAR UNITS

These units were the first Belgian EMUs to feature 2+2 seating in second class. Another innovation is the use of polyester sides and front nose which are glued onto the main body. They are designed for eventual one-person operation and rear-view mirrors are fitted which are flush with the side of the vehicle when not in use. They are officially known as Sprinters, but their unusual front end appearance has led to them being nicknamed "Snorkels". Used on local trains Brussels–Charleroi and other local services around Brussels, Antwerpen, Hasselt and Leuven including Leuven to St. Niklaas.

AB + AB (MCO–DTCO).

Wheel Arrangement: Bo-Bo + 2-2.
Built: 1988–91.
Builder–Mech. Parts: BN.
Builder–Elec. Parts: ACEC.
Traction Motors: 4 x 172 kW type AE121N.
Accommodation: 16/72 1T + 24/86.
Weight: 59 + 48 tonnes.
Length over Couplers: 26.40 + 26.40 m.
Max. Speed: 120 km/h.

901	FSRE	914	FSRE	927	FSRE	940	FSRE
902	FSRE	915	FSRE	928	FSRE	941	FSRE
903	FSRE	916	FSRE	929	FSRE	942	FSRE
904	FSRE	917	FSRE	930	FSRE	943	FSRE
905	FSRE	918	FSRE	931	FSRE	944	FSRE
906	FSRE	919	FSRE	932	FSRE	945	FSRE
907	FSRE	920	FSRE	933	FSRE	946	FSRE
908	FSRE	921	FSRE	934	FSRE	947	FSRE
909	FSRE	922	FSRE	935	FSRE	948	FSRE
910	FSRE	923	FSRE	936	FSRE	949	FSRE
911	FSRE	924	FSRE	937	FSRE	950	FSRE
912	FSRE	925	FSRE	938	FSRE	951	FSRE
913	FSRE	926	FSRE	939	FSRE	952	FSRE

TYPE AM54P   2-CAR UNITS

These units were converted at Mechelen Works from type AM54 during 1987/88 and have been designed to handle mail carried in containers. They have roller shutter doors and can carry a total of 86 containers. Used all over the network.

D + D (DMP–DMBP).

Wheel Arrangement: A1-1A + A1-1A.
Built: 1954–56.
Builder–Mech. Parts: BN (961), Ragheno (962/4/8–70/2), Fam/Germain, one car each (others).
Builder–Elec. Parts: ACEC, SEMG.
Traction Motors: 4 x 155 kW.
Weight: 42 + 44 tonnes.

Length over Couplers: 22.985 + 22.985 m.
Max. Speed: 130 km/h.

ⓑ   27

961	(080)	**P**	NK
962	(085)	**P**	NK
964	(086)	**P**	NK
965	(117)	**P**	NK
966	(123)	**P**	NK

967	(118)	**P**	NK
968	(074)	**P**	NK
969	(091)	**P**	NK
970	(093)	**P**	NK
971	(128)	**P**	NK

972	(084)	**P**	NK
973	(120)	**P**	NK
974	(110)	**P**	NK
975	(111)	**P**	NK

▲ Class AM54P Postal EMU No. 962 at Merelbeke depot on 26/09/1999.   **Adrian Norton**

1.2. ELECTRIC LOCOMOTIVES

Note: All electric locomotives are in the standard blue livery with yellow stripes unless stated otherwise. The standard voltage is 3000 V d.c.

CLASS 11   Bo-Bo

These dual voltage locos are a development of Class 21. They are used on the Brussels–Amsterdam service. The SNCB provides the locos for these push–pull Inter-City services and the NS provides the coaching stock. Originally planned to be numbered 1101–1112, the higher numbers were eventually decided on to avoid conflicting with the NS 1100 class. Thyristor control.

Built: 1985–6.
Systems: 1500 V/3000 V d.c.
Builder-Mechanical Parts: BN.
Builder-Electrical Parts: ACEC.
Traction Motors: 4 x LE622S frame mounted.
One Hour Rating: 3310 kW.   **Weight**: 85 tonnes.
Maximum Tractive Effort: 234 kN.   **Length over Buffers**: 18.65 m.
Driving Wheel Dia.: 1250 mm.   **Max. Speed**: 140 km/h.

Electro-pneumatic braking. Rheostatic braking.

1181	B	FKR	1184	B	FKR	1187	B	FKR	1190	B	FKR
1182	B	FKR	1185	B	FKR	1188	B	FKR	1191	B	FKR
1183	B	FKR	1186	B	FKR	1189	B	FKR	1192	B	FKR

CLASS 12   Bo-Bo

With the introduction of dual-voltage EMUs on services between Antwerpen and Lille these locomotives are now mainly used on freight trains between Merelbeke and Lille La Delivrance, Muizen–Frethun, and services from France to Liège via Charleroi and Namur. Thyristor control.

Built: 1986.
Systems: 3000 V d.c., 25 kV a.c. 50 Hz.
Builder-Mechanical Parts: BN.
Builder-Electrical Parts: ACEC.
Traction Motors: 4 x LE622S frame mounted.
One Hour Rating: 3310 kW.   **Weight**: 85 tonnes.
Maximum Tractive Effort: 234 kN.   **Length over Buffers**: 18.65 m.
Driving Wheel Dia.: 1250 mm.   **Max. Speed**: 160 km/h.

Electro-pneumatic braking. Rheostatic braking.

1201	FKR	1204	FKR	1207	FKR	1210	FKR
1202	FKR	1205	FKR	1208	FKR	1211	FKR
1203	FKR	1206	FKR	1209	FKR	1212	FKR

CLASS 13   Bo-Bo

These sixty dual-voltage locomotives were ordered together with 20 for CFL. They are a development of SNCF Class 36000. The first ten were built in Belfort, France with the remainder being built at the Bombardier Eurorail plant at Brugge. They are general purpose machines with a capability of 200 km/h but their 25 kV capability will see them working on such routes as Liège–Luxembourg and the newly-electrified Namur–Athus route as well as into France on Stockem–Thionville–Metz workings. The usual teething problems have beset the class and the first ten have returned to works to receive modifications which have been incorporated into later production.

Built: 1997 onwards.
Systems: 3000 V d.c., 25 kV a.c. 50 Hz.
Builder-Mechanical Parts: Bombardier.
Builder-Electrical Parts: Alstom.
Traction Motors: 4 x PXA4339B frame mounted.
One Hour Rating: 5200 kW.   **Weight**: 90 tonnes.
Maximum Tractive Effort: 288 kN.   **Length over Buffers**: 19.11 m.
Driving Wheel Dia.: 1160 mm.   **Max. Speed**: 200 km/h.
Class Specific Livery: S White with blue stripe below and red stripe above bodyside grilles.

Electro-pneumatic braking. Rheostatic braking.

1301	S	FKR	1316	S	FKR	1331	S		1346	S	
1302	S	FKR	1317	S	FKR	1332	S		1347	S	
1303	S	FKR	1318	S	FKR	1333	S		1348	S	
1304	S	FKR	1319	S	FKR	1334	S		1349	S	
1305	S	FKR	1320	S	FKR	1335	S		1350	S	
1306	S	FKR	1321	S		1336	S		1351	S	
1307	S	FKR	1322	S		1337	S		1352	S	
1308	S	FKR	1323	S		1338	S		1353	S	
1309	S	FKR	1324	S		1339	S		1354	S	
1310	S	FKR	1325	S		1340	S		1355	S	
1311	S	FKR	1326	S		1341	S		1356	S	
1312	S	FKR	1327	S		1342	S		1357	S	
1313	S	FKR	1328	S		1343	S		1358	S	
1314	S	FKR	1329	S		1344	S		1359	S	
1315	S	FKR	1330	S		1345	S		1360	S	

CLASS 15   Bo-Bo

These are triple voltage locos for through workings to the NS and SNCF systems. The class were used on EC/IC/TEE services between Paris, Brussels and Amsterdam, but in 1988 they were banned from the NS, Class 25.5 being used instead between Brussels and Amsterdam. The introduction of TGV Nord and Thalys services has made these locos mostly redundant and they were transferred from Oostende to Kinkempois. They are used on peak services around Brussels. The pantograph at No. 1 end is for d.c. and that at No. 2 end is for a.c.

Built: 1962.
Systems: 1500/3000 V d.c., 25 kV a.c. 50 Hz.
Builder-Mechanical Parts: BN.
Builder-Electrical Parts: ACEC.
Traction Motors: 4 x ES541 frame mounted.
One Hour Rating: 2780 kW.   **Weight**: 77.7 tonnes.
Maximum Tractive Effort: 170 kN.   **Length over Buffers**: 17.75 m.
Driving Wheel Dia.: 1250 mm.   **Max. Speed**: 160 km/h.

Electro-pneumatic braking.

Originally numbered 150.001–003/011/012.

1501	NK	1503	NK	1504	NK	1505	NK
1502	NK						

CLASS 16   Bo-Bo

When introduced these locos brought a bold new styling to the SNCB and an electric blue livery instead of the dark green then prevailing. These are true international locos and can work on four systems. The introduction of "Thalys" services between Paris and Köln has taken away some of their work, but the class is still much in evidence on the Oostende–Köln service. 1601/2 have been repainted into "Memling" livery sponsored by the model railway company Märklin whose name also appears on the locomotives. No. 1 end has two pantographs, one for 15 kV a.c. and one for 1500/3000 V d.c. whilst No. 2 end has the 25 kV a.c. pantograph.

Built: 1966.
Systems: 1500/3000 V d.c., 15 kV a.c. $16^2/_3$ Hz, 25 kV a.c. 50 Hz.
Builder-Mechanical Parts: BN.
Builder-Electrical Parts: ACEC.
Traction Motors: 4 x ES541 frame mounted.
One Hour Rating: 2780 kW.   **Weight**: 82.6 tonnes.
Maximum Tractive Effort: 196 kN.   **Length over Buffers**: 16.65 m.
Driving Wheel Dia.: 1250 mm.   **Max. Speed**: 160 km/h.

Electro-pneumatic braking.

Originally numbered 160.001–004/021–024.

1601	M	FSD	1603	FSD	1605	FSD	1607	FSD
1602	M	FSD	1604	FSD	1606	FSD	1608	FSD

CLASS 20 Co-Co

These thyristor controlled locos are the most powerful on SNCB and have had a chequered career with varying defects over the years which still give problems. The main use is on the Oostende–Brussels–Luxembourg artery (passenger) as well as Stockem–Antwerpen (freight).

Built: 1975–77.
Builder-Mechanical Parts: BN.
Builder-Electrical Parts: ACEC.
Traction Motors: 6 x LE772G frame mounted.
One Hour Rating: 5150 kW.
Maximum Tractive Effort: 314 kN.
Driving Wheel Dia.: 1250 mm.

Weight: 110 tonnes.
Length over Buffers: 19.50 m.
Max. Speed: 160 km/h.

Electro-pneumatic braking. Separately excited rheostatic braking.

2001	MKM	2007	MKM	2013	MKM	2019	MKM
2002	MKM	2008	MKM	2014	MKM	2021	MKM
2003	MKM	2009	MKM	2015	MKM	2022	MKM
2004	MKM	2010	MKM	2016	MKM	2023	MKM
2005	MKM	2011	MKM	2017	MKM	2024	MKM
2006	MKM	2012	MKM	2018	MKM	2025	MKM

CLASS 21 Bo-Bo

These are similar to class 27 but lower powered. Used on push-pull trains with M4 or M5 stock and freights. 2130 was converted to prototype dual-voltage (3000 V d.c./25 kV a.c.) loco 1901 as a development stage for Class 13. It has now been converted back to standard.

Built: 1984–1987.
Builder-Mechanical Parts: BN.
Builder-Electrical Parts: ACEC.
Traction Motors: 4 x LE622S frame mounted.
One Hour Rating: 3310 kW.
Maximum Tractive Effort: 234 kN.
Driving Wheel Dia.: 1250 mm.

Weight: 84 tonnes.
Length over Buffers: 18.65 m.
Max. Speed: 160 km/h.

Rheostatic braking.
Converted at Salzinnes to asynchronous-motored dual-voltage loco 1901.

2101	FSD	2116	FSD	2131	FSD	2146	FSD
2102	FSD	2117	FSD	2132	FSD	2147	FSD
2103	FSD	2118	FSD	2133	FSD	2148	FSD
2104	FSD	2119	FSD	2134	FSD	2149	FSD
2105	FSD	2120	FSD	2135	FSD	2150	FSD
2106	FSD	2121	FSD	2136	FSD	2151	FNDM
2107	FSD	2122	FSD	2137	FSD	2152	FNDM
2108	FSD	2123	FSD	2138	FSD	2153	FNDM
2109	FSD	2124	FSD	2139	FSD	2154	FNDM
2110	FSD	2125	FSD	2140	FSD	2155	FNDM
2111	FSD	2126	FSD	2141	FSD	2156	FNDM
2112	FSD	2127	FSD	2142	FSD	2157	FNDM
2113	FSD	2128	FSD	2143	FSD	2158	FNDM
2114	FSD	2129	FSD	2144	FSD	2159	FNDM
2115	FSD	2130	FSD	2145	FSD	2160	FNDM

CLASS 22 Bo-Bo

A general purpose locomotive found all over the network. 2239–2250 were originally dual voltage (1500/3000 V d.c.) but are now standard with the first batch. 2249/50 are used for banking at Liège Guillemins.

Built: 1953–54.

Builder-Mechanical Parts: Niv.
Builder-Electrical Parts: SEMG/ACEC.
Traction Motors: 4 x CF729 axle-hung.
One Hour Rating: 1880 kW.
Maximum Tractive Effort: 196 kN.
Driving Wheel Dia.: 1262 mm.

Weight: 87 tonnes.
Length over Buffers: 18.00 m.
Max. Speed: 130 km/h.

Originally numbered 122.001–038/201/212.

2201	FGH	2214	FGH	2227	FGH	2239	FGH
2202	FGH	2215	FGH	2228	FGH	2240	FGH
2203	FGH	2216	FGH	2229	FGH	2241	FGH
2204	FGH	2217	FGH	2230	FGH	2242	FGH
2205	FGH	2218	FGH	2231	FGH	2243	FGH
2206	FGH	2220	FGH	2232	FGH	2244	FGH
2207	FGH	2221	FGH	2233	FGH	2245	FGH
2208	FGH	2222	FGH	2234	FGH	2246	FGH
2209	FGH	2223	FGH	2235	FGH	2247	FGH
2210	FGH	2224	FGH	2236	FGH	2248	FGH
2211	FGH	2225	FGH	2237	FGH	2249	NK
2212	FGH	2226	FGH	2238	FGH	2250	NK
2213	FGH						

CLASS 23   Bo-Bo

Another mixed traffic loco at work all over the system mainly on freight. Can work in multiple with others of the same class and Class 26.

Built: 1955–57.
Builder-Mechanical Parts: BN.
Builder-Electrical Parts: ACEC/SEMG.
Traction Motors: 4 x CF729 axle-hung.
One Hour Rating: 1880 kW.
Maximum Tractive Effort: 196 kN.
Driving Wheel Dia.: 1262 mm.

Weight: 92 tonnes.
Length over Buffers: 18.00 m.
Max. Speed: 130 km/h.

Regenerative braking.

Originally numbered 123.001–083.

2383 was fitted with special equipment for banking at Liège. It was renumbered 124.001 and then 2401 before becoming 2383.
§ Has side portholes on bottom of bodyside and ventilation grilles as on class 27.

2301	FNDM	2323	FKR	2344	FKR	2364	FSD
2302 §	FNDM	2324	FKR	2345	FKR	2365	FSD
2303	FNDM	2325	FKR	2346	FKR	2366	FSD
2304	FNDM	2326	FKR	2347	FKR	2367	FSD
2305	FNDM	2327	FKR	2348	FKR	2368	FSD
2306	FNDM	2328	FKR	2349	FKR	2369	FSD
2308	FNDM	2329	FKR	2350	FKR	2370	FSD
2309	FNDM	2330	FKR	2351	FSD	2371	FSD
2310	FNDM	2331	FKR	2352	FSD	2372	FSD
2311	FNDM	2332	FKR	2353	FSD	2373	FSD
2312	FNDM	2333	FKR	2354	FSD	2374	FSD
2313	FNDM	2334	FKR	2355	FSD	2375	FSD
2314	FNDM	2335	FKR	2356	FSD	2376	FSD
2315	FNDM	2336	FKR	2357	FSD	2377	FSD
2316	FNDM	2337	FKR	2358	FSD	2378	FSD
2317	FNDM	2338	FKR	2359	FSD	2379	FSD
2318	FNDM	2339	FKR	2360	FSD	2380	FSD
2319	FNDM	2340	FKR	2361	FSD	2381	FSD
2320	FNDM	2341	FKR	2362	FSD	2382	FSD
2321	FKR	2342	FKR	2363	FSD	2383	FSD
2322	FKR	2343	FKR				

CLASS 25 Bo-Bo

This class are push-pull fitted for use on trains around Antwerpen using M2 stock. 2504 was rebuilt from 2557 (2521) in 1979.

Built: 1960–61.
Builder-Mechanical Parts: BN.
Builder-Electrical Parts: ACEC/SEM.
Traction Motors: 4 x CF729 axle-hung.
One Hour Rating: 1880 kW.
Maximum Tractive Effort: 196 kN.
Driving Wheel Dia.: 1262 mm.
Weight: 84 tonnes.
Length over Buffers: 18.00 m.
Max. Speed: 130 km/h.

Originally numbered 125.001–014.

2501	FNDM	2505	FNDM	2509	FNDM	2512	FNDM
2502	FNDM	2506	FNDM	2510	FNDM	2513	FNDM
2503	FNDM	2507	FNDM	2511	FNDM	2514	FNDM
2504	FNDM	2508	FNDM				

CLASS 25.5 Bo-Bo

Formerly numbered 2515–22, these locos were modified in 1973/4 to dual voltage for working the push & pull Brussels–Amsterdam service for which they received an additional headlamp and a special dark blue livery. Note that only one pantograph is fitted. These locos have been replaced on these duties by Class 11. They are not compatible with the new Benelux push-pull stock. They are used on freights between Antwerpen, Muizen and Leuven to Kijfhoek yard, also between Maastricht and Sittard.

Built: 1960–61.
Systems: 1500/3000 V d.c.
Builder-Mechanical Parts: BN.
Builder-Electrical Parts: ACEC/SEM.
Traction Motors: 4 x CF729 axle-hung.
One Hour Rating: 1880 kW.
Maximum Tractive Effort: 196 kN.
Driving Wheel Dia.: 1262 mm.
Weight: 85 tonnes.
Length over Buffers: 18.00 m.
Max. Speed: 130 km/h.
Class-Specific Livery: S Old Benelux push-pull livery. dark blue with a yellow stripe.

Originally numbered 125.015–016, 140.001–006 (later 125.101–106).
Note: After an accident in 1979, 2557 and 2504 changed identities.

2551	(2515)	S	FNDM	2554	(2518)	S	FNDM	2557	(2521)	S	FNDM
2552	(2516)	S	FNDM	2555	(2519)	S	FNDM	2558	(2522)	S	FNDM
2553	(2517)	S	FNDM	2556	(2520)	S	FNDM				

CLASS 26 B-B

These locos feature monomotor bogies by Schneider and have two gear ratios giving maximum speeds of 100/130 km/h. Seen all over Belgium, the class is fitted for multiple working with other members of the class and with Class 23 for heavy freights.

Built: 1964–71.
Builder-Mechanical Parts: BN.
Builder-Electrical Parts: ACEC.
Traction Motors: 2 x 2ES508 frame mounted.
One Hour Rating: 2580 kW.
Maximum Tractive Effort: 235 kN.
Driving Wheel Dia.: 1150 mm.
Weight: 83 tonnes.
Length over Buffers: 17.25 m.
Max. Speed: 130 km/h.

Originally numbered 126.001–005, 126.101–130.

2601	LNC	2607	LNC	2613	LNC	2620	LNC
2602	LNC	2608	LNC	2614	LNC	2621	LNC
2603	LNC	2609	LNC	2615	LNC	2622	LNC
2604	LNC	2610	LNC	2617	LNC	2623	LNC
2605	LNC	2611	LNC	2618	LNC	2624	LNC
2606	LNC	2612	LNC	2619	LNC	2625	LNC

2626	LNC	2629	LNC	2632	LNC	2634	LNC
2627	LNC	2630	LNC	2633	LNC	2635	LNC
2628	LNC	2631	LNC				

CLASS 27   Bo-Bo

Developed after experience with Class 20, these were the first of the 1980s generation of electric locomotives and heralded a new era, being more powerful than their predecessors. Chopper control. Flexicoil suspension. They are used throughout the network on both passenger and freight work.

Built: 1981–1984.
Builder-Mechanical Parts: BN.
Builder-Electrical Parts: ACEC.
Traction Motors: 4 x LE921S frame mounted.
One Hour Rating: 4380 kW.   **Weight**: 85 tonnes.
Maximum Tractive Effort: 234 kN.   **Length over Buffers**: 18.65 m.
Driving Wheel Dia.: 1250 mm.   **Max. Speed**: 160 km/h.

Electro-pneumatic braking. Rheostatic braking.

2701	NK	2716	NK	2731	NK	2746	NK
2702	NK	2717	NK	2732	NK	2747	NK
2703	NK	2718	NK	2733	NK	2748	NK
2704	NK	2719	NK	2734	NK	2749	NK
2705	NK	2720	NK	2735	NK	2750	NK
2706	NK	2721	NK	2736	NK	2751	NK
2707	NK	2722	NK	2737	NK	2752	NK
2708	NK	2723	NK	2738	NK	2753	NK
2709	NK	2724	NK	2739	NK	2754	NK
2710	NK	2725	NK	2740	NK	2755	NK
2711	NK	2726	NK	2741	NK	2756	NK
2712	NK	2727	NK	2742	NK	2757	NK
2713	NK	2728	NK	2743	NK	2758	NK
2714	NK	2729	NK	2744	NK	2759	NK
2715	NK	2730	NK	2745	NK	2760	NK

1.3. DIESEL MULTIPLE UNITS
CLASS 41   2-CAR UNITS

These are new units under construction and will bring new standards of comfort to Belgian branch line services as they have air conditioning, good seating, information displays etc. besides replacing existing DMUs of Classes 44 & 45 they will also replace diesel locomotive-operated push-pull trains making many Class 62 locos + M2 stock surplus. They will be used on IR trains Antwerpen–Neerpelt; L trains Libramont–Virton/Dinant, Charleroi–Couvin, Gent–Eeklo. Gent–Ronse, Gent–Grammont and P trains Aalst–Burst.

AB–B (DMC–DMS).

Built: 2000–2002.
Builder: Alstom Spain.
Wheel Arrangement: 2-B + B-2.
Engine: One of 485 kW per car.
Transmission: Hydraulic. Voith.
Length over Couplers: 24.80 + 24.80 m.　　**Weight:** 93 tonnes.
Max. Speed: 120 km/h.　　**Accommodation:** 12/138 2T.

4101	W	4121	W	4141	W	4161	W
4102	W	4122	W	4142	W	4162	W
4103	W	4123	W	4143	W	4163	W
4104	W	4124	W	4144	W	4164	W
4105	W	4125	W	4145	W	4165	W
4106	W	4126	W	4146	W	4166	W
4107	W	4127	W	4147	W	4167	W
4108	W	4128	W	4148	W	4168	W
4109	W	4129	W	4149	W	4169	W
4110	W	4130	W	4150	W	4170	W
4111	W	4131	W	4151	W	4171	W
4112	W	4132	W	4152	W	4172	W
4113	W	4133	W	4153	W	4173	W
4114	W	4134	W	4154	W	4174	W
4115	W	4135	W	4155	W	4175	W
4116	W	4136	W	4156	W	4176	W
4117	W	4137	W	4157	W	4177	W
4118	W	4138	W	4158	W	4178	W
4119	W	4139	W	4159	W	4179	W
4120	W	4140	W	4160	W	4180	W

CLASS 44   SINGLE UNITS

Used on branch lines. The FKR units work Aalst–Burst whilst the MKM units work the Virton–Libramont and Libramont–Dinant routes.

B (DMS).

Built: 1954.
Builder: Germain, rebuilt 1975–78 by CWFM.
Wheel Arrangement: B-2.
Engine: 2 x GM 6V71N of 118 kW each at 1800 r.p.m.
Transmission: Hydraulic. Voith.
Length over Couplers: 23.80 m.　　**Weight:** 54 tonnes.
Max. Speed: 100 km/h.　　**Accommodation:** –/93 1T.

Originally numbered 604.01–10.

4402	W	FKR	4404	W	MKM	4406	W	MKM	4408	W	MKM
4403	D	FKR	4405	W	FKR	4407	W	MKM	4410	D	MKM

CLASS 45   SINGLE UNITS

These units can be found on the Virton–Bertrix–Libramont and Dinant–Libramont routes.

B (DMS).

Built: 1954–55.
Builder: Germain, rebuilt 1974–78 by CWFM.
Wheel Arrangement: 1A–A1. **Engine:** 2 x GM 6V71N of 118 kW each at 1800 r.p.m.
Transmission: Hydraulic. Voith.
Length over Couplers: 23.80 m.   **Weight:** 54 tonnes.
Max. Speed: 100 km/h.   **Accommodation:** –/93 1T.

Originally numbered 605.01–10.

| 4501 | **D** | MKM | 4504 | **D** | MKM | 4506 | **W** | MKM | 4509 | **D** | MKM |
| 4502 | **D** | MKM | 4505 | **W** | MKM | 4508 | **D** | MKM | 4510 | **D** | MKM |

CLASS 49   SINGLE UNIT

The last survivor of a class that once totalled 50. It is used for crew training trips from Antwerpen.

B (DMS).

Built: 1942.
Builder: Germain.
Wheel Arrangement: 1A–A1.
Engine: Brossel 8D120B of 113 kW.
Transmission: Mechanical.
Length over Couplers: 15.98 m.   **Weight:** 22.7 tonnes.
Max. Speed: 66 km/h.   **Accommodation:** –/77 1T.

Originally numbered 553.12

4903 **D**   FNDM(D) |

▲ Class 45 single units DMU No. 4510 in red and yellow livery at Kinkempois depot on 25/09/1999.
Adrian Norton

1.4. MAIN LINE DIESEL LOCOMOTIVES

Note: All diesel locomotives are in yellow and green livery except where stated otherwise.

CLASS 51   Co-Co

This class of mixed traffic locos is found all over the network except in the Liège and Luxembourg areas where Class 55 is used. They are mostly used on freights. Many of the class at Antwerpen stand spare available for traffic from the docks on an as required basis. This traffic finds them working, often in pairs, from Antwerpen to Montzen/Aachen West and Liège. All are scheduled to be withdrawn by 2005.

Built: 1961–63.
Builder-Mech. Parts: Cockerill.
Builder-Elec. Parts: ACEC/SEM.
Engine: Cockerill/Baldwin 10-608A of 1435 kW at 650 rpm.
Transmission: Electric. Six axle-hung traction motors.
Train Heating: None. (s Steam. Vapor OK4616). (NB None-boilered locos have a dot next to the number).
Weight: 117 tonnes (5101–5152) 113.2 tonnes (5154–93).
Maximum Tractive Effort: 272 kN.   **Length over Buffers:** 20.16 m.
Driving Wheel Dia.: 1010 mm.   **Max. Speed:** 120 km/h.

Multiple working fitted.

Originally numbered 200.001–093.

5101		FHS	5121	LNC	5143	FHS	5168	s FNDM
5102		FNDM	5122	FHS	5145	FHS	5170	FNDM
5103	s	FHS	5123	LNC	5146	LNC	5172	FNDM
5104		LNC	5125	FNDM	5147	LNC	5173	FNDM
5105		FHS	5127	FHS	5148	LNC	5174	FNDM
5107	s	FKR	5128	FKR	5149	s LNC	5175	FNDM
5108	s	FKR	5129	FHS	5150	s LNC	5177	FNDM
5109	s	FKR	5130	FNDM	5152	FHS	5178	FNDM
5110		FNDM	5131	LNC	5154	FNDM	5179	FHS
5111	s	FKR	5132	FKR	5156	s FNDM	5180	FNDM
5112		FKR	5133	FNDM	5157	FNDM	5181	FNDM
5114		FHS	5134	FNDM	5158	FNDM	5182	FNDM
5115		FNDM	5135	LNC	5162	FNDM	5183	FHS
5116		FKR	5136	FHS	5164	FNDM	5185	FHS
5117		LNC	5138	FHS	5166	FNDM	5186	FNDM
5118	s	FKR	5141	FHS	5167	FNDM	5193	FHS
5120		LNC	5142	FHS				

CLASS 52   Co-Co

Classes 52, 53 and 54 are part of a large European family of locomotives. The design originated as Nohab/GM and similar locomotives are found in Denmark (Classes MX and MY), Hungary (Class M61) and Norway (Class Di3). Class 52 can be found mainly on freight between Namur and Athus via Virton, but also on a return Bertrix–Namur passenger train Monday–Friday. The class can also be found on summer tourist trains in the Ardennes region and have also been seen working freights along the Liège–Namur–Charleroi–La Louvière route. After many complaints from crews new cabs were fitted to all locos which substantially altered their appearance. Since the restructuring of passenger services several locos which lost their boilers some time ago were reclassified to Class 53. All three classes are soon to be replaced by electric locomotives on the Namur–Athus route after which most will be surplus, Some may be retained for works trains on new high speed routes but are expected to be withdrawn by 2005.

Built: 1955.
Builder-Mech. Parts: AFB.
Builder-Elec. Parts: GM.
Engine: GM 16-567C of 1265 kW at 835 rpm.
Transmission: Electric. Six axle-hung Smit D19 traction motors.
Train Heating: None (s Steam. Vapor OK4616).
Weight: 108 tonnes.

Maximum Tractive Effort: 245 kN.   **Length over Buffers**: 18.85 m.
Driving Wheel Dia.: 1010 mm.   **Max. Speed**: 120 km/h.

Multiple working fitted. Rheostatic braking.
The original 5201–13 were originally numbered 202.001–013.

5201	s	MKM	5211		MKM	5215	(5302)	MKM
5205	s	MKM	5212	s	MKM	5216	(5317)	MKM
5209		MKM	5214	(5307)	MKM	5217	(5318)	MKM

CLASS 53   Co-Co

These are similar to Class 52 but have no train heating. Similar freight use to Class 52. Several class 52s lost their boilers and were renumbered to Class 53. All are fitted with new cabs.

Built: 1955.
Builder-Mech. Parts: AFB.
Builder-Elec. Parts: GM.
Engine: GM 16-567C of 1265 kW at 835 rpm.
Transmission: Electric. Six axle-hung Smit D19 traction motors.
Train Heating: None.   **Weight**: 106.6 tonnes.
Maximum Tractive Effort: 245 kN.   **Length over Buffers**: 18.85 m.
Driving Wheel Dia.: 1010 mm.   **Max. Speed**: 120 km/h.

Rheostatic braking. Multiple working fitted.
The original 5301–19 were originally numbered 203.001–019.

5301		MKM	5307	(5206)	MKM	5314		MKM
5302	(5203)	MKM	5308		MKM	5315		MKM
5303		MKM	5309		MKM	5316		MKM
5304		MKM	5311		MKM	5318	(5208)	MKM
5305		MKM	5312		MKM	5319		MKM
5306		MKM	5313		MKM	5320	(5210)	MKM

CLASS 54   Co-Co

Similar to Class 52, but no rheostatic braking and an additional headlight. More often used on passenger than Class 52.

Built: 1955–57.
Builder-Mech. Parts: AFB.
Builder-Elec. Parts: GM.
Engine: GM 16-567C of 1265 kW at 835 rpm.
Transmission: Electric. Six axle-hung traction motors.
Train Heating: None (s Steam. Vapor OK4616).
Weight: 108 tonnes.
Maximum Tractive Effort: 245 kN.   **Length over Buffers**: 18.85 m.
Driving Wheel Dia.: 1010 mm.   **Max. Speed**: 120 km/h.

Multiple working fitted.

Originally numbered 204.001–007.

5401	s	MKM	5403	s	MKM	5407		MKM

CLASS 55   Co-Co

Most of the class is based at Liège for freight use but a few locos there are fitted with e.t.h. for working the Liège–Luxembourg trains and are painted in blue & yellow livery instead of the standard yellow & green. This route is scheduled to be electrified during 2000 making these locomotives redundant. Locos at Schaarbeek are fitted with TVM430 cab signalling and adapter Couplers for TGV rescue work on the high speed lines and have TGV Couplers. They are outstationed at Ath. Their livery has an extra red band. These TVM-fitted locos are the only ones expected to survive beyond 2005.

Built: 1961–62.
Builder-Mech. Parts: BN.

Builder-Elec. Parts: ACEC/SEMG.
Engine: GM 16-567C of 1435 kW at 835 rpm.
Transmission: Electric. Six axle-hung ACEC D57 traction motors.
Train Heating: None (s Steam. Vapor OK4616, e Electric. ACEC 300 kW alternator).
Weight: 110 tonnes.
Maximum Tractive Effort: 272 kN.   **Length over Buffers**: 19.55 m.
Driving Wheel Dia.: 1010 mm.   **Max. Speed**: 120 km/h.

Rheostatic braking. Multiple working fitted.
t Fitted with TVM 430 cab signalling.

Originally numbered 205.001–042.

5501	t	FSR	5511	t	FSR	5524		NK	5533		NK
5502		NK	5512	t	FSR	5525		NK	5534		NK
5503		NK	5513	s	NK	5526	s	NK	5535		NK
5504		NK	5514	t	FSR	5527		NK	5536	s	NK
5505	Y e	NK	5515	Y e	NK	5528	s	NK	5537		NK
5506	t	FSR	5517		NK	5529	Y e	NK	5538		NK
5507		NK	5518	s	NK	5530		NK	5539		NK
5508	s	NK	5519	Y e	NK	5531	Y e	NK	5540	Y e	NK
5509	t	FSR	5521		NK	5532		NK	5541	s	NK
5510	Y e	NK	5523	Y e	NK						

CLASS 59   Bo-Bo

This class has been lucky! Most were already withdrawn when the need for construction trains on the French high speed line from Paris to Lille gave them a reprieve. This work has been finished but the locomotives have been saved again and now they are moving over to Kinkempois depot for use on construction trains on the Brussels–Aachen route. Their main operating base at the time of writing is at Voroux-Goreux.

Built: 1954–55.
Builder-Mech. Parts: Cockerill/BM/Niv.
Builder-Elec. Parts: ACEC.
Engine: Cockerill/Baldwin 608A of 1280 kW at 625 rpm.
Transmission: Electric. Four axle-hung traction motors.
Train Heating: None.   **Weight**: 84 tonnes.
Maximum Tractive Effort: 196 kN.   **Length over Buffers**: 16.18 m.
Driving Wheel Dia.: 1118 mm.   **Max. Speed**: 120 km/h.

Originally numbered 201.005–050.

5905	G	NK	5926		NK	5941		NK	5947		NK
5916		NK	5936		NK	5946	G	NK	5950		NK
5917		NK	5939		NK						

CLASS 62   Bo-Bo

A mixed traffic locomotive whose use on passenger trains is likely to cease within two to three years as the new Class 41 DMUs arrive. Some locomotives have been transferred to Infrastructure department use and these could linger in traffic a little longer. Five locos have been sold to private operator ACTS in the Netherlands. Note that "Infra" locomotives are maintained by the depots concerned but normally stable in the engineers' own yards and sidings or at construction sites.

Built: 1961–66.
Builder-Mech. Parts: BN.
Builder-Elec. Parts: ACEC.
Engine: GM 12-567C of 1050 kW at 835 rpm.
Transmission: Electric. Four ACEC DN41.1 axle-hung traction motors.
Train Heating: None (s Steam. Vapor OK4616).
Weight: 78.6 tonnes.
Maximum Tractive Effort: 212 kN.   **Length over Buffers**: 16.79 m.
Driving Wheel Dia.: 1010 mm.   **Max. Speed**: 120 km/h.
Multiple working fitted.

Originally numbered 212.101–231.

6201		FKR	6234	s	LNC	6264	s	FKR	6298	s	FHS
6202	s	FKR	6235	s	FKR	6266		LNC(D)	6299	s	FHS
6203		FKR(D)	6236	s	FKR	6267	s	FHS	6301		FKR
6204	s	FKR	6237	s	FKR	6268	s	FHS	6302	G	NK
6207	s	FHS	6238	s	FHS	6269	G	NK	6303		FKR(D)
6210		NK	6240		FHS	6271	s	LNC	6304	s	FKR
6211		NK	6241		NK(D)	6273		LNC(D)	6305		NK(D)
6212	s	FKR	6242		LNC(D)	6274		NK	6306		FKR
6213	s	LNC	6243		LNC	6275		LNC(D)	6307	s	FKR
6214	s	LNC	6244	G	FKR	6277	s	LNC	6309		NK(D)
6215		NK(D)	6245	s	FHS	6278	s	LNC	6311	s	FKR
6216		FKR	6246	s	FHS	6281	s	FHS	6312		FHS(D)
6217	s	LNC	6247	s	FKR	6282	s	LNC	6313	s	FKR
6218	s	LNC	6248	s	FKR	6283		FHS	6314	G	LNC(D)
6219	G s	FKR	6249	s	FKR	6284	G s	LNC	6315	s	FKR
6220	s	FKR	6250		FHS	6285	s	LNC	6316		LNC(D)
6221	s	LNC	6251	s	FHS	6286		LNC(D)	6317		FHS(D)
6222	s	FKR	6252		FKR(D)	6287		NK(D)	6319		NK
6223		FHS	6253	s	FHS	6288	s	LNC	6320		LNC(D)
6224	s	LNC	6254	G s	LNC	6289	G	NK(D)	6322		FKR
6225	s	FKR	6255	s	FHS	6291	s	FHS	6323	G	NK
6227		NK	6256	s	FKR	6292	s	FKR	6324		NK
6228	s	FKR	6257		NK(D)	6293		NK	6326		FHS(D)
6229	s	FKR	6260	s	NK	6294	s	FHS	6328		NK
6230		FKR	6261	s	FHS	6295	s	FHS	6329		NK(D)
6231		FHS	6262		LNC	6296	s	FHS	6330		FHS(D)
6233	s	FKR	6263	G	NK	6297	s	FHS	6331		NK

▲ Vintage Belgian diesels 5939 + 5947 at work at the Ste Henriette LGV construction base in France in January 1992. **David Haydock**

▲ Class 84 No. 8470 at Antwerpen Dam depot on 26/09/1999.　　　**Adrian Norton**

▼ Class 91 No. 9108 at Scharbeek on 25/09/1996.　　　**Guy Clarke**

1.5. DIESEL SHUNTING LOCOMOTIVES

Note: Many locomotives carry a name on the cabside. This is the radio call sign for the locomotive. Names are duplicated within the class but not at individual depots. A locomotive being transferred thus may get a new name if this is already in use at its new depot. The list of "named" locomotives is not complete and in some cases actual observations have shown that the depot records are not correct!

CLASS 70   Bo-Bo
This class is used on trip freights around Antwerpen.

Built: 1954.
Builder-Mech. Parts: BM.
Builder-Elec. Parts: ACEC.
Engine: ABC 6DXC of 550 kW at 750 r.p.m.(7001/2). ABC 8DUS of 515 kW at 650 r.p.m. (7003/5/6). Cockerill CO240 6-cylinder of 570 kW (7004).
Transmission: Electric. Four axle-hung traction motors.
Train Heating: None.   **Weight:** 85 tonnes.
Maximum Tractive Effort: 196 kN.   **Length over Buffers:** 12.15 m.
Driving Wheel Dia.: 1070 mm.   **Max. Speed:** 50 km/h.

Originally numbered 270.001–6.

7001	FNDM	ARTEMIS	7004	FNDM	HERMES
7002	FNDM	ATHENA	7005	FNDM	HERCULES
7003	FNDM	ATLAS			

CLASS 71   B-B
Rebuilt from 6602–03 in 1980 at FAZ. Used for hump shunting duties in the departure yard at Antwerpen Noord, plus local trips. Fitted with automatic couplers.

Built: 1962–63.
Builder: ABR.
Engine: ABC 6DXC 100-750A of 662 kW at 750 r.p.m.
Transmission: Hydraulic. Voith L217.
Train Heating: None.   **Weight:** 74 tonnes.
Maximum Tractive Effort: 197 kN.   **Length over Buffers:** 13.44 m.
Driving Wheel Dia.: 1010 mm.   **Max. Speed:** 50 km/h shunting/80 km/h main line.

Originally numbered 222.002–3.

| 7102 | FNDM | COLIBRI | 7103 | FNDM | CONDOR |

CLASS 73   C
General purpose shunters, sometimes used on trip freights.

Built: 1965–67 7301–35; 1973–74 7336–75; 1976–77 7376–95.
Builder: BN (ABR 7326–7335).
Engine: Cockerill 6TH695SA (7301–25), 6T240CO (7326–95) of 550 kW at 950 r.p.m.
Transmission: Hydraulic. Voith L217u.
Train Heating: None.   **Weight:** 56 tonnes.
Maximum Tractive Effort: 211 kN.   **Length over Buffers:** 11.17 m (7301–35),
                                                                  11.40 m (7336–95).
Driving Wheel Dia.: 1262 mm.   **Max. Speed:** 30 km/h shunting/60 km/h main line.

a Auto-couplers for shunting.
m Multiple working fitted for use in hump yards.

7301–35 were originally numbered 273.001–035.

7301	LNC	Alabama	7306	LNC	Artémis
7302	LNC	Albatros	7307	LNC	Etna
7303	LNC	Albi	7308	LNC	
7304	LNC	Alpha	7309	LNC	Atlanta
7305	LNC	Anapurna	7310	LNC	Atlas

7311		LNC	Arizona	7354		FKR	JIVARO
7312		LNC	Arkansas	7355		FKR	FLORAC
7313		LNC	Bakou	7356		FKR	NEVADA
7314		LNC	Bameko	7357	a	FHS	CARGO
7315		LNC	Bangkok	7358		FKR	MAZURKA
7316		LNC		7359		FKR	ALABAMA
7317		LNC	Bilbao	7360		LNC	Erato
7318		LNC		7361		LNC	Etna
7319		LNC	Borneo	7362		FKR	MONACO
7320		LNC	Bravo	7363		FKR	VEGA
7321		LNC	Buffalo	7364		FKR	NEW YORK
7322		LNC		7365	a	FHS	ATLAS
7323		LNC		7366		FHS	BRAVO
7324		LNC	Capri	7367		FKR	BILBAO
7325		LNC	Cargo	7368		FKR	Hermes
7326	m	LNC	Chicago	7369		FKR	Hercule
7327	m	LNC	Cobra	7370		FHS	ALPHA
7328	m	LNC	Colibri	7371	a	FHS	CAPRI
7329	m	LNC	Colorado	7372		FHS	DELTA
7330	m	LNC	Columbia	7373	a	FHS	COBRA
7331	m	LNC	Condor	7374		FHS	NAPOLI
7332	m	LNC	Cordoba	7375	a	FHS	ETNA
7333	m	LNC	Cosmos	7376		FNDM	METEOOR
7334	m	LNC	Cuzco	7377		FNDM	MIMOSA
7335	m	LNC	Dakar	7378		FNDM	MISTRAL
7336		FHS	MEXICO	7379		FNDM	NIAGARA
7337		FKR	MALAGA	7380		FNDM	OMEGA
7338		MKM	ALBI	7381		NK	ATHOS
7339		MKM	BRAVO	7382		NK	KATAR
7340		MKM		7383		NK	ATLAS
7341		MKM		7384		NK	OMEGA
7342		MKM		7385		NK	OSAKA
7343		LNC	Dakota	7386		FNDM	ONTARIO
7344		LNC	Delta	7387		FNDM	PAPYRUS
7345		LNC	Albi	7388		FNDM	PIRANA
7346		LNC	Domino	7389		FNDM	RUBIS
7347		LNC	Echo	7390		FNDM	SAFFIER
7348		LNC	Edelweiss	7391		FNDM	EDELWEISS
7349		LNC		7392		FNDM	TANGO
7350		FKR	SAFFIER	7393		FNDM	KENIA
7351		FKR	ECHO	7394		FNDM	TRIPOLI
7352		FKR	MIMOSA	7395		FNDM	LIMA
7353		FKR	FOXTROT				

CLASS 74   C

Shunters used in pairs around Antwerpen docks.

Built: 1977.
Builder: BN/CFC.
Engine: ABC 6DXS of 550 kW at 750 r.p.m.
Transmission: Hydraulic. Voith L217u.
Train Heating: None.   **Weight:** 59 tonnes.
Maximum Tractive Effort: 196 kN.   **Length over Buffers:** 11.40 m.
Driving Wheel Dia.: 1262 mm.   **Max. Speed:** 30 km/h shunting/60 km/h main line.

Multiple working within class and with Class 82.

7401	FNDM	POLKA	7406	FNDM	SIRIUS
7402	FNDM	MARS	7407	FNDM	SALAMBO
7403	FNDM	TANGO	7408	FNDM	URANUS
7404	FNDM	OSIRIS	7409	FNDM	KIMONO
7405	FNDM	MAZURKA	7410	FNDM	MIKADO

CLASS 75 B-B

Originally main-line locos of class 65, these were downgraded to shunters in 1982–83 when their steam boilers and water tanks were removed. Similar in outline to Class 62. They are now used for heavy trip working around Antwerpen Docks.

Built: 1965.
Builder: BN.
Engine: GM 12-567D-1 of 1075 kW at 835 r.p.m.
Transmission: Hydraulic. Voith L216 rsb.
Train Heating: None.
Maximum Tractive Effort: 191 kN.
Driving Wheel Dia.: 1118 mm.
Weight: 79 tonnes.
Length over Buffers: 16.79 m.
Max. Speed: 82 km/h shunting/120 km/h main line.

Originally numbered 203.001–006 then 6501–6.

7501	FNDM	ALABAMA	7504	FNDM	COLORADO
7502	FNDM	ARIZONA	7505	FNDM	DAKOTA
7503	FNDM	ARKANSAS	7506	FNDM	KANSAS

CLASS 76 Bo-Bo

When Belgian railways planned the building of their high speed line from the French frontier to Brussels it found that it would not have enough locomotives for the ballast trains so they bought second hand NS Class 2200s. The high speed line has been completed for some time now, but SNCB/NMBS are finding these locos very useful on trip work around the docks at Antwerpen. The locomotives may well see further use on ballast trains as major work is now underway on the high speed links from Brussels to Aachen and Rotterdam. They work from Antwerpen and other places as required. They receive heavy repairs at NedTrain's Tilburg Works.

Built: 1955–58.
Builder: Schneider (7603–5/13/24/5), Allan (others).
Engine: Stork Schneider Superior 40C-Lx-8 of 670 kW at 1100 r.p.m.
Transmission: Electric. Four Heemaf TM98 traction motors.
Train Heating: None.
Maximum Tractive Effort: 181 kN.
Driving Wheel Dia.: 950 mm.
Weight: 72 tonnes.
Length over Buffers: 14.10 m.
Max. Speed: 100 km/h.
Class-Specific Livery: S NS grey and yellow.
Non-Standard Livery: N NS brown.

7601	(2277)	S	FSR	7610	(2266)	S	FSR	7618	(2205)	S	FSR
7602	(2259)	S	FSR	7611	(2244)	S	FSR	7619	(2213)	S	FSR
7603	(2327)	S	FSR	7612	(2247)	S	FSR	7620	(2214)	S	FSR
7604	(2309)	S	FSR	7613	(2318)	S	FSR	7621	(2274)	S	FSR
7605	(2308)	S	FSR	7614	(2285)	S	FSR	7622	(2238)	S	FSR
7606	(2305)	S	FSR	7615	(2283)	S	FSR	7623	(2258)	S	FSR
7607	(2292)	S	FSR	7616	(2261)	S	FSR	7624	(2362)	S	FSR
7608	(2275)	N	FSR	7617	(2219)		FSR	7625	(2306)	S	FSR
7609	(2273)	S	FSR								

CLASS 77 B-B

Ordered in June 1997, these locomotives are for freight train and shunting use. They will allow many of the older main-line and shunting locomotives to be withdrawn. The class is based on the Vossloh (former Siemens/MaK) type G1200 but adapted for Belgian conditions. It is understood that final assembly will be done at Bombardier Eurorail in Brugge. Ten of the locos will have BSI couplers for working with EMUs at Gent, Zeebrugge and Oostende. Eighteen will be fitted with radio controls for working at Antwerpen Noord (8) and Stockem, Arlon and Athus (10) and twenty will have Dutch ATB for working onto the NS. The rest will be general purpose locomotives based at NK and FNDM.

Built: 1999 onwards.
Builders: Vossloh/Bombardier.
Engine: ABC type 60ZC-1000 of 1150 kW at 1000 r.p.m.
Transmission: Hydraulic. Voith L4r4zseU2a.
Train Heating: None.
Weight: 90 tonnes.

Maximum Tractive Effort: 232/291 kN.   **Length over Buffers**: 15.50 m.
Driving Wheel Dia.: 1000 mm.   **Max. Speed**: 100/60 km/h.
Multiple Working: Up to three locos may work in multiple.
Class Specific Livery: S White with yellow solebars, handrails and ends, blue stripe at bottom of cab and narrow red stripe on bonnets.

7701	S	FNDM	ALIBI	7746	S
7702	S	FNDM	ALPHA	7747	S
7703	S	FNDM	BAKOE	7748	S
7704	S	FNDM	BAMAKO	7749	S
7705	S	FNDM	BANGKOK	7750	S
7706	S	FNDM	BARRACUDA	7751	S
7707	S	FNDM	BILBAO	7752	S
7708	S	FNDM	BORNEO	7753	S
7709	S		BRAVO	7754	S
7710	S		BUFFALO	7755	S
7711	S		CALCUTTA	7756	S
7712	S		CALYPSO	7757	S
7713	S		CAPRI	7758	S
7714	S		CARGO	7759	S
7715	S		CHICAGO	7760	S
7716	S		COBRA	7761	S
7717	S		COLUMBIA	7762	S
7718	S		CORDOBA	7763	S
7719	S		DAKAR	7764	S
7720	S		DELTA	7765	S
7721	S		DIAMANT	7766	S
7722	S		DOMINO	7767	S
7723	S		ECHO	7768	S
7724	S		EDELWEISS	7769	S
7725	S		EL PASO	7770	S
7726	S		FLORAC	7771	S
7727	S		GRANADA	7772	S
7728	S		JAVA	7773	S
7729	S			7774	S
7730	S			7775	S
7731	S			7776	S
7732	S			7777	S
7733	S			7778	S
7734	S			7779	S
7735	S			7780	S
7736	S			7781	S
7737	S			7782	S
7738	S			7783	S
7739	S			7784	S
7740	S			7785	S
7741	S			7786	S
7742	S			7787	S
7743	S			7788	S
7744	S			7789	S
7745	S			7790	S

CLASS 80   C

General purpose shunter used around Brussels. A version of the DB Class 360 (V60) built under licence. 8043–8069 have much larger fuel tanks than 8001–42. Many withdrawn locos have been sold abroad, particularly to Italian track maintenance firms. More withdrawals are likely as Class 77s enter service.

Built: 1960–1963.
Builder: BN (ABR 8025–40).
Engine: Maybach GTO6A of 480 kW at 1400 r.p.m.
Transmission: Hydraulic. Voith L37z Ub.
Train Heating: None.   **Weight**: 52 tonnes.
Maximum Tractive Effort: 173 kN.   **Length over Buffers**: 10.360 m.

Driving Wheel Dia.: 1262 mm.   **Max. Speed**: 30 km/h shunting/60 km/h main line.

* Compressed air dryer for shunting Eurostar rakes at Forest depot.
Originally numbered 260.001–069.

8001	*	FSR	ATLANTA	8047	FSR	ATLAS
8002	*	FSR		8049	FSR	
8006		FSR	ARIZONA	8050	FSR	
8009		FSR		8051	FSR	BAKOU
8011		FSR		8052	FSR	
8012		FSR		8053	FSR	
8020	*	FSR		8055	FSR	
8025		FSR		8058	FSR	
8031		FSR		8059	FSR	
8032	*	FSR		8061	FSR	BRAVO
8033	*	FSR		8062	FSR	
8034		FSR		8064	FSR	
8035		FSR		8065	FSR	
8036		FSR		8066	FSR	
8040		FSR		8067	FSR	
8045		FSR		8068	FSR	
8046		FSR		8069	FSR	

CLASS 82   C

General purpose shunters, sometimes used for trip workings. FNDM multiple fitted locos are used in pairs for trips around Antwerpen Docks.

Built: 1965/6 8201–55; 1972/3 8256–75.
Builder: ABR (BN 8241–45/8256–75).
Engine: ABC 6DXS of 480 kW at 750 r.p.m.
Transmission: Hydraulic. Voith L217u.
Train Heating: None.   **Weight**: 57 (59 m, 56 s) tonnes.
Maximum Tractive Effort: 191 kN.   **Length over Buffers**: 11.170 (11.320 s) m.
Driving Wheel Dia.: 1262 mm.   **Max. Speed**: 60 km/h.

m Fitted for multiple working within class and with Class 74 around Antwerpen.
8275 was rebuilt in 1977 to a slave unit by the removal of the cab.

8201–55 were originally numbered 262.001–055.

8201	FKR	METEOOR	8227	NK	BOLERO
8202	FKR	MICHIGAN	8228	NK	DOMINO
8203	NK	TOLEDO	8229	NK	BUFFALO
8204	FKR	NEBRASKA	8230	NK	ALPHA
8205	NK	CAPRI	8231	NK	COLORADO
8206	FKR	MANITOBA	8232	FKR	BOLERO
8207	FKR	MISSOURI	8233	FKR	NIAGARA
8208	FKR	MIAMI	8234	NK	CONDOR
8209	FKR	ALPHA	8235	NK	PALMA
8210	FKR	ONTARIO	8236	FKR	URANUS
8211	FKR	NAPOLI	8237	NK	KASAI
8212	NK	HERMES	8238	NK	BORNEO
8213	NK	CARGO	8239	NK	DAKAR
8214	FKR	ATLANTA	8240	NK	DAKOTA
8215	NK	TIRANO	8241	FKR	MARS
8216	NK	COBRA	8242	FKR	ALBATROS
8217	NK	BAKOU	8243	FKR	MIRANDA
8218	NK	ALBI	8244	FKR	MIKADO
8219	NK	ATLANTA	8245	NK	DELTA
8220	NK	TÓPASE	8246	FKR	BORNEO
8221	NK	COLIBRI	8247	FKR	EL PASO
8222	NK		8248	NK	ETNA
8223	NK	BRAVO	8249	FKR	MONTANA
8224	NK	SIRIUS	8250	FKR	MEXICO
8225	NK	PEKIN	8251	FKR	ETNA
8226	NK	RUBIS	8252	NK	ERATO

8253	NK	LIMA		8265	m FNDM	NEW YORK
8254	NK	IRIS		8266	m FNDM	OSAKA
8255	NK	POLKA		8267	m FNDM	PALMA
8256	m FNDM	KATAR		8268	m FNDM	PEKING
8257	m FNDM	KENIA		8269	m FNDM	PORTO-RICO
8258	m FNDM	LIMA		8270	m FNDM	RIMINI
8259	m FNDM	MALAGA		8271	m FNDM	SUMATRA
8260	m FNDM	MEXICO		8272	m FNDM	TIRANA
8261	m FNDM	MONACO		8273	m FNDM	TOLEDO
8262	m FNDM	NAPOLI		8274	m FNDM	TORONTO
8263	m FNDM	NEBRASKA		8275	m FNDM	TRIPOLI
8264	m FNDM	NEVADA				

CLASS 84   C

General purpose shunters. 8461–70 were renumbered from 8526–8535 respectively. Withdrawals are likely to start again as Class 77s enter service.

Built: 1962–64 (8426–60); 1959/60 rebuilt 1968–79 (8461–70).
Builders: ABR (*BM).
Engine: ABC 6DUS (*6DXS) of 405 kW at 680 r.p.m.
Transmission: Hydraulic. Voith L37u (L37ub 8426–60).
Train Heating: None.
Weight: 55.8 (*57.3) tonnes.
Maximum Tractive Effort: 157 kN.   **Length over Buffers**: 10.650 (10.150*) m.
Driving Wheel Dia.: 1262 mm.   **Max. Speed**: 30 km/h shunting/50 km/h main line.

Originally numbered 250.004–025, 250.101–135, 252.026–035.

8426	FKR(D)	8440	FNDM(D)	8453	FNDM(D)	8463	* FNDM
8428	FNDM(D)	8441	FNDM(D)	8454	FNDM(D)	8464	* FNDM
8429	FKR(D)	8443	LNC(D)	8455	FNDM(D)	8465	* FNDM(D)
8431	FKR(D)	8444	NK(D)	8456	FNDM(D)	8466	* FNDM
8432	FKR(D)	8447	NK(D)	8457	FSR(D)	8467	* FNDM
8433	FNDM(D)	8448	NK(D)	8458	FSR(D)	8468	* FNDM
8434	FKR(D)	8450	LNC(D)	8460	FSR(D)	8469	* FNDM
8435	LNC(D)	8451	FNDM(D)	8461	* FNDM	8470	* FNDM
8437	FKR(D)	8452	FNDM(D)	8462	* FNDM		

CLASS 85   C

Used for general purpose shunting around Antwerpen, plus Essen, Muizen and Mechelen works. Now in the process of withdrawal as a result of the arrival of Class 77.

Built: 1956–57.
Builder: FUF.
Engine: ABC 6DXS of 405 kW at 680 r.p.m.
Transmission: Voith L37u.
Train Heating: None.   **Weight**: 57.3 tonnes.
Maximum Tractive Effort: 157 kN.   **Length over Buffers**: 10.000 m.
Driving Wheel Dia.: 1262 mm.   **Max. Speed**: 30 km/h shunting/50 km/h main line.

Originally numbered 252.001–025.

8501	FNDM			8514	FNDM	FLORAC
8502	FNDM	BAKOU		8515	FNDM	GRANADA
8503	FNDM			8516	FNDM	JAVA
8504	FNDM			8517	FNDM	ALPHA
8506	FNDM	BUFFALO		8518	FNDM	BAMAKO
8507	FNDM	CALCUTTA		8519	FNDM	BARRACUDA
8509	FNDM	CHICAGO		8520	FNDM	BRAVO
8510	FNDM	COLUMBIA		8521	FNDM	CALYPSO
8511	FNDM	CORDOBA		8522	FNDM	CARGO
8512	FNDM	DAKAR		8524	FNDM	DELTA
8513	FNDM	EL PASO		8525	FNDM	DIAMONT

CLASS 91   B

This class was originally numbered 9001-60 and was rebuilt in the late 1970s wi more powerful th engines and in some cases lengthened frames (marked *) ready for automatic Couplers! Many have been made spare by changes in freight workings and have been transferred to departmental use. Those in traffic stock are used for shunting at small stations and yards. Some are used as loco depot pilots. Many withdrawn locomotives are still stored at depots awaiting scrapping.

Built: 1961-64.
Builders: Cockerill (9101-10), ABR (9111-9135), BN (9136-60).
Engine: GM 12V71N of 245 kW at 1800 r.p.m.
Transmission: Hydraulic. Esco Power Twin Disc 11500 HS390.
Train Heating: None   **Weight**: 33.8 (35*) tonnes.
Maximum Tractive Effort: 90 kN. **Length over Buffers**: 6.625 m (8.055 m.*)
Driving Wheel Dia.: 920 mm.   **Max. Speed**: 20 km/h shunting/40 km/h main line.

Originally numbered 230.001-010/101-150.

9101	FKR(D)		9135	*	MKM	
9105	FSR(D)		9136	*	FKR	
9107	FSR	MIAMI	9137	*	LNC	
9108	FKR(D)		9138	*	FKR(D)	
9109	FKR		9140		LNC(D)	
9110	FKR		9142		FSR(D)	
9111	LNC		9144	*	LNC	
9112	LNC		9146	*	NK	
9115	LNC	MIKADO	9147	*	NK	
9116	* LNC(D)		9148	*	MKM	
9117	LNC	Mimosa	9149		LNC(D)	
9118	LNC		9150		FKR(D)	
9119	FSR(D)		9151		NK	
9121	FSR(D)		9152		FKR	
9122	LNC(D)		9153		MKM	
9123	FKR		9154		LNC(D)	
9124	FMS(D)		9155	*	NK	
9126	* LNC		9156	*	NK	
9128	LNC(D)		9157		FNDM	MONTANA
9130	* LNC		9158	*	NK	
9131	FAZ(D)		9159	*	MKM	
9132	FKR		9160		FKR	
9134	LNC					

CLASS 92   C

Only 9209 remains is use as a works pilot at Salzinnes works. Many withdrawn locomotives remain at depots and engineers yard waiting to call to the scrapyard

Built: 1960.
Engine: SEM 6K113HS of 255 kW at 1300 r.p.m.
Builder: BN.
Transmission: Hydraulic. Voith L37u.
Train Heating: None.   **Weight**: 50.5 tonnes.
Maximum Tractive Effort: 147 kN. **Length over Buffers**: 10.40 m.
Driving Wheel Dia.: 1262 mm.   **Max. Speed**: 20 km/h shunting/40 km/h main line.

Originally numbered 232.009.

9209   FAZ(D) |

1.6. SELF-PROPELLED DEPARTMENTAL STOCK

This series consists mainly of overhead line inspection units. Full details of these are not available. They are found in separate sheds belonging to the traction supply department.

ES200 SERIES
Built new 1971–72.

ES201	FCR	ES205	LL	ES209	NK		ES211 FNR
ES204 **R** FKR		ES207 **R** FMS		ES210	FR		

ES400 SERIES
Conversions from class 43 DMUs.

* Unpowered.

ES401 (4307)	FSR	ES404 (4319)	**Y** LL	ES407 (4320)	FLV
ES402 (4325)	FMS	ES405 (4326) *	**Y** GNS	ES409 (4309)	FR
ES403 (4328)	FTY	ES406 (4306)	FGSP	ES410 (4315)	FVS

ES4600/4900 SERIES
Converted from class 46/49 DMUs and not renumbered.

4612	FVS	4901	FVS	4911	FLV

ES500 SERIES
In generally requipping itself, Belgian Railways acquired some new overhead line units which are similar to ÖBB Class X 552. The arrival of these new units has allowed older ES 100 and ES 200 cars to be withdrawn.

Built: 1996–99.
Builder: Matisa, Roma, Italy.
Wheel Arrangement: B–2.
Engine: Deutz BF8M1015C of 330 kW.
Auxilary Engine: Deutz BF6M1012 of 93 kW.
Transmission: Hydraulic. Voith T211 rzz.
Weight in Full Working Order: 55 tonnes.
Length over Buffers: 16.04 m.
Wheel Diameter: 840 mm.
Max. Speed: 100 km/h.

ES501	**Y** ATH	ES505	**Y** FNR	ES509	**Y** FSR	ES513	**Y** FLV
ES502	**Y** GNS	ES506	**Y** FCR	ES510	**Y** FMS	ES514	**Y** FGSP
ES503	**Y** FGSP	ES507	**Y** FSR	ES511	**Y** LJ	ES515	**Y** NK
ES504	**Y** GNS	ES508	**Y** NK	ES512	**Y** FLV		

▲ Break unit 391, in the "Memling" livery which is now standard for the class, at De Panne forming the 12.50 to Gent on 20/08/1997. **Peter Fox**

▼ A refurbished Class AM64 EMU in the new livery on display at Brussels Midi. **Courtesy SNCB/NMBS**

h

▲ Class AM75 EMU 809 approaches Antwerpen Centraal on 22/11/1996. **Pete Moody**

▼ Class AM86 "Snorkel" EMU No. 904, is seen on a Roosendaal (NL) to Antwerpen stopping train service at Nispen (NL) on 17/10/1999. **Quintus Vosman**

▲ AM96 EMUs 451 and 443 leave Knock with an Antwerpen–Lille service on 12/03/1998.
Alex Dasi-Sutton

▼ Class 11 No. 1192, is seen hauling a Benelux push pull train on an Amsterdam–Brussels service through Delft on 28/04/1999. The first coach is in normal NS Intercity livery rather than the special yellow and red livery of the rest of the set. This is one of a number of coaches which are fitted with through control wiring for use on this service in emergency. **Quintus Vosman**

▲ Class 12 No. 1211 heads through De Pinte with a freight on 31/07/1998.   **W.J. Freebury**

▼ A publicity photo of the first Class 13, No. 1301.   **Courtesy SNCB/NMBS**

▲ Class 15 No. 1504 at Kinkempois depot on 25/09/1999.   **Adrian Norton**
▼ Class 16 No. 1604 at Brugge on 19/06/1999 with an Oostende–Köln working.   **Pete Moody**

▲ Class 20 locomotives are mainly used on the Brussels–Luxembourg line. The photo shows 2005 at Luxembourg with the 13.30 Basel–Brussels on 11/09/1997.   **Colin J. Marsden**

▼ Class 21 No. 2139 arrives at Gent St. Pieters on 26/07/1997 with an Oostende–Eupen service formed of 111 stock. In the background is sister loco 2155.   **David Haydock**

▲ A pair of Class 23s, 2304 and 2362, seen creeping around the back of Leuven station on 30/08/1999. **Brian Garvin**

▼ Dual voltage Class 25.5 loco 2551 hauls a container service from Belgium to the port of Rotterdam (Kijfhoek yard) through Dordrecht on 09/07/1999. **Quintus Vosman**

▲ Class 26 No. 2617 at Antwerpen on 22/11/1996. **Pete Moody**

▼ Class 27 No. 2715 at Tournai on 25/04/1998 having arrived on a service from Schaarbeek.
Colin J. Marsden

▲ DMU 4406 in the short-lived blue and yellow livery at Virton with the 16.20 to Bertrix. **W.J. Freebury**

▼ The first of the Class 41 DMUs No. 4101 is seen during its first tests in Belgium.   **Max Delie**

▲ Class 51 No. 5118 at Sas van Gent near Terneuzen on 26/09/1999. **Adrian Norton**

▼ Class 52 No. 5201 at Dinant with the 11.51 departure for Houyet on 14/07/1999. This train is provided for the use of kayak riders. **W.J. Freebury**

▲ During several summer weekends, an NS Haarlem to Maastricht train is extended to Luxembourg city via Liège and Troisvierges. Belgian Class 55 No. 5531 is seen at Drauffelt (LUX) on 04/07/1999 hauling the Dutch stock through the Luxembourg hills. One of the coaches is an IC+. This service will, in future be electric-hauled.   **Quintus Vosman**

▼ Class 62 No. 6287 at Kinkempois depot on 25/09/1999.   **Adrian Norton**

▲ 7001 heads an Along Different Lines special formed of Type K1 stock in the port of Antwerpen on 13/04/1996. **David Haydock**

▼ 7102 at the head of the Along Different Lines "Antwerpen Docker II" tour at BASF sidings on 17/10/1998. **Keith Preston**

▲ Shunter 7335 runs light from Gent Noord yard to Gent Zeehaven on 22/09/1998. This loco carries the name FLORAC which is used as a radio call sign.   **David Haydock**

▼ Class 75 No. 7504 at Antwerpen Dam depot on 26/09/1999.   **Adrian Norton**

▲ The Belgian Class 76 are former NS Class 2200. 7608 and 7610 are seen at Antwerpen dam depot on 26/09/1999, 7608 being in the old NS red livery whilst 7610 is in current NS livery.
Adrian Norton

▼ The same ADL train as the one shown in the upper photograph on page 60 being hauled by 7001 is seen with "master and slave" shunter 8274 & 8275.
David Haydock

▲ New departmental unit ES 410 at Kinkempois depot on 25/09/1999. **Adrian Norton**

▼ Refurbished type M4 open second 52102 at Schaarbeek on 25/09/1999. Note the crossed out number on the end. **Adrian Norton**

▲ Type l6 couchette 14605 in the special couchette livery at Oostende on 26/09/1999.   **Adrian Norton**

▼ One of the new type l11 open firsts 11820 at Oostende in the formation of a Köln train on 26/09/1999.   **Adrian Norton**

1.7. LOCO-HAULED COACHING STOCK

Developments. There have been major changes to Belgian hauled stock since the last edition of Benelux Railways. Type IO Trans Europe Express stainless steel stock was withdrawn from the Amsterdam–Brussels–Paris services with the introduction of Thalys TGVs. Some has been sold to Gabon. 1960s Type I4 stock has been withdrawn completely whilst I11 stock, the hauled version of Type AM96 EMUs have been introduced on the Oostende–Eupen/Köln and Antwerpen–Charleroi routes. The result is that some Type I6 and I10 former international stock has been cascaded to internal peak hour services. Type I11 is built for 200 km/h operation which will be possible when the Leuven–Liège high-speed line is completed and when the Brussels–Oostende line is upgraded.

In 1994, SNCB/NMBS bought 80 second-hand coaches from SNCF for peak-only services. These were classified Type K4 and helped replace all Type K3 coaches. The French coaches were not a great success due to their narrow doors and Belgian Railways have hired the whole fleet to NS. As they are still owned by Belgian Railways they are shown in this section.

In 1997, refurbishment of Type M4 stock started. The work is relatively limited and does little to improve the austere interiors although the new exterior livery is a big improvement. Continuing introductions of new stock are allowing slow withdrawal of Type M2 stock which was downgraded from 140 to 125 km/h in June 1995 following bogie problems. Diesel-hauled stock will be replaced by Class 41 DMUs from 2000.

The next new stock will be 210 Type M6 double-deck coaches to be delivered from May 2001 to July 2003. These will be to a similar high standard to Type I11, with 2+2 seating in both classes, and will be used mainly on longer distance peak services. Each set will have 6 coaches with a total seating capacity of 788, consisting of one non-smoking first class car with 124 seats, four non-smoking second class cars with 140 seats each and one smoking composite driving trailer with accommodation for handicapped persons and bicycles with 25 first and 30 second class seats per car.

Type M5 double-deck stock will be refurbished – in principle from early 2000 to early 2002 - and confined to shorter distance peak trains, replacing most remaining Type M2 coaches.

Numbering. All Belgian stock has the official UIC number painted on the side of the coach in the centre, and its 'old' number, duly crossed out, either on the bottom left-hand corner or on the end of the vehicle. All stock has an 'old' number, including new stock being delivered! Old numbers are used in this section, with a note on the UIC series in the class details.

Types. There are three basic categories of hauled stock in Belgium: Type I stock is for international use with 2+1 seating in open firsts, 2+2 seating in open seconds and 6 seats for both first and second class compartments. I stock is now also being used on non-international services. Type K stock has small doors at coach ends for boarding. Type M stock is of an open design and has larger doors placed closer to the middle of the train. Seating in both K and M stock is 2+2 in first class and 2+3 in second. Until now, both the latter types have been to a lower standard than in most other European countries but M6 stock should be a major improvement. M4 stock is used on several InterCity services whilst M2 stock is restricted to peak-hour services except on diesel-hauled services where it is to be replaced by Class 41 DMUs. In addition to the above some pre-war Type L stock still exists and is reserved for "historic" trains.

Liveries. Livery on historic K1 and L stock is plain dark green. M4/5 stock was introduced in a maroon livery lined in white and M2 stock has now all been repainted in this livery. Refurbished M4 stock is being repainted in the new pale grey livery with red doors and blue trim and this is also being applied to refurbished Type I stock. Prior to Type I11, all Type I stock was turned out in orange with a white stripe. A small number of international coaches were painted in the "Memling" livery (for service on the train of that name which ran from Oostende to Dortmund). This livery is similar to that on "Break" EMUs. Couchettes are dark blue with a pink band. Coaches are in red livery unless otherwise shown.

1.7.1. INTERNATIONAL STOCK
Ex-WAGONS LITS SLEEPING CAR TYPE T2

Built: 1974–75.
Bogies: Minden-Deutz M6.
Accommodation: 18 2-berth compartments.
Heating: Air conditioned.
Computer Numbers: 71 88 75 70 156–161.

Builder: CF.
Length over Buffers: 26.40 m.
Weight: 61 tonnes.
Max. Speed: 160 km/h.

5108	5109	5110	5151	5152	5153

TYPE I6 — CORRIDOR FIRST

Built: 1977.
Bogies: Fiat Y0270.S.
Accommodation: 54/– 2T.
Heating: Electric.
Computer Numbers: 61 88 19 70 601–620.

Builder: BN.
Length over Buffers: 26.40 m.
Weight: 43 tonnes.
Max. Speed: 160 km/h.

11601	0	11605	0	11609	M	11612	N	11615	0
11602	M	11606	0	11610	M	11613	M	11616	0
11603	0	11607	0	11611	0	11614	M	11617	0
11604	M	11608	N						

11618 M / 11619 M / 11620 0

TYPE I10 — OPEN FIRST

Built: 1988.
Bogies: Fiat Y0270.S.
Accommodation: 66/– 2T.
Heating: Electric.
Computer Numbers: 51 88 11 70 001–015.

Builder: BN.
Length over Buffers: 26.40 m.
Weight: 41 tonnes.
Max. Speed: 160 km/h.

11701	0	11704	0	11707	0	11710 0	11712 0	11714 0
11702	0	11705	0	11708	0	11711 0	11713 0	11715 0
11703	0	11706	0	11709	0			

TYPE I11 — OPEN FIRST

Built: 1995–98.
Bogies: ANF type 36.
Accommodation: 60/– 2T.
Heating: Electric.
Computer Numbers: 61 88 10 90 001–036.

Builder: Bombardier.
Length over Buffers: 26.40 m.
Weight: 45 tonnes.
Max. Speed: 200 km/h.

Push-pull fitted.

11801	W	11807	W	11813	W	11819	W	11825	W	11831	W
11802	W	11808	W	11814	W	11820	W	11826	W	11832	W
11803	W	11809	W	11815	W	11821	W	11827	W	11833	W
11804	W	11810	W	11816	W	11822	W	11828	W	11834	W
11805	W	11811	W	11817	W	11823	W	11829	W	11835	W
11806	W	11812	W	11818	W	11824	W	11830	W	11836	W

TYPE I6 — CORRIDOR SECOND

Built: 1977–78.
Bogies: Fiat Y0270.S.
Accommodation: –/66 2T 1W.
Heating: Electric.
Computer Numbers: 61 88 21 70 601–659.

Builder: BN.
Length over Buffers: 26.40 m.
Weight: 43 tonnes.
Max. Speed: 160 km/h.

Note: Some of these vehicles have been converted to couchettes and numbered in the 146XX series.

12601	M	12604	M	12607	M	12609	0	12611	M	12614	0
12603	M	12605	0	12608	M	12610	M	12613	0	12615	0

12616 M	12621 O	12629 O	12636 O	12643 N	12653 O
12617 N	12622 O	12630 O	12638 O	12648 M	12654 O
12618 O	12625 O	12631 O	12640 O	12650 M	12656 M
12619 O	12626 O	12634 O	12641 O	12651 O	12658 N
12620 M	12627 O	12635 O	12642 O	12652 N	12659 O

TYPE I10   OPEN SECOND

Built: 1987–88.
Bogies: Fiat Y0270.S.
Accommodation: –/86 2T.
Weight: 41 tonnes. (42.5 tonnes 12746–79).
Heating: Electric. 12746–79 are air conditioned.
Computer Numbers: 51 88 21 70 001–045, 61 88 21 70 046–079.

Builder: BN.
Length over Buffers: 26.40 m.
Max. Speed: 160 km/h.

12701 O	12715 O	12728 O	12741 O	12754 O	12767 O
12702 O	12716 O	12729 O	12742 O	12755 O	12768 O
12703 O	12717 O	12730 O	12743 O	12756 O	12769 O
12704 O	12718 O	12731 O	12744 O	12757 O	12770 O
12705 O	12719 O	12732 O	12745 O	12758 O	12771 O
12706 O	12720 O	12733 O	12746 O	12759 O	12772 O
12707 O	12721 O	12734 O	12747 M	12760 O	12773 O
12708 O	12722 O	12735 O	12748 O	12761 M	12774 M
12709 O	12723 O	12736 O	12749 O	12762 O	12775 O
12710 O	12724 O	12737 O	12750 O	12763 O	12776 O
12711 O	12725 O	12738 O	12751 O	12764 O	12777 M
12712 O	12726 O	12739 O	12752 O	12765 O	12778 M
12713 O	12727 O	12740 O	12753 O	12766 O	12779 M
12714 O					

TYPE I10   BISTRO CAR

Built: 1988. Converted from second.
Bogies: Fiat Y0270.S
Accommodation: –/37 2T.
Weight: 48 tonnes.
Heating: Electric. Air conditioned.
Computer Numbers: 61 88 88 80 080-1.

Builder: BN.
Length over Buffers: 26.40 m.
Max. Speed: 160 km/h.

12780   M

TYPE I11   OPEN SECOND

Built: 1995–98.
Bogies: ANI type 30.
Accommodation: –/80 2T.
Heating: Electric.
Computer Numbers: 61 88 20 90 001–106.

Builder: Bombardier.
Length over Buffers: 26.40 m.
Weight: 45 tonnes.
Max. Speed: 200 km/h.

Push-pull fitted.

12801 W	12816 W	12831 W	12846 W	12861 W	12876 W
12802 W	12817 W	12832 W	12847 W	12862 W	12877 W
12803 W	12818 W	12833 W	12848 W	12863 W	12878 W
12804 W	12819 W	12834 W	12849 W	12864 W	12879 W
12805 W	12820 W	12835 W	12850 W	12865 W	12880 W
12806 W	12821 W	12836 W	12851 W	12866 W	12881 W
12807 W	12822 W	12837 W	12852 W	12867 W	12882 W
12808 W	12823 W	12838 W	12853 W	12868 W	12883 W
12809 W	12824 W	12839 W	12854 W	12869 W	12884 W
12810 W	12825 W	12840 W	12855 W	12870 W	12885 W
12811 W	12826 W	12841 W	12856 W	12871 W	12886 W
12812 W	12827 W	12842 W	12857 W	12872 W	12887 W
12813 W	12828 W	12843 W	12858 W	12873 W	12888 W
12814 W	12829 W	12844 W	12859 W	12874 W	12889 W
12815 W	12830 W	12845 W	12860 W	12875 W	12890 W

12891	W	12894	W	12897	W	12900	W	12903	W	12905	W
12892	W	12895	W	12898	W	12901	W	12904	W	12906	W
12893	W	12896	W	12899	W	12902	W				

TYPE I5   SECOND COUCHETTE

Built: 1967.
Bogies: Schlieren 25.
Accommodation: /60 (60 berths) 2T 3W.
Heating: Electric or dual.
Computer Numbers: 51 88 50 70 501–545.

Builder:
Length over Buffers: 26.40 m.
Weight: 47 tonnes.
Max. Speed: 160 km/h.

14501	C	14509	C	14517	C	14525	C	14532	C	14539	C
14502	C	14510	C	14518	C	14526	C	14533	C	14540	C
14503	C	14511	C	14519	C	14527	C	14534	C	14541	C
14504	C	14512	C	14520	C	14528	C	14535	C	14542	C
14505	C	14513	C	14521	C	14529	C	14536	C	14543	C
14506	C	14514	C	14522	C	14530	C	14537	C	14544	C
14507	C	14515	C	14523	C	14531	C	14538	C	14545	C
14508	C	14516	C	14524	C						

TYPE I6   SECOND COUCHETTE

Built: 1977–78. Converted from corridor second.
Builder: BN.
Bogies: Fiat Y0270.S.
Accommodation: –/66 (66 berths) 2T 1W.
Heating: Electric.
Computer Numbers: 61 88 50 70 601–615.

Length over Buffers: 26.40 m.
Weight: tonnes.
Max. Speed: 160 km/h.

14601	(12602)	C	14606	(12628)	C	14611	(12644)	C
14602	(12606)	C	14607	(12632)	C	14612	(12646)	C
14603	(12612)	C	14608	(12633)	C	14613	(12649)	C
14604	(12623)	C	14609	(12637)	C	14614	(12655)	C
14605	(12624)	C	14610	(12639)	C	14615	(12657)	C

TYPE IR   "RESTO" RESTAURANT CAR

Built: 1970–71. Formerly SNCF "Gril-Express" type Vru coaches. Acquired by SNCB/NMBS in 1993. Refurbished by CIWLT Oostende 1994.
Builder: CIMT/B&L.
Bogies: Y28F.
Accommodation: 40 unclassified.
Heating: Electric.
Computer Numbers: 61 88 88 70 001–004.

Length over Buffers: 24.50 m.
Weight: 57 tonnes.
Max. Speed: 160 km/h.

16001	(61 87 88 90 142-8)	N		16003	(61 87 88 90 126-5)	N
16002	(61 87 88 90 140-6)	N		16004	(61 87 88 90 146-9)	N

TYPE ID   BRAKE VAN

Built: 1978.
Bogies: Fiat YO 332.
Accommodation: None.
Heating: Electric.
Computer Numbers: 51 88 95 70 901–934.

Builder: BN.
Length over Buffers: 26.40 m.
Weight: 39 tonnes.
Max. Speed: 160 km/h.

b - Adapted for carriage of cycles.

17401	O		17406	O b	17413	O	17420	O b	17426	N	17431	O b
17402	O b		17407	O	17414	N	17421	O b	17427	N	17432	O b
17403	N		17408	O b	17417	O	17424	O	17428	N	17433	O b
17404	N		17411	O	17418	O b	17425	N	17429	O	17434	O b
17405	O		17412	N	17419	N						

TYPE I1

Built: 1933.
Bogies: Schlieren 27.
Accommodation: None.
Heating: Electric.
Class-Specific Livery: S Painted as required.
Computer Numbers: 60 88 99 40 025–030/035–037.

EXHIBITION VEHICLES

Builder:
Length over Buffers: 22.30 m.
Weight: 45 tonnes.
Max. Speed: 140 km/h.

Note: These vehicles are based at Schaarbeek.

17805	S	17807	S	17809	S	17815	S	17816	S	17817	S
17806	S	17808	S	17810	S						

TYPE I6

Built: 1978.
Bogies: Fiat 31.
Accommodation: None.
Heating: Electric. Air conditioned.
Computer Number: 61 88 89 70 002-6.

BAR

Builder:
Length over Buffers: 26.40 m.
Weight: 48 tonnes.
Max. Speed: 160 km/h.

17902 **0**

TYPE I11

Built: 1995–98.
Bogies: ANF type 36.
Accommodation: –/58 1T.
Heating: Electric.
Computer Numbers: 61 88 80 90 001–021.
Push-pull fitted.

DRIVING OPEN SECOND

Builder: Bombardier.
Length over Buffers: 26.40 m.
Weight: 45 tonnes.
Max. Speed: 200 km/h.

19801	W	19805	W	19809	W	19813	W	19816	W	19819	W
19802	W	19806	W	19810	W	19814	W	19817	W	19820	W
19803	W	19807	W	19811	W	19815	W	19818	W	19821	W
19804	W	19808	W	19812	W						

1.7.2. TYPE K STOCK
TYPE K1   OPEN FIRST

Museum stock for use on historic trains.

Built: 1934–35.
Builder: BM/BND.
Bogies: Pennsylvania.   **Length over Buffers:** 23.32 m.
Accommodation: 64/– 1T.   **Weight:** 43.1 tonnes.
Heating: Electric.   **Max. Speed:** 140 km/h.
Computer Numbers: 50 88 18 40 005–123.

21005 G	21008 G	21015 G	21023 G	21029 G	21038 G
21007 G	21012 G	21017 G	21026 G	21030 G	21123 G

TYPE K4   SEMI-OPEN FIRST

Ex SNCF type USI A4t4. These vehicles have four compartments in the centre with open sections at the ends. On hire to NS. Note: Numbers in parentheses are former SNCF numbers.

Built: 1964–73.
Builder: ANF.
Bogies: Y28D.   **Length over Buffers:** 25.09 m.
Accommodation: 54/– 2T.   **Weight:** 38 tonnes.
Heating: Electric.   **Max. Speed:** 140 km/h.
Computer Numbers: 50 88 18 37 401–414.

21501	(50 87 28-37 015-8)	21508	(50 87 28-77 123-1)
21502	(50 87 28-37 016-6)	21509	(50 87 28-77 125-6)
21503	(50 87 38-37 033-9)	21510	(50 87 28-77 126-4)
21504	(50 87 28-77 103-3)	21511	(50 87 28-77 127-2)
21505	(50 87 28-77 109-0)	21512	(50 87 28-77 128-0)
21506	(50 87 28-77 112-4)	21513	(50 87 28-77 132-2)
21507	(50 87 28-77 117-3)	21514	(50 87 28-77 134-8)

TYPE K4   OPEN SECOND

Ex SNCF type USI B10t. On hire to NS. Note: Numbers in parentheses are former SNCF numbers.

Built: 1964–73.
Builder: ANF.
Bogies: Y28D.   **Length over Buffers:** 25.09 m.
Accommodation: –/80 2T.   **Weight:** 36 tonnes.
Heating: Electric.   **Max. Speed:** 140 km/h.
Computer Numbers: 50 88 20 37 301–355, except 22505/16/29 which are 50 88 20 38 405/416/429.

22501	(50 87 20-37 308-5)	22519	(50 87 20-70 923-9)
22502	(50 87 20-37 309-3)	22520	(50 87 20-70 929-6)
22503	(50 87 20-37 316-8)	22521	(50 87 20-70 930-4)
22504	(50 87 20-37 321-8)	22522	(50 87 20-70 934-6)
22505	(50 87 20-37 324-2)	22523	(50 87 20-70 978-3)
22506	(50 87 20-37 326-7)	22524	(50 87 20-70 979-1)
22507	(50 87 20-37 335-8)	22525	(50 87 20-70 981-7)
22508	(50 87 20-37 362-2)	22526	(50 87 20-70 985-8)
22509	(50 87 20-37 363-0)	22527	(50 87 20-70 987-4)
22510	(50 87 20-37 365-5)	22528	(50 87 20-70 989-0)
22511	(50 87 20-37 370-5)	22529	(50 87 20-71 002-1)
22512	(50 87 20-37 376-2)	22530	(50 87 20-74 013-5)
22513	(50 87 20-37 377-0)	22531	(50 87 20-74 014-3)
22514	(50 87 20-37 381-2)	22532	(50 87 20-74 019-2)
22515	(50 87 20-37 394-5)	22533	(50 87 20-74 021-8)
22516	(50 87 20-37 401-8)	22534	(50 87 20-74 023-4)
22517	(50 87 20-37 455-4)	22535	(50 87 20-74 038-2)
22518	(50 87 20-70 874-4)	22536	(50 87 20-74 050-7)

22537	(50 87 20-74 055-6)		22547	(50 84 20-74 778-6)
22538	(50 87 20-74 062-2)		22548	(50 84 20-74 779-4)
22539	(50 84 20-74 732-3)		22549	(50 84 20-74 780-2)
22540	(50 84 20-74 734-9)		22550	(50 84 20-74 784-4)
22541	(50 84 20-74 735-6)		22551	(50 84 20-74 786-9)
22542	(50 84 20-74 739-8)		22552	(50 84 20-74 787-7)
22543	(50 84 20-74 740-6)		22553	(50 87 20-77 799-6)
22544	(50 84 20-74 747-1)		22554	(50 87 20-77 852-3)
22545	(50 84 20-74 774-5)		22555	(50 87 20-77 857-2)
22546	(50 84 20-74 776-0)			

TYPE K4   COMPARTMENT SECOND

Ex SNCF type USI B10. These vehicles have a guard's compartment. On hire to NS.
Note: Numbers in parentheses are former SNCF numbers.

Built: 1964–73.
Builder: De Dietrich.
Bogies: Y24A.   **Length over Buffers**: 24.50 m.
Accommodation: –/72 2T.   **Weight**: 43 tonnes.
Heating: Electric.   **Max. Speed**: 140 km/h.
Computer Numbers: 50 88 82 37 401–415.

29501	(50 87 20-71 700-0)		29509	(50 87 20-71 762-0)
29502	(50 87 20-71 706-7)		29510	(50 87 20-71 763-8)
29503	(50 87 20-71 738-0)		29511	(50 87 20-71 765-3)
29504	(50 87 20-71 742-2)		29512	(50 87 20-71 766-1)
29505	(50 87 20-71 746-3)		29513	(50 87 20-71 770-3)
29506	(50 87 20-71 750-5)		29514	(50 87 20-71 775-2)
29507	(50 87 20-71 751-3)		29515	(50 87 20-71 788-5)
29508	(50 87 20-71 752-1)			

1.7.3. TYPE L SLAM DOOR STOCK
Museum stock for use on historic trains.

TYPE L   OPEN FIRST
Built: 1933.   **Builder:**
Bogies: **Length over Buffers:** 19.30 m.
Accommodation: 64/– 2T.   **Weight:** 38 tonnes.
Heating: Steam.   **Max. Speed:** 120 km/h.
Computer Numbers: 50 88 18 26 413-9.

31107 **G** | 31113 **G** |

TYPE L   OPEN SECOND
Built: 1933–34.   **Builder:** HSP.
Bogies: **Length over Buffers:** 19.30 m.
Accommodation: –/97 2T   **Weight:** 47 tonnes.
Heating: Steam.   **Max. Speed:** 120 km/h.
Computer Numbers: 50 88 20 26 435–568.

32035 **G** | 32037 **G** | 32049 **G** | 32076 **G** | 32143 **G** | 32168 **G**

TYPE L   COMPOSITE
Built: 1933.   **Builder:**
Bogies: **Length over Buffers:** 19.30 m.
Accommodation: **Weight:**   tonnes.
Heating: Steam.   **Max. Speed:** 120 km/h.
Computer Numbers: 50 88 37 26 402–6.

33002 **G** | 33006 **G** |

TYPE L   BRAKE FIRST
Built: 1933.   **Builder:** Ragheno.
Bogies: **Length over Buffers:** 19.30 m.
Accommodation: 38/– 2T   **Weight:**   tonnes.
Heating: Steam.   **Max. Speed:** 120 km/h.
Computer Numbers: 50 88 81 26 405-7.

38005 **G** |

TYPE L   BRAKE SECOND
Built: 1933.   **Builder:**
Bogies: **Length over Buffers:** 19.30 m.
Accommodation: **Weight:**   tonnes.
Heating: Steam.   **Max. Speed:** 120 km/h.
Computer Numbers: 50 88 82 26 425-4.

39025 **G** |

1.7.4. TYPE M1 & M2 STOCK
TYPE M2   OPEN FIRST

Built: 1958–60.   **Builder**: BN/Ragheno/St. Eloi.
Bogies: Schlieren type 23.   **Length over Buffers**: 24.00 m.
Accommodation: 68/– 1T.   **Weight**: 34.5 tonnes.
Heating: Dual.   **Max. Speed**: 125 km/h.
Computer Numbers: 50 88 18 48 (38 e) 601–635.

e Electric heating only.

41001	e	41007		41012	e	41018		41023		41031	e
41003	e	41008		41014		41020		41025		41033	
41004	e	41009		41016		41021		41026		41034	
41005		41011		41017		41022		41029		41035	

TYPE M1   OPEN SECOND
Museum stock for use on historic trains.

Built: 1937.
Builder: AFB.
Bogies: Pennsylvania.   **Length over Buffers**: 22.76 m.
Accommodation: –/94 1T.   **Weight**: 43.9 tonnes.
Heating: Steam.   **Max. Speed**: 120 km/h.
Computer Numbers: 50 88 29 26 605/30/43/44/52.
Push-pull fitted.

42014	42062	42094	42097	42128

TYPE M2   OPEN SECOND

Built: 1958–60.   **Builder**: BN/Ragheno/St. Eloi.
Bogies: Schlieren type 23.   **Length over Buffers**: 24.00 m.
Accommodation: –/106 1T.   **Weight**: 33.6 tonnes.
Heating: Dual.   **Max. Speed**: 125 km/h.
Computer Numbers: 50 88 20 48 (38 e) 601–950.

e Electric heating only.
p Push-pull fitted.

42301		42329		42358		42390	e	42421		42455	
42303	e	42330		42362	e	42391		42422	e	42456	
42305		42331		42363	e	42392	e	42424	e	42457	
42306		42333		42364	p	42393		42425		42458	
42307		42334		42367		42394	p	42426		42459	p
42308		42335		42369		42395		42429		42460	
42311	p	42337		42370	p	42396		42430		42461	
42312		42338		42371		42398		42431		42462	e
42313		42340		42373		42400		42434	e	42463	
42314	e	42341		42374	e	42401	e	42435	e	42464	
42315		42342		42375	p	42402		42436		42465	
42317		42343		42376		42403	p	42437		42466	
42318		42344		42377		42404		42439		42467	
42319		42345		42378	p	42407		42440		42468	
42320	e	42346		42379		42408		42441		42469	
42321		42348	p	42380		42410		42446	e	42472	
42322		42349	p	42381	e	42412		42447	e	42473	
42323		42351		42382	e	42414		42448		42474	
42324		42352		42383		42415		42450	e	42475	
42325		42354		42384		42416		42451		42476	
42326		42355	e	42386		42418		42452		42477	
42327		42356		42387		42419	e	42453		42478	
42328		42357		42389	e	42420	p	42454		42479	

42483	e	42508		42534		42566		42592		42617	
42484		42510		42536	p	42567		42595	e	42621	
42485		42511	e	42539		42568		42596	e	42623	e
42486		42513		42540		42569	e	42598		42627	
42487		42514		42541		42570		42599		42629	
42490		42515		42543	e	42572		42600		42631	p
42491		42516		42547		42573	e	42601	e	42633	e
42492		42517	e	42548		42574	p	42602		42635	e
42493		42518		42549	p	42575		42603		42636	e
42494	p	42519	p	42550		42576	p	42604		42637	
42495		42520	p	42551		42578		42605		42638	p
42496	p	42522		42552		42579		42606		42639	
42500	p	42523		42554		42580		42608	e	42640	
42501		42524		42555		42581		42610		42642	p
42502	p	42526	e	42558	p	42583		42611		42645	p
42503		42528		42559		42586	p	42612	e	42647	p
42504		42530	e	42562		42587		42613		42648	
42505		42531	p	42563		42590	p	42614		42649	p
42506		42532		42564	p	42591		42616		42650	e

TYPE M1   OPEN COMPOSITE

Museum stock for use on historic trains.

Built: 1937.
Builder: BND.
Bogies: Pennsylvania.
Accommodation: 38/36 1T.
Heating: Steam.
Computer Numbers: 50 88 38 26 624-7.
Push-pull fitted.

Length over Buffers: 22.76 m.
Weight: 42.2 tonnes.
Max. Speed: 120 km/h.

43045 **G** |

TYPE M2   OPEN COMPOSITE

Built: 1958–60.
Bogies: Schlieren type 23.
Accommodation: 36/47 1T.
Heating: Dual.
Computer Numbers: 50 88 39 48 (38 e) 601–704.

Builder: BN/Ragheno/St. Eloi.
Length over Buffers: 24.00 m.
Weight: 34.4 tonnes.
Max. Speed: 125 km/h.

e Electric heating only.
p Push-pull fitted.

43201	p	43221		43239		43257	e	43272	e	43287	
43202	e	43222	p	43240	e	43258		43273		43288	
43203		43223		43241		43259		43274		43290	e
43204	e	43224		43242		43260	e	43275	p	43291	p
43205		43225		43243		43261		43276		43292	
43207		43226		43244	e	43262		43277		43293	
43208		43227		43246		43263	e	43278		43294	
43210		43229	p	43248		43264		43279		43295	p
43212		43230	p	43249		43265		43280	e	43297	p
43213	p	43231		43250		43266		43281	p	43299	e
43214	p	43233	e	43251	e	43267	e	43282	p	43300	
43216	e	43234	p	43252	p	43268		43283		43301	
43217	p	43235		43253		43269		43284		43302	
43218	p	43236		43254	e	43270	e	43285	p	43303	p
43219		43237		43256		43271		43286	p	43304	
43220		43238									

TYPE M1   DRIVING BRAKE OPEN SECOND

Push-pull driving trailer. Museum stock for use on historic trains. **Built:** 1937.
Builder: Seneffe.
Bogies: Pennsylvania.   **Length over Buffers:** 22.76 m.
Accommodation: –/77 1T.   **Weight:** 41.9 tonnes.
Heating: Steam.   **Max. Speed:** 125 km/h.
Computer Number: 50 88 82 26 649-9.

49108   **G** |

TYPE M2   BRAKE OPEN SECOND

Built: 1958–60.   **Builder:** BN/Ragheno/St. Eloi.
Bogies: Schlieren type 23.   **Length over Buffers:** 24.00 m.
Accommodation: –/75 1T.   **Weight:** 32.4 tonnes.
Heating: Dual.   **Max. Speed:** 125 km/h.
Computer Numbers: 50 88 82 48 (38 e) 601–716.

e Electric heating only.
p Converted to push-pull driving trailer.

49201		49219	e	49241	p	49261	e	49279		49300	
49202		49220		49242		49262		49281		49301	
49203		49221		49243		49263		49283		49302	
49204		49222	e	49244		49264	p	49284	p	49303	
49205		49223		49246		49265		49285	p	49304	
49206	e	49225		49247		49266	p	49288		49306	
49207		49227		49249		49268		49289		49307	p
49208		49228		49251		49269		49292	p	49308	
49209		49230		49252	p	49270		49293	p	49309	
49211	p	49231		49253	e	49271	p	49294		49310	
49212	p	49232	p	49254		49273		49295	e	49311	
49213		49233		49256	e	49274	p	49296		49313	
49214		49235		49257		49275		49297		49314	
49215		49238		49258	e	49276		49298	p	49315	
49216		49239		49259		49277		49299		49316	p
49218	e	49240		49260	e	49278					

TYPE M2   DRIVING BRAKE OPEN SECOND

Built: 1958–60. Push-pull driving trailer.
Builder: BN.
Bogies: Schlieren type 23.   **Length over Buffers:** 24.00 m.
Accommodation: –/74 1T.   **Weight:** 32.4 tonnes.
Heating: Dual.   **Max. Speed:** 120 km/h.
Computer Numbers: 50 88 87 48 (38 e) 601–615.

e Electric heating only.

49901	e	49904	e	49907	e	49910	e	49911	49914
49903		49906							

(B)

1.7.5. TYPE M4 & M5 STOCK
TYPE M4   OPEN FIRST

Built: 1979–80.
Bogies: Fiat type Y32.
Accommodation: 80/– 1T (r 72/– 1T).
Heating: Electric.
Computer Numbers: 50 88 19 78 001–050.

Builder: BN.
Length over Buffers: 24.26 m.
Weight: 38 tonnes.
Max. Speed: 160 km/h.

p Push-pull fitted.
r Refurbished.

51001		51010		51019		51027		51035	N pr	51043	N pr
51002	N r	51011		51020		51028		51036	p	51044	N pr
51003		51012	N r	51021		51029		51037	N pr	51045	p
51004		51013		51022		51030	N r	51038	N pr	51046	N pr
51005		51014		51023	N r	51031		51039	p	51047	N pr
51006		51015		51024		51032		51040	N pr	51048	p
51007		51016		51025		51033		51041	p	51049	N pr
51008		51017		51026		51034	N pr	51042	p	51050	p
51009		51018	N r								

TYPE M5   OPEN FIRST

Push-pull fitted double-deck stock.

Built: 1986–87.
Builder: BN.
Bogies: .
Accommodation: 142/– 2T.
Heating: Electric.
Computer Numbers: 50 88 16 38 001–015.

Length over Buffers: 26.40 m.
Weight: 44 tonnes.
Max. Speed: 140 km/h.

51501	51504	51507	51510	51512	51514
51502	51505	51508	51511	51513	51515
51503	51506	51509			

TYPE M4   OPEN SECOND

Built: 1980–83.
Bogies: Fiat type Y32.
Accommodation: –/104 1T.
Heating: Electric.
Computer Numbers: 50 88 20 78 001–430.

Builder: BN.
Length over Buffers: 24.26 m.
Weight: 39 tonnes.
Max. Speed: 160 km/h.

p Push-pull fitted.
r Refurbished.

52001		52017		52033		52049	N r	52065		52081	
52002		52018		52034		52050		52066		52082	
52003		52019		52035		52051		52067	N r	52083	N r
52004	N r	52020		52036	N r	52052		52068	N r	52084	
52005		52021		52037		52053		52069		52085	
52006		52022	N r	52038	N r	52054		52070		52086	
52007		52023		52039		52055		52071		52087	
52008	N r	52024	N r	52040		52056		52072		52088	
52009		52025		52041		52057		52073		52089	
52010		52026		52042		52058	N r	52074		52090	
52011	N r	52027		52043		52059		52075	N r	52091	
52012	N r	52028		52044		52060		52076		52092	
52013	N r	52029		52045		52061		52077		52093	
52014		52030		52046		52062		52078		52094	
52015	N r	52031		52047		52063		52079		52095	
52016	N r	52032		52048	N r	52064	N r	52080		52096	

No.		No.		No.		No.		No.		No.	
52097		52154		52210	N r	52266	p	52321	N pr	52376	N pr
52098	N r	52155		52211		52267	p	52322	p	52377	N pr
52099		52156		52212	N r	52268	N pr	52323	N pr	52378	N pr
52100		52157		52213		52269	N pr	52324	N pr	52379	N pr
52101		52158		52214		52270	N pr	52325	p	52380	N pr
52102	N r	52159		52215		52271	N pr	52326	p	52381	N pr
52103		52160		52216		52272	p	52327	N pr	52382	p
52104		52161	N r	52217		52273	N pr	52328	N pr	52383	N pr
52105		52162		52218		52274	N pr	52329	N pr	52384	N pr
52106		52163		52219		52275	N pr	52330	N pr	52385	N pr
52107	N r	52164		52220	N r	52276	N pr	52331	N pr	52386	p
52108		52165		52221		52277	N pr	52332	N pr	52387	N pr
52109		52166		52222	N r	52278	N pr	52333	N pr	52388	p
52110		52167		52223		52279	p	52334	p	52389	p
52111		52168		52224		52280	p	52335	N pr	52390	N pr
52112		52169		52225		52281	N pr	52336	N pr	52391	N pr
52113		52170		52226	N r	52282	N pr	52337	p	52392	N pr
52114		52171		52227		52283	p	52338	N pr	52393	N pr
52115		52172		52228		52284	p	52339	N pr	52394	N pr
52116	N r	52173		52229		52285	p	52340	p	52395	N pr
52117		52174		52230	N r	52286	N pr	52341	N pr	52396	N pr
52118		52175		52231		52287	p	52342	N pr	52397	N pr
52119	N r	52176	N r	52232		52288	N pr	52343	p	52398	N pr
52120		52177		52233		52289	N pr	52344	N pr	52399	p
52121		52178	N r	52234		52290	N pr	52345	N pr	52400	N pr
52122	N r	52179		52235		52291	p	52346	N pr	52401	N pr
52123		52180		52236		52292	N pr	52347	N pr	52402	p
52124		52181		52237		52293	N pr	52348	N pr	52403	p
52125		52182		52238	N r	52294	N pr	52349	N pr	52404	p
52126		52183		52239	N r	52295	p	52350	N pr	52405	N pr
52127		52184	N r	52240		52296	N pr	52351	N pr	52406	N pr
52128		52185	N r	52241		52297	N pr	52352	p	52407	N pr
52129		52186		52242		52298	N pr	52353	N pr	52408	N pr
52130		52187		52243		52299	N pr	52354	N pr	52409	N pr
52131		52188		52244		52300	p	52355	N pr	52410	N pr
52132		52189		52245		52301	N pr	52356	N pr	52411	N pr
52133		52190		52246	N r	52302	N pr	52357	N pr	52412	p
52134		52191	N r	52247		52303	N pr	52358	N pr	52413	N pr
52135		52192		52248	p	52304	p	52359	N pr	52414	p
52136	N r	52193		52249	N pr	52305	N pr	52360	N pr	52415	N pr
52137		52194		52250	N pr	52306	N pr	52361	N pr	52416	N pr
52138		52195	N r	52251	p	52307	p	52362	N pr	52417	N pr
52139		52196		52252	N pr	52308	p	52363	N pr	52418	N pr
52140		52197		52253	N pr	52309	p	52364	p	52419	N pr
52141		52198		52254	p	52310	p	52365	N pr	52420	p
52142		52199		52255	N pr	52311	N pr	52366	N pr	52421	N pr
52143		52200		52256	N pr	52312	N pr	52367	N pr	52422	N pr
52144		52201		52257	p	52313	p	52368	N pr	52423	N pr
52145		52202		52258	N pr	52314	N pr	52369	p	52424	N pr
52146		52203		52259	p	52315	N pr	52370	p	52425	N pr
52147		52204		52260	N pr	52316	p	52371	p	52426	N pr
52148		52205		52261	N pr	52317	N pr	52372	N pr	52427	N pr
52149		52206	N r	52262	N pr	52318	N pr	52373	N pr	52428	N pr
52150	N r	52207		52263	p	52319	N pr	52374	p	52429	N pr
52152		52208		52264	N pr	52320	p	52375	N pr	52430	N pr
52153		52209	N r	52265	N pr						

TYPE M5   OPEN SECOND

Push-pull fitted double-deck stock.

Built: 1986–87.
Builder: BN .
Bogies: .   **Length over Buffers**: 26.40 m.

Accommodation: –/146 2T.
Heating: Electric.
Computer Numbers: 50 88 26 38 001–097.

Weight: 43.8 tonnes.
Max. Speed: 140 km/h.

52501	52518	52534	52550	52566	52582
52502	52519	52535	52551	52567	52583
52503	52520	52536	52552	52568	52584
52504	52521	52537	52553	52569	52585
52505	52522	52538	52554	52570	52586
52506	52523	52539	52555	52571	52587
52507	52524	52540	52556	52572	52588
52508	52525	52541	52557	52573	52589
52509	52526	52542	52558	52574	52590
52510	52527	52543	52559	52575	52591
52511	52528	52544	52560	52576	52592
52512	52529	52545	52561	52577	52593
52513	52530	52546	52562	52578	52594
52514	52531	52547	52563	52579	52595
52515	52532	52548	52564	52580	52596
52516	52533	52549	52565	52581	52597
52517					

TYPE M4   BRAKE OPEN FIRST

Built: 1982.
Bogies: Fiat type Y32.
Accommodation: 56/– 1T.
Heating: Electric.
Computer Numbers: 50 88 81 78 001–033.

Builder: BN
Length over Buffers: 24.26 m.
Weight: 37.2 tonnes.
Max. Speed: 160 km/h.

58001		58007		58013		58019	58024		58029	
58002		58008	N r	58014		58020	58025		58030	
58003		58009		58015		58021	58026		58031	
58004	N r	58010		58016		58022	58027		58032	
58005		58011	N r	58017	N r	58023	58028	N r	58033	
58006		58012		58018	N r					

TYPE M4   DRIVING BRAKE OPEN FIRST

Built: 1983. Push-pull driving trailer.
Builder: BN.
Bogies: Fiat type Y32.
Accommodation: 48/– 1T.
Heating: Electric.
Computer Numbers: 50 88 81 78 034–065.

Length over Buffers: 24.26 m.
Weight: 39 tonnes.
Max. Speed: 160 km/h.

58034	N r	58040		58046		58051	N r	58056		58061	N r
58035	N r	58041		58047	N r	58052		58057	N r	58062	N r
58036	N r	58042	N r	58048		58053	N r	58058	N r	58063	N r
58037		58043	N r	58049	N r	58054	N r	58059	N r	58064	N r
58038	N r	58044	N r	58050	N r	58055	N r	58060	N r	58065	
58039	N r	58045	N r								

TYPE M4   BRAKE OPEN SECOND

Built: 1983–84.
Bogies: Fiat type Y32.
Accommodation: –/64 1T.
Heating: Electric.
Computer Numbers: 50 88 82 78 001–035 (k 50 88 87 78 001–035.

Builder:
Length over Buffers: 24.26 m.
Weight: 39.5 tonnes.
Max. Speed: 160 km/h.

k With compartment for catering trolley.
p Converted to push-pull driving trailer.

59901		59903		59905		59907	N r	59909		59911	k
59902		59904		59906		59908		59910		59912	k

59913	N r	59917		59921		59925		59929	N pk	59933	N pk
59914		59918	k	59922		59926	pk	59930	pk	59934	pk
59915	k	59919	k	59923	k	59927	pk	59931	N pk	59935	pk
59916		59920		59924		59928	pk	59932	N pk		

TYPE M5   DRIVING OPEN SECOND

Double-deck push-pull driving trailer.

Built: 1986–87.
Builder: BN.
Bogies: .   **Length over Buffers:** 26.85 m.
Accommodation: –/118 2T.   **Weight:** 49.3 tonnes.
Heating: Electric.   **Max. Speed:** 140 km/h.
Computer Numbers: 50 88 82 38 001–018.

59951	59954	59957	59960	59963	59966
59952	59955	59958	59961	59964	59967
59953	59956	59959	59962	59965	59968

▲ Type M5 double-deck second No. 52521 at Schaarbeek on 25/09/1999.   **Adrian Norton**

1.7.6. MISCELLANEOUS STOCK
GENERATOR VANS

Built: 1933–34.
Bogies: Pennsylvania.
Weight: 46 tonnes.
Computer Numbers: 50 88 92 66 907/911.

Length over Buffers: 15.60 m.
Max. Speed: 120 km/h.

77019 | 77023 |

MISCELLANEOUS DEPARTMENTAL STOCK

11	60 88 99 70 011-6	Traction department test coach
13	60 88 99 70 013-2	Traction department test coach
41	60 88 99 10 041-6	Cinema coach
51	60 88 99 69 051-5	Emergency vehicle
52	60 88 99 69 052-3	Emergency vehicle
53	60 88 99 69 053-1	Emergency vehicle
54	60 88 99 69 054-9	Emergency vehicle
55	60 88 99 69 055-6	Emergency vehicle
56	60 88 99 29 056-3	Emergency vehicle
57	60 88 99 00 057-4	Emergency vehicle
61	60 88 99 69 101-9	Signalling school coach
62	60 88 99 69 102-7	Signalling school coach
63	60 88 99 69 103-5	Signalling school coach
64	60 88 99 69 104-3	Signalling school coach
65	60 88 99 69 105-0	Signalling school coach
201	60 88 99 29 201-5	Infrastructure dept. coach (track renewal).
202	60 88 99 29 202-3	Infrastructure dept. coach (track renewal).
203	60 88 99 29 203-1	Infrastructure dept. coach (track renewal).
204	60 88 99 29 204-9	Infrastructure dept. coach (track renewal).
205	60 88 99 29 205-6	Infrastructure dept. coach (track renewal).
206	60 88 99 29 206-4	Infrastructure dept. coach (mess coach).
207	60 88 99 29 207-2	Infrastructure dept. coach (mess coach).
208	60 88 99 29 208-0	Infrastructure dept. coach (staff dormitory).
209	60 88 99 29 209-8	Infrastructure dept. coach (staff dormitory).
210	60 88 99 29 210-6	Infrastructure dept. coach
211	60 88 99 29 211-4	Infrastructure dept. coach
212	60 88 99 29 212-2	Infrastructure dept. coach
213	60 88 99 29 213-0	Infrastructure dept. coach
214	60 88 99 29 214-8	Infrastructure dept. coach
215	60 88 99 29 215-5	Infrastructure dept. coach
216	60 88 99 29 216-3	Infrastructure dept. coach
217	60 88 99 29 217-1	Infrastructure dept. coach
218	60 88 99 29 218-9	Infrastructure dept. coach
223	60 88 99 48 223-6	Infrastructure dept. coach
224	60 88 99 29 224-7	Infrastructure dept. coach
226	60 88 99 29 226-2	Infrastructure dept. coach
601	60 88 99 80 001-5	Infrastructure dept. test coach
602	60 88 99 89 002-4	Infrastructure dept. test coach

1.7.7. WAGONS-LITS COACHING STOCK
PULLMAN RESTAURANT CAR
Built: 1925–7. Used in Pullman Orient Express.
Builder: Reggio (BRCW*).
Bogies: **Length over Buffers:** 23.45 m.
Accommodation: 56 (42§).   **Weight:**   tonnes.
Heating: Electric.
Max. Speed: 160 km/h.

Computer Numbers: 61 88 88 08 70 019/024/026/027.
c – Air conditioned.

| 2869 | | 2973 | | 2976 | | 2979 | |

PULLMAN SHOWER CAR
Built: 1926 for Flèche D'Or. Rebuilt for La Scala Opera tour and now used in Pullman Orient Express.
Builder: BRCW.
Bogies: **Length over Buffers:** 23.45 m.
Accommodation: –.   **Weight:**   tonnes.
Heating:
Max. Speed: 160 km/h.

4013   51 88 09 70 013-2

PULLMAN CAR
Built: 1929 for Côte d'Azur. Used in "Pullman Orient Express".
Builder: EIC.
Bogies: **Length over Buffers:** 23.45 m.
Accommodation: **Weight:**   tonnes.
Heating: Electric.
Max. Speed: 160 km/h.

4148	51 88 09 70 148-6	Bar/disco.
4151	61 88 09 70 151-8	Pullman bar ex 'Mistral'.
4159	51 88 09 70 159-3	Pullman bar.
4160	51 88 09 70 160-1	Lounge car.

RESTAURANT CAR
Built: 1955 incorporating parts of damaged cars. Vestibule and outer doors at one end only.
Builder: Breda.
Bogies: Pennsylvania.   **Length over Buffers:** 23.45 m.
Accommodation: 48 unclassified.   **Weight:** 52.6 tonnes.
Heating: Coal with through electric wiring.
Max. Speed: 160 km/h.
Computer Numbers: 61 88 08 70 267-3.

| 4013 | **0** | | 4148 | **0** | | 4151 | **0** | | 4159 | **0** | | 4160 | **0** | | 4267 | **0** |

SLEEPING CAR TYPE AB30
Built: 1955–6. Budd-patent stainless steel bodies. Air conditioned.
Builder: CF (4530–43), Ansaldo (4554).
Bogies: Schlieren.   **Length over Buffers:** 24.00 m.
Accommodation: 20 berths.   **Weight:** 44 tonnes.
Heating: Electric.   **Max. Speed:** 160 km/h.
Computer Numbers: 71 88 70 70 015/014/012/013/011.

| 4530 | **U** | | 4531 | **U** | | 4532 | **U** | | 4543 | **U** | | 4554 | **U** | |

SLEEPING CAR TYPE MU

Built: 1967.
Builder: Donauwörth
Bogies: Minden-Deutz M4.
Length over Buffers: 26.40 m.
Accommodation: 12 3-berth compartments.
Weight: 61 tonnes.
Heating: Air conditioned.
Max. Speed: 160 km/h.
Computer Numbers: 61 88 72 71 314–319/323/326, 71 88 72 70 615–619.

4744	4747	4750	4753	4756	4794
4745	4748	4751	4754	4792	4795
4746	4749	4752	4755	4793	4796

A NOTE ON WAGONS-LITS SLEEPING CARS

Modern Wagons-Lits sleeping cars are painted dark blue and come in two types as follows:

Type MU (Modern Universal)

These vehicles have conventional three-berth compartments and can be used as first class one- or two berth compartments or second class three-berth compartments. The lower berth hinges back to form three seats. A door can be unlocked between adjacent compartments for pairs of first class passengers booking single berth compartments.

Type T2 (Tourist 2-berth)

These vehicles have an odd arrangement of upper and lower compartments arranged alternately. The lower compartments have two berths one above the other with the lower berth folding back to form seats. The upper compartments feature a step up from the corridor and permanent seats on the left hand side which protrude back into the next lower compartment on the left. The berths are arranged one above the lower berth to the left and one above the lower berth to the right.

All compartments have a wash basin with a chamber pot in a compartment underneath.

▲ CIWLT Type MU sleeping car No. 4794 at Schaarbeek on 25/09/1999. **Adrian Norton**

2. NETHERLANDS RAILWAYS (NS)

The Dutch name for the Netherlands Railways is NV Nederlandse Spoorwegen (NS). The NS is a relatively small system and approximately two thirds of all routes are electrified at 1500 V d.c. with overhead wire collection. Language presents no problem, since most Dutch people speak good English, but restaurant menus are often in Dutch only, so a dictionary or phrase book can still be useful. Different numbering series were used for locos and multiple units, but with re-numbering and condemnations, numbers do not now duplicate.

NV Nederlandse Spoorwegen is a holding company with legally seperated business units. The units are divided into commercially orientated and government orientated units. The commercially oriented units are united in NS Groep NV and are:

NS Reizigers (NS passengers). Responsible for operation of almost all passenger services in the Netherlands.

NS Internationaal. Responsible for operation of international passenger services.

Railion Benelux. This is the NS's freight train operator which has is to be amalgamated with DB Cargo, the German Railways' freight arm. Formerly **NS Cargo.**

NedTrain. The operator of NS's workshops. Formerly **NS Materieel** (NS rolling stock).

NS Stations. Operates the commercial space in the stations, like shops etc.

NS Vastgoed. A property company.

NS Financial services. A leasing company based in Dublin, which leases DMUs to two regional TOC's, i.e. Syntus and NoordNed.

There are also other minor commercial business units e.g. NS Aansluitingen BV, which owns the property of almost all private freight links between companies/industrial plants and the railway lines.

The three government orientated and financed business units are:

Railned. makes decisions on the capacity of the railnetwork/ timetables, makes studies on rail traffic for the Ministry of Transport (for new investments), and is the major player on railway safety.

NS Railinfrabeheer. Responsible for the maintenance and the extension of the Dutch railway network.

NS Verkeersleiding. Traffic control.

These units are to be lifted out of NS holdings and transferred to the State sometime in 2001.

There are also two infrastructure companies which are also wholly-owned subsidiaries of the NS. These are **NBM Rail** and **Volker Stevin Rail & Traffic**

In addition, the private company **Strukton Materieel** also owns a number of shunters and 2200 Class diesel locos. NS has shares in this.

PASSENGER TRAINS

The NS timetable is almost entirely regular interval with most routes having half-hourly services and many routes four trains per hour.

There are now three types of train category on the NS. Intercity, stoptreinen and sneltreinen. Stoptreinen are stopping trains and are generally either EMUs or push-pull double-decker sets. Intercity trains are generally either Koploper EMUs or are loco-hauled, but IRM units are also used on some services. Principal Intercity routes are:

Amsterdam–Den Haag HS–Rotterdam–Dordrecht–Roosendaal–Antwerpen Centraal–Brussels. These are push-pull trains with SNCB dual-voltage Class 11 electric locos and ICR3 stock. Through trains to Paris are now operated by Thalys units.

Haarlem–Amsterdam–Utrecht–'s-Hertogenbosch–Eindhoven–Sittard–Maastricht. These trains are loco hauled with either Class 1700 or 1800. In summer the Maastricht services convey a bicycle brake. Stock is mainly ICR with some Plan W. Some sets have one or two double-deckers at the Maastricht end.

Den Haag CS–Rotterdam–Dordrecht–Tilburg–Eindhoven–Heerlen/Venlo. Also loco-hauled with Class 1700/1800. The stock is plan ICR with most trains having 3 or 4 Belgian type K4 coaches in the formation. These are ex-SNCF vehicles, painted in SNCB/NMBS livery with NS logos! Because the total number of loco-hauled coaches required to operate ½-hourly services on Haarlem–Eidhoven/Maastricht and Den Haag–Heerlen/Venlo is greater than the number posessed by the NS, these coaches will continue to be used until the new batch of IRM units just ordered are delivered (or until the NS manages to scrounge some stock from somewhere else).

Amsterdam/Hoofddorp or Den Haag CS/Rotterdam–Amersfoort–Enschede and Amsterdam/Schiphol or Den Haag CS/Rotterdam CS–Amersfoort–Zwolle–Groningen/Leeuwarden. Because these trains split and join they are operated by Plan Z 3 or 4-car "Koploper" units.

Den Helder–Amsterdam–Utrecht–Arnhem–Nijmegen. These trains also detach portions and are operated by ICM 3 or 4-car "Koploper" units.

Amsterdam–Den Haag HS–Rotterdam–Dordrecht–Roosendaal–Vlissingen. These are formed of Plan IRM double-deck EMUs.

Amsterdam–Utrecht–Arnhem–Emmerich–Düsseldorf–Köln. These are: **EC** (Eurocity) services which are formed of DB IC stock. Two services run to or from Switzerland formed of SBB stock.

Schiphol–Amsterdam–Amersfoort–Hengelo–Bad Bentheim–Hannover–Berlin. These are formed of DB Interregio stock.

DEPOTS & WORKSHOPS

NS depots (*onderhoudsbedrijven*) are responsible for day-to-day maintenance of vehicles and the particular depots which normally carry out such maintenance are shown as allocations in this section. Please note, however that loco-hauled Intercity coaches which are shown as Leidschendam would normally be maintained at Amsterdam Zaanstraat if operating on the Haarlem–Maastricht service. The Belgian-owned type K4 coaches which are on loan are, however, all maintained at Leidschendam as they operate only on the Den Haag CS–Heerlen/Venlo service. These depots are now known as "Nedtrain Services".

The main workshops (revisiebedrijven) are at Haarlem (for all units) and Tilburg (for all locos and the power units of DMUs and Amersfoort (for wagons). They have recently been renamed "Overhaul and Refurbishment Haarlem, Tilburg and Amersfoort" in an attempt to obtain repair contracts from foreign railways where Dutch is not spoken.

There are many places where EMUs stable, but the main locations where units and some locos will be found are: Alkmaar, Amersfoort, Arnhem, Botlek*, Den Haag , Den Helder, Eindhoven, Groningen, Heerlen, Hengelo, Hoofddorp, Kijfhoek Yard*, Leeuwarden, Lelystad, Maastricht, Maasvlaakte*, Nijmegen, Roosendaal, Rotterdam CS, Sittard, Utrecht, Venlo, Vlissingen, Waalhaven Zuid*, Zwolle and Zutphen. (* – locos only).

DEPOT CODES

There are no official depot codes in the Netherlands, but the following unofficial depot codes are used in this section:

AZ	Amsterdam Zaanstraat
AM	Amsterdam Zaanstraat, Zwolle and Maastricht (maintained at any of these)
FO	Feijenoord (Rotterdam)
LD	Leidschendam-Voorburg (Den Haag)
MT	Maastricht
ON	Onnen
TB	Tilburg
WG	Watergraafsmeer (Amsterdam)
ZL	Zwolle

(S) after the code denotes the vehicle is stored, (X) that it is sold for scrap (N) that it is leased to NoordNed and (Y) that it is leased to Syntus.

COMPANY CODES FOR LOCOMOTIVES

Company codes are shown for locomotives as follows:

C	Railion Benelux (formerly NS Cargo)
M	NedTrain (formerly NS Materieel)
N	NBM Rail
P	NS Railpro
R	NS Reizigers
S	Strukton Materieel
V	Volker Stevin Rail & Traffic

LIVERY CODES

The following livery codes are used in this section. Where no code is shown against the individual vehicle, it is assumed that NS electric locomotives (except Class 1100) are yellow, diesel locomotives (and electric locomotives of Class 1100) are grey/yellow and NS multiple units are yellow with three blue "lozenges" on the side. Where two colours are shown, the first colour mentioned is the colour on the lower half of the body.

A	Advertising livery.
B	Benelux push-pull livery (yellow & bordeaux red).
D	Dark blue (overnight train livery).
I	NS Intercity livery (yellow & blue).
N	NoordNed (green with red blob on ends).
O	Non-standard livery (refer to text).
P	Post office red.
R	Raspberry red (NS Cargo/Railion Benelux).
V	Railion Benelux (DB Verkehrsrot).
Y	Plain yellow.
+	IC+ livery (dark blue).

2.1. DIESEL SHUNTING LOCOMOTIVES
In this section the last known location is given in the last column.

CLASS 200   B

These small locomotives known as "Siks" (goats) are to be found on light duties in freight yards and engineers locations throughout the NS system. They were originally painted dark green with cast number plates. Many of them are now out of use.

Built: 1934–51.
Builder: Werkspoor (281–306 built by NS Zwolle Works).
Engine: Stork R153 of 63 kW at 1050 r.p.m.
Transmission: Electric. Two Heemaf TM6 or Smit GT 322/7 axle-hung traction motors.
Train Heating: None.   **Weight in Full Working Order:** 21 (23 c) tonnes.
Maximum Tractive Effort: 39 kN.   **Length over Buffers:** 7.22 m.
Driving Wheel Dia.: 1000 mm.   **Max. Speed:** 65 km/h.

c Fitted with telescopic crane.

203	.	V	Deventer	283		V	Breda. To be scrapped.
207		M	TB	284	c	S	Kijfhoek
208		V		285		S	Zutphen
209		S	Roosendaal	286		P	WG
210		V	Hengelo	288		S	Zwolle
211		M	MT	290		C	TB. To be scrapped.
213		N	Eindhoven	291		S	Dordrecht
214		V	Almelo	292		M	Amersfoort
215		C	To be scrapped	296		M	FO
217		N	Eindhoven	297		V	
219		C	MT. To be scrapped.	298		C	Tilburg West
222		S	Maarsen	299		N	
223		S	Maarsen	300		C	ON. To be scrapped.
226		C	WG. To be scrapped.	301		M	Haarlem Works
227	c	N	Tilburg	302		C	To be scrapped.
229		C	To be scrapped.	303		C	FO
230		C	TB. To be scrapped.	307		V	
232		V		308		N	TB
234		S		309	c	S	Zwolle
235		C	To be scrapped.	312		C	To be scrapped.
238		S	Maastricht	313		C	To be scrapped.
241		C	Geldermalsen.	314		S	Nijmegen
242	c	S	Amersfoort	315		V	
243		M	Amersfoort	318		N	Den Haag
244		S	Zwolle	319		P	Feijenoord
245		P	Crailoo	320		S	
246	c	V	Alkmaar	322		C	To be scrapped.
247		C	Breda.	323		V	Deventer
248	c	S	Sittard	324		C	On hire to Shell Moerdijk
250	c	S	Groningen	325		C	To be scrapped.
252	c	N	's-Hertogenbosch	326		S	Terneuzen
253		S	Maastricht	328		S	
254		S	Kijfhoek Yard	329		V	Zwolle
255		M	TB	330		N	Feijenoord
257		M	MT	332		N	Feijenoord
260		S		334		M	Haarlem Works
263		V	WG	335		P	TB
265	c	V	Zwolle	336		C	To be scrapped.
267		S	Sittard	337		C	
270		P	Utrecht	338		M	LD
271		S	Amsterdam Westhaven	339		M	TB
274	c	N	Tilburg	340		S	Arnhem
276		V	Hengelo	341		C	Zwolle
279		P	Utrecht	342		V	
281		V		343		S	Zwolle

344	N	Eindhoven	357	M		Hengelo
345	C	To be scrapped.	358	N		Lage Zwaluwe
346	S	Zwolle	359	S		Venlo
347	N	's-Hertogenbosch	360	c	V	
348	N	Boxtel	361	c	S	Amsterdam Westhaven
349	S	Dordrecht	362	c	S	Kijfhoek
350	C		363	N		Feijenoord
351	C	Eindhoven	366	S		
352	N	Rotterdam Noord	368	c	V	Zwolle

CLASS 600   C

Instantly recognisable to the British eye, based on the BR Class 08, these locomotives perform similar duties. Again, many of these are out of use.

Built: 1950–57.
Builder: EE.
Engine: English Electric 6KT of 294 kW at 680 r.p.m.
Transmission: Electric. Two EE 506 4B axle-hung traction motors.
Train Heating: None.   **Weight in Full Working Order:** 47 tonnes.
Maximum Tractive Effort: 143 kN.   **Length over Buffers:** 9.07 m.
Driving Wheel Dia.: 1230 mm.   **Max. Speed:** 30 km/h.

603	C	(S)	Breda	644	C	(S)	TB
604	C	(S)	TB	647	C		On hire to M at Haarlem
608	C	(S)		648	C		Haarlem
610	C	(S)	Breda	650	R		WG
617	C	(S)	Breda	651	C	(S)	Breda
618	A		TB	653	R		's-Hertogenbosch
619	C	(S)	Breda	655	C	(S)	FO
622	C	(S)	Breda	656	C	(S)	TB
623	C	(S)	ZL	657	C		Utrecht
624	C	(S)	Breda	658	C	(S)	TB
628	C	(S)	TB	660	C		On hire to M at LD
629	R		MT	661	A	(S)	TB
631	C	(S)	TB	662	M		ZL.
635	C	(S)	TB	663	C	(S)	WG
639	R		MT	664	R		Den Haag CS
641	C	(S)	FO				

Fitted with Radio Remote Control & Renumbered.

671	(601)	R		WG	683	(621)	R		Den Haag
672	(602)	C	(S)	Breda	684	(626)	R		Heerlen
673	(605)	C		On hire to M at Amersfoort	685	(627)	R		WG
674	(606)	R		Den Haag CS	686	(0)	C		Zeeuws Vlaanderen
675	(607)	C	(S)	MT	687	(632)	R		TB
676	(611)	R		MT	688	(634)	R		MT
677	(612)	R		WG	689	(652)	R		Venlo
678	(613)	C		TB	690	(654)	R		Den Haag
679	(614)	R		MT	691	(642)	R		Venlo
680	(615)	R	(S)	TB	692	(649)	R		WG
681	(616)	C	(S)	TB	693	(659)	C	(S)	TB
682	(620)	C	(S)	WG					

2.2. ELECTRIC LOCOMOTIVES

CLASS 1100   Bo-Bo

These locomotives are based on the SNCF Class BB 8100 dating from 1949, modified with spring-borne traction motors. Alterations by the NS have included the fitting of roller bearings and larger sleeve-type buffers as carried by Class 1600. From 1978 new nose-ends were fitted. 1101–50 were originally liveried in turquoise blue, but this gave way in 1954 to dark blue with polished raised metal bands. From 1971 the locos started to be repainted in grey and yellow livery. All locos are now stored out of use. At the time of writing 1111 was at TB, 1117/27/47/49 at Breda, 1122/42/44/60 at WG and the rest at MT.

Built: 1950–56. (Rebuilt by NS 1978–82).
Builder-Mech. Parts: Alsthom.
Builder-Elec. Parts: Alsthom.
Traction Motors: 4 x Alsthom TA628A frame-mounted.
One Hour Rating: 2030 kW.   **Weight**: 83 tonnes.
Maximum Tractive Effort: 152 kN.   **Length over Buffers**: 14.110 m.
Driving Wheel Dia.: 1250 mm.   **Max. Speed**: 135 km/h.

1107	C	MT(S)	1122	C	MT(S)	1145	C	MT(S)
1110	C	MT(S)	1127	C	MT(S)	1147	C	MT(S)
1111	C	MT(S)	1132	C	MT(S)	1149	C	MT(S)
1113	C	MT(S)	1136	C	MT(S)	1152	C	MT(S)
1115	C	MT(S)	1142	C	MT(S)	1160	C	MT(S)
1117	C	MT(S)	1144	C	MT(S)			

CLASS 1300   Co-Co

The impressive-looking Class 1300 are based on the SNCF Class CC 7100 which includes in its ranks CC 7107, the co-world speed record holder (331 km/h attained in 1955). The class had a major refurbishment programme in the 1980s. At the time of writing all locos had been stored by Railion, but have now been sold to NS Reizigers and most are expected to re-enter service soon.

Built: 1952–56.
Builder-Mech. Parts: Alsthom.
Builder-Elec. Parts: Alsthom.
Traction Motors: 6 x Alsthom TA 628A frame mounted.
One Hour Rating: 3045 kW.   **Weight**: 111 tonnes.
Maximum Tractive Effort: 226 kN.   **Length over Buffers**: 18.952 m.
Driving Wheel Dia.: 1250 mm.   **Max. Speed**: 135 km/h.

p 'Elbow' style pantographs instead of the standard 'box' type.

1301		R	MT	DIEREN	1310	p	R	MT	BUSSUM
1302		R	MT	WOERDEN	1311		R	MT	BEST
1304		R	MT	CULEMBOURG	1312		R	MT	ZOETERMEER
1305		R	MT	ALPHEN AAN DER RIJN	1313	p	R	MT(S)	UITGEEST
1306	p	R	MT	BRUMMEN	1314		R	MT	HOORN
1307	p	R	MT	ETTEN-LEUR	1315		R	MT	TIEL
1308		R	MT	NUNSPEET	1316		R	MT	GELDERMALSEN
1309		R	MT	SUSTEREN					

CLASS 1600   B-B

These locomotives are based on the SNCF Class BB 7200 designed for a maximum speed of 200 km/h (limited at present to 160 km/h). The locos work freight trains over all principal routes.

Built: 1981–83.
Builder-Mech. Parts: Alsthom.
Builder-Elec. Parts: Alsthom.
Traction Motors: 2 x Alsthom TAB 674 C4 frame mounted.
One Hour Rating: 4400 kW.   **Weight**: 83 tonnes.
Maximum Tractive Effort: 294 kN.   **Length over Buffers**: 17.48 m.
Driving Wheel Dia.: 1250 mm.   **Max. Speed**: 160 km/h.

All push-pull fitted.

1601	C MT	AMSTERDAM		1618	C MT	ALMELO
1602	C MT	Schiphol		1619	C MT	MAASTRICHT
1603	C MT	ZUTPHEN		1620	C MT	ARNHEM
1604	C MT	DORDRECHT		1621	C MT	DEVENTER
1605	C MT	BREDA		1622	C MT	HAARLEM
1606	C MT	HARDERWIJK		1623	C MT	HILVERSUM
1607	C MT	VLISSINGEN		1624	C MT	ALKMAAR
1608	C MT	'S-HERTOGENBOSCH		1625	C MT	SITTARD
1609	C MT	HOOFDDORP		1626	C MT	MEPPEL
1610	C MT	HENGELO		1627	C MT	GOUDA
1611	C MT	VENLO		1628	C MT	APELDOORN
1612	C MT	GOES		1629	C MT	EDE
1613	C MT	ROERMOND		1630	C MT	ZWOLLE
1614	C MT	SCHIEDAM		1631	C MT	VOORBURG
1615	C MT	ZANDVOORT		1632	C MT	NIJMEGEN
1616	C MT	OLDENZAAL		1633	C MT	BERGEN OP ZOOM
1617	C MT	ASSEN				

CLASS 1700 B-B

This class is virtually identical to the Class 1600, the main difference being the fact that they have thyristor control. As built the locos had auto-couplers on one end for use with the double-decker DD-AR stock as "virtual EMUs". However 50 of them have been replaced with the new mDDM double-deck power cars and have had the auto-couplers removed. The braking system is not suitable for freight train use.

Built: 1990–94.
Builder-Mech. Parts: GEC-Alsthom.
Builder-Elec. Parts: GEC-Alsthom.
Traction Motors: 2 x Alsthom TAB 674 C4 frame mounted.
One Hour Rating: 4400 kW. **Weight**: 83 tonnes.
Maximum Tractive Effort: 294 kN. **Length over Buffers**: 17.48 m.
Driving Wheel Dia.: 1250 mm. **Max. Speed**: 160 km/h.

k Fitted with auto-coupler at one end.

1701	k	R LE			1728	k	R LE	
1702	k	R LE			1729	k	R LE	
1703	k	R LE			1730	k	R LE	
1704	k	R LE			1731	k	R LE	PURMEREND
1705	k	R LE	DALFSEN		1732		R MT	ZEVENBERGEN
1706	k	R LE			1733		R MT	
1707	k	R LE			1734		R MT	
1708	k	R LE			1735		R MT	SOEST
1709	k	R LE			1736		R MT	GILZE-RIJEN
1710	k	R LE			1737		R MT	
1711	k	R LE	EMMEN		1738		R MT	DUIVENDRECHT
1712	k	R LE			1739		R MT	DAALEN
1713	k	R LE			1740		R MT	BARN
1714	k	R LE	VEENENDAAL		1741		R MT	PUTTEN
1715	k	R LE			1742		R MT	
1716	k	R LE			1743		R MT	WOLVEGA
1717	k	R LE			1744		R MT	WIJCHEN
1718	k	R LE			1745		R MT	
1719	k	R LE	VOORHOUT		1746		R MT	CASTRICUM
1720	k	R LE	BEILEN		1747		R MT	
1721	k	R LE			1748		R MT	
1722	k	R LE			1749		R MT	
1723	k	R LE			1750		R MT	
1724	k	R LE	Anna Paulowna		1751		R MT	
1725	k	R LE			1752		R MT	
1726	k	R LE			1753		R MT	
1727	k	R LE			1754		R MT	DIEMEN

1755	R	MT		1769	R	MT	
1756	R	MT		1770	R	MT	
1757	R	MT		1771	R	MT	Abcoude
1758	R	MT		1772	R	MT	
1759	R	MT		1773	R	MT	ENKHUIZEN
1760	R	MT	AKKRUM	1774	R	MT	GRAMSBERGEN
1761	R	MT		1775	R	MT	
1762	R	MT		1776	R	MT	
1763	R	MT		1777	R	MT	
1764	R	MT		1778	R	MT	
1765	R	MT		1779	R	MT	
1766	R	MT		1780	R	MT	
1767	R	MT		1781	R	MT	
1768	R	MT	Boomsterhiem				

CLASS 1600 B-B

Class continued. NS Reizigers locos. Renumbered from 1634–1658.

1834	R	MT	LELYSTAD	1847	R	MT	DELFT
1835	R	MT	ENSCHEDE	1848	R	MT	VALKENBURG
1836	R	MT	HEERENVEEN	1849	R	MT	OSS
1837 **R**	R	MT	AMERSFOORT	1850	R	MT	DEN HAAG
1838	R	MT	GRONINGEN	1851	R	MT	TILBURG
1839	R	MT	LEIDEN	1852	R	MT	UTRECHT
1840	R	MT	STEENWIJK	1853	R	MT	DEN HELDER
1841	R	MT	ALMERE	1854	R	MT	GELEEN
1842	R	MT	WEERT	1855	R	MT	EINDHOVEN
1843	R	MT	HEERLEN	1856	R	MT	HOOGEVEEN
1844	R	MT	ROOSENDAAL	1857	R	MT	ROTTERDAM
1845	R	MT	MIDDELBURG	1858	R	MT	ZAANDAM
1846	R	MT	LEEUWARDEN				

2.3. MAIN-LINE DIESEL LOCOMOTIVES

CLASS 2200   Bo-Bo

These locos which have a cab at one end are now nearly all stored. The remaining ones work in the Terneuzen area.

Built: 1955–58.
Builder: Allan (2201–2300), Schneider (2301–2350).
Engine: Stork Schneider Superior 40C-Lx-8 of 670 kW at 1100 rpm.
Transmission: Electric. 4 Heemaf TM98 traction motors.
Train Heating: None.   **Weight in Full Working Order:** 72 tonnes.
Maximum Tractive Effort: 181 kN.   **Length over Buffers:** 14.100 m.
Driving Wheel Dia.: 950 mm.   **Max. Speed:** 100 km/h.

2201	(0)		C	(S)	2224	(2227)	C	(S)	2264	(0)		C	(S)
2202	(0)		C	(S)	2225	(0)	C	(S)	2274	(0)		C	(S)
2203	(0)		C	FO	2228	(2223)	C	(S)	2278	(0)	s	C	(S)
2204	(0)		C	(S)	2235	(0)	C	(S)	2293	(0)		C	(S)
2207	(0)		C		2239	(0)	C	(S)	2310	(0)		C	(S)
2209	(0)		C	(S)	2241	(0)	C	(S)	2311	(0)		C	(S)
2210	(2237)		C	(S)	2245	(0)	C	(S)	2319	(0)		C	(S)
2211	(0)		C	(S)	2246	(0)	C	(S)	2320	(0)		C	(S)
2212	(0)		C	FO	2249	(0)	C	(S)	2323	(0)		C	(S)
2215	(0)		C	FO(S)	2256	(0)	C	(S)	2330	(0)		C	(S)
2221	(2236)		C	(S)	2260	(0)	C	(S)	2336	(0)		C	(S)
2223	(2278)		C	(S)	2263	(0)	C	(S)					

Fitted with Radio Remote Control & Renumbered.

2351	(2267)	s	C	(S)	2367	(2295)	C	(S)	2376	(2335)		C	
2352	(2268)		C	(S)	2368	(2296)	C	(S)	2377	(2338)		C	(S)
2353	(2303)		C	(S)	2369	(2297)	C	(S)	2378	(2339)		C	(S)
2354	(2304)	s	C	(S)	2370	(2298)	C	(S)	2379	(2343)		C	(S)
2361	(2230)		C	(S)	2371	(2300)	C	(S)	2380	(2344)	s	C	(S)
2363	(2252)		C	(S)	2372	(2307)	C	(S)	2381	(2346)		C	(S)
2364	(2290)		C	(S)	2373	(2317)	C	(S)	2382	(2348)		C	(S)
2365	(2291)		C	(S)	2374	(2324)	C	(S)	2384	(2342)	R	C	FO
2366	(2294)		C	(S)	2375	(2332)	C	(S)					

CLASS 6400   Bo-Bo

Thyristor-controlled locomotives for freight and shunting use.

Built: 1988–94.
Builder: MaK.
Engine: MTU 12V396 TC 13 of 1180 kW at 1800 r.p.m.
Transmission: 4 x three phase BBC traction motors.
Train Heating: None (e Electric).   **Weight in Full Working Order:** 80 tonnes.
Maximum Tractive Effort: 290 kN.   **Length over Buffers:** 14.40 m.
Driving Wheel Dia.: 1000 mm.   **Max. Speed:** 120 km/h.

b Fitted with Belgian ATP for working into Belgium.
d Fitted with German ATP (Indusi) for working into Germany.

6401		C	ZL	Mijndert	6412	C	FO	Hans
6402		C	ZL	Marinus	6413	C	FO	Foeke
6403		C	ZL	Gijs	6414	C	FO	Sander
6404		C	ZL	Jo	6415	C	FO	Rens
6405		C	ZL	Jan	6416	C	FO	Arie
6406		C	ZL	Tonnie	6417	C	FO	Bob
6407		C	ZL	Henk	6418	C	FO	John
6408	V	C	ZL	Gerard	6419	C	ZL	Willem
6409		C	ZL	Herman	6420	C	ZL	Horst
6410		C	ZL	Toon	6421	C	ZL	Sebe
6411		C	FO	Oliver	6422	C	ZL	Wim

Nr					Naam
6423			C	ZL	Chris
6424			C	ZL	Dirk
6425			C	ZL	Chris
6426			C	ZL	Niko
6427			C	ZL	Hans
6428			C	ZL	Dirk
6429			C	ZL	Hans
6430			C	ZL	Jan Adrianus
6431			C	ZL	Antonius
6432			C	ZL	Hendrikus
6433			C	ZL	Han
6434			C	ZL	Henk
6435			C	ZL	Joop
6436			C	ZL	Willem
6437			C	ZL	Arie
6438			C	ZL	Henk
6439			C	ZL	Geert
6440			C	ZL	Jaap
6441			C	ZL	Joyce
6442			C	ZL	
6443			C	ZL	
6444			C	ZL	Eeltje
6445			C	ZL	Wijbo
6446			C	ZL	Jo
6447			C	ZL	Maurits
6448			C	ZL	Rein
6449			C	ZL	John
6450			C	ZL	Hanja
6451			C	ZL	Daan
6452			C	ZL	Rein
6453			C	ZL	Frans
6454	R		C	ZL	Wim
6455			C	ZL	Klaas-Abel
6456			C	ZL	
6457			C	ZL	
6458			C	ZL	Harry
6459			C	ZL	Anton
6460			C	ZL	Leo
6461		e	C	ZL	
6462		e	C	ZL	Olga
6463		e	C	ZL	Theo
6464		e	C	ZL	Jan
6465		e	C	ZL	Lammert
6466			C	ZL	
6467			C	ZL	
6468			C	ZL	
6469			C	ZL	
6470			C	ZL	
6471			C	ZL	

Nr					Naam
6472			C	ZL	
6473			C	ZL	
6474			C	ZL	
6475			C	ZL	
6476			C	ZL	
6477			C	ZL	
6478			C	ZL	
6479			C	ZL	
6480			C	ZL	
6481			C	ZL	Lies
6482			C	ZL	
6483			C	ZL	
6484			C	ZL	
6485			C	FO	
6486			C	FO	
6487			C	FO	
6488			C	FO	Gerard
6489			C	FO	
6490			C	FO	
6491			C	FO	
6492			C	FO	
6493			C	FO	Joke
6494		d	C	FO	
6495	V	d	C	FO	
6496	V	d	C	FO	
6497	V	d	C	FO	
6498		d	C	FO	
6499		d	C	FO	
6500			C	FO	
6501			C	FO	Edo
6502			C	FO	
6503			C	FO	
6504			C	FO	
6505			C	FO	
6506			C	FO	
6507			C	FO	
6508			C	FO	
6509			C	FO	
6510			C	FO	
6511	R		C	FO	
6512	R	b	C	FO	
6513	R	b	C	FO	
6514	R	b	C	FO	
6515	R	b	C	FO	
6516	R	b	C	FO	
6517	R	b	C	FO	
6518	R	b	C	FO	
6519	R	b	C	FO	
6520	R	b	C	FO	

2.4. DIESEL MULTIPLE UNITS

Note: In this section, units marked (N) are on lease to Noordned and units marked (Y) are leased to Syntus.

CLASS DEIII (PLAN U)   3-CAR UNITS

Known as "red devils" when new because of their original red livery (and because their predecessors were known as "blue angels"), the remaining units work non-electrified lines around Zutphen and Arnhem. They are similar in apearance to the "Mat'64" EMUs. 19 sets are to be refurbished for a further five years service. Some of the stored units are at WG in use as a noise barrier.

mBDk+B+ABk (DMBSO–TSO–DTCso).

Built: 1960–63.
Builder: Werkspoor.
Wheel Arrangement: Bo–Bo + 2–2 + 2–2.
Engine: SACM MGO-12-BSHR of 735 kW at 1400 r.p.m.
Transmission: Electric. Smit GT 38/224 or Metropolitan Vickers MV 139.
Accommodation: –/40 + –/88 2T + 24/40 2T.
Weight: 66 + 35 + 35 tonnes.
Length over couplings: 25.17 + 24.09 + 25.17 m.
Max. Speed: 130 km/h.

111	ZL(S)	120	ZL(S)	130	ZL	141	ZL
112	ZL	121	ZL	131	ZL(S)	142	ZL
113	ZL(Y)	122	ZL	133	ZL	146	ZL(S)
114	ZL(Y)	123	ZL(S)	134	ZL	147	ZL
115	ZL(Y)	125	ZL(Y)	135	ZL	148	ZL(S)
116	ZL	126	ZL	136	ZL(S)	149	ZL(S)
117	ZL	127	ZL(S)	137	ZL	150	ZL
118	ZL	128	ZL	139	ZL(S)	151	ZL
119	ZL	129	ZL(S)	140	ZL(S)	152	ZL

3100/3200 CLASSES (DHI & DHII):

These units represented a change in policy for the NS at the end of the seventies when the closure of the northern NS secondary lines was under discussion. The power equipment was based on that used to modernise the DEII units, i.e. a Cummins engine, but Voith hydraulic transmission was used. The engine and transmission system was copied by BR for their new DMUs which were known as Sprinters, the name also being pinched from the NS! A new body style was adopted with flat ends with one-piece windscreens. The units work on branch lines out of Groningen and Leeuwarden, and carry the logo 'Wadloper'. This is because the area between the Dutch mainland along the Frisian and Groningen shore and the islands has called the Waddenzee (Wadden sea) The word "loper" means "walker". All sets have now been refurbished with new seating. The number of fixed seats has been reduced in favour of more standee/bike space with tip-up seating. The units have now also been fitted with cowcatchers.

CLASS DHI   SINGLE UNITS

mBk (DMSO).

Built: 1983.
Builder: Duewag.
Wheel Arrangement: 2–B.
Engine: Cummins NT855R4 of 210 kW at 2100 r.p.m.
Transmission: Hydraulic. Voith T211r.
Accommodation: –/34 1T.
Weight: 36 tonnes.
Length over couplings: 22.31 m.
Max. Speed: 100 km/h.
Disc brakes. Magnetic track brakes.

3101	ZL	3104	ZL(N)	3107	ZL(N)	3110	ZL(N)
3102	ZL	3105	ZL(N)	3108	ZL(N)	3111	ZL(N)
3103	ZL	3106	ZL(N)	3109	ZL(N)	3112	ZL(N)

| 3113 | ZL(N) | 3115 | ZL(N) | 3117 | ZL(N) | 3119 | ZL(N) |
| 3114 | ZL(N) | 3116 | ZL(N) | 3118 | ZL(N) | | |

CLASS DHII   2-CAR UNITS

mBk + mBk (DMSO–DMSO).

Built: 1981–82.
Builder: Duewag.
Wheel Arrangement: 2–B+B–2.
Engine: Cummins NT855R4 of 210 kW of 2100 r.p.m. (one per car).
Transmission: Hydraulic. Voith T211r.
Accommodation: –/52 + –/48 1T.
Weight: 35 + 35 tonnes.
Length over couplings: 21.72 + 21.72 m.
Max. Speed: 100 km/h.

Disc brakes. Magnetic track brakes.

3201	ZL(N)	3209	ZL	3217	ZL(N)	3225	ZL(N)
3202	ZL(N)	3210	ZL	3218	ZL(N)	3226	ZL(N)
3203	ZL(N)	3211	ZL(N)	3219	ZL(N)	3227	ZL(N)
3204	ZL(N)	3212	ZL(N)	3220	ZL(N)	3228	ZL(N)
3205	ZL(N)	3213	ZL(N)	3221	ZL(N)	3229	ZL(N)
3206	ZL(N)	3214	ZL(N)	3222 N	ZL(N)	3230	ZL(N)
3207	ZL	3215	ZL(N)	3223	ZL(N)	3231	ZL(N)
3208	ZL	3216	ZL(N)	3224	ZL(N)		

Note: 3201 is named "MATTHIAS".

CLASS DM'90   2-CAR UNITS

mBk+mABk (DMSO–DMCO).

These new units were introduced to replace the remaining 1950s and 1960s-built DMUs. Assembly was at the Duewag plant in Germany with Talbot providing the bodies and SIG the bogies. These new units have underfloor engines like DHI and DHII. They can only work on lines which have been modified with new generation ATB, i.e. Groningen–Leeuwarden, Leeuwarden–Stavoren, Zwolle–Kampen, Zwolle–Enschede, Nijmegen–Venlo–Roermond, Arnhem–Winterswijk and Heerlen–Aachen. Other lines are being modified to allow DM'90 to run on them.

Built: 1995–1999.
Builder: Duewag/Talbot/SIG.
Wheel Arrangement: 2–B + B–2.
Engine: Cummins NT855R4 of 320 kW at 2000 r.p.m.
Transmission: Hydraulic. Voith 211 rzzc.
Accommodation: –/48 1T + 24/37 1T.
Weight: 47 + 48 tonnes.
Length over couplings: 26.17 + 26.17 m.
Max. Speed: 140 km/h.

Disc brakes. Magnetic track brakes.
-d Modified with retractible steps and Indusi for working to Aachen, Germany.

3401	ZL	3415	ZL	3428	ZL	3441	ZL
3402	ZL	3416	ZL	3429	ZL	3442	ZL
3403	ZL	3417	ZL	3430	ZL	3443	ZL
3404	ZL	3418	ZL	3431	d MT	3444	ZL
3405	ZL	3419	ZL	3432	d MT	3445	ZL
3406	ZL	3420	ZL	3433	d MT	3446	ZL(N)
3407	ZL	3421	ZL	3434	ZL	3447	ZL(N)
3408	ZL	3422	ZL	3435	ZL	3448	ZL(N)
3409	ZL	3423	ZL	3436	ZL	3449	ZL(N)
3410	ZL	3424	ZL	3437	ZL	3450	ZL(Y)
3411	ZL	3425	ZL	3438	ZL	3451	ZL(Y)
3412	ZL	3426	ZL	3439	ZL	3452	ZL(Y)
3413	ZL	3427	ZL	3440	ZL	3453	ZL(Y)
3414	ZL						

2.5. ELECTRIC MULTIPLE UNITS

All NS EMUs are gangwayed within the unit only, except for the Plan Z "Koploper" units. All are disc-braked except for Plan V,T and mP which have tread brakes. All have power-operated sliding or folding doors. The various builds of NS EMUs can easily be recognised by their front-end design as follows:

1946 stock ('Mat 46') had a round front and a characteristic green livery. All 1946 stock is now withdrawn from capital stock.

1954 stock ('Mat 54') had a large 'dog head' and was designed for Inter-City and stopping services. Known as "Hondekoppen" (dog-noses). All now withdrawn from capital stock.

1964 stock ('Mat 64') has a shorter bonnet with the outer cab windows pointed. It is used mainly on stopping services.

Sprinters were built between 1972 and 1976 and have a slightly sloping front end which curves in at the bottom.

Railhoppers have ends which slope outwards down to a point below the windscreen and then inwards.

Koplopers were built between 1977 and 1993 and have gangwayed ends with a roof cab.

Regio Runners are double-deck units with a distinctive front-end design.

EMUs are often referred to by their formation code as follows:
EL EMU, D includes guard's/luggage area (dienst), P Post area. 2, 3 or 4 No. of cars.
Example: ELD-2 is a two car EMU with guard's/luggage accommodation.

PLAN V1, V2 & V3   2-CAR UNITS

Mat'64. These sets work stoptreinen and sneltreinen all over the NS network. They operate as a common fleet with all other Plan V stock.

mABDk + mBk (DMBCO–DMSso).

Built: 1966–68.
Builder-Mech. Parts: Werkspoor.
Builder-Elec. Parts: Smit.
Wheel Arrangement: 2–Bo + Bo–2.
Traction Motors: 4 x Heemaf of 145 kW.
Accommodation: 24/24 1T + –/64 1T.
Weight: 43 + 42 tonnes.
Length over couplings: 26.07 + 26.07 m.
Max. Speed: 140 km/h.

401–415 are plan V1, 416–430 are plan V2 and 431–438 are plan V3.

401	AM	411	AM	421	AM	430	AM
402	AM	412	AM	422	AM	431	AM
403	AM	413	AM	423	AM	432	AM
404	AM	414	AM	424	AM	433	AM
405	AM	415	AM	425	AM	434	AM
406	AM	416	AM	426	AM	435	AM
407	AM	417	AM	427	AM	436	AM
408	AM	418	AM	428	AM	437	AM
409	AM	419	AM	429	AM	438	AM
410	AM						

PLAN V4, V5 & V6   2-CAR UNITS

1964 stock. These sets are similar to 401–438 but were built without luggage compartments.

mABk + mBk (DMCso–DMSso).

Built: 1969–70.
Builder-Mech. Parts: Werkspoor (441–461), Talbot (462–483).
Builder-Elec. Parts: Smit.
Wheel Arrangement: 2–Bo + Bo–2.
Traction Motors: 4 x Heemaf 145 kW.
Accommodation: 24/40 1T + –/78.
Weight: 43 + 42 tonnes.

Length over couplings: 26.07 + 26.07 m.
Max. Speed: 140 km/h.

441–461 are V4, 462–471 are V5 and 472–483 are V6.

441	AM	452	AM	463	AM	474	AM
442	AM	453	AM	464	AM	475	AM
443	AM	454	AM	465	AM	476	AM
444	AM	455	AM	466	AM	477	AM
445	AM	456	AM	467	AM	478	AM
446	AM	457	AM	468	AM	479	AM
447	AM	458	AM	469	AM	480	AM
448	AM	459	AM	470	AM	481	AM
449	AM	460	AM	471	AM	482	AM
450	AM	461	AM	472	AM	483	AM
451	AM	462	AM	473	AM		

PLAN TT   4-CAR UNIT

Mat'64. Prototype four-car unit for Plan T (see below).

Bk + mAD + mB + Bk (DTSso–MBFso–MSO–DTSso).

Built: 1961.
Builder-Mech. Parts: Werkspoor.
Builder-Elec. Parts: Smit.
Wheel Arrangement: 2–2 + Bo–Bo + Bo–Bo + 2–2.
Traction Motors: 8 x Heemaf 150 kW.
Accommodation: –/80 1T + 41/– 1T + –/80 1T + –/80 1T.
Weight: 38 + 46 + 44 + 35 tonnes.
Length over couplings: 25.70 + 24.27 + 24.27 + 25.70 m.
Max. Speed: 140 km/h.

501	AZ	

PLAN T   4-CAR UNITS

These four-car units were originally designed for Intercity use for which they were fitted with pantries and a buffet area. They are now being refurbished with new seating with the pantry, restaurant and luggage areas removed. They operate over a limited area in and around the Randstad in particular between Den Haag CS and Hoorn.

Bk + mBD + mAB + Bk (DTSso–MBSO(K)–MCso–DTSo).

Built: 1964–65.
Builder-Mech. Parts: Werkspoor.
Builder-Elec. Parts: Smit.
Wheel Arrangement: 2–2 + Bo–Bo + Bo–Bo + 2–2.
Traction Motors: 8 x Heemaf 150 kW.
Accommodation: –/80 1T + 24S 22 buffet 1T + 42/24 1T + –/80 1T.
Weight: 39 + 47 + 46 + 36 tonnes.
Length over couplings: 26.07 + 24.93 + 24.93 + 26.07 m.
Max. Speed: 140 km/h.

r Refurbished with new seating. Accommodation –/80 + –/76 1T + 42/24 1T + –/80.

502	r	AZ	510	r	AZ	518		AZ	525		AZ
503	r	AZ	511	r	AZ	519		AZ	526		AZ
504	r	AZ	512		AZ	520		AZ	527		AZ
505	r	AZ	513	r	AZ	521		AZ	528		AZ
506	r	AZ	514		AZ	522		AZ	529	r	AZ
507	r	AZ	515	r	AZ	523		AZ	530		AZ
508	r	AZ	516		AZ	524		AZ	531		AZ
509	r	AZ	517	r	AZ						

PLAN V7   2-CAR UNITS

1964 stock. Similar to other plan V units, but built with post compartment.

mAbk + mBPk (DMCso–DMPSO).

Built: 1970–72.
Builder-Mech. Parts: Werkspoor.
Builder-Elec. Parts: Smit.
Wheel Arrangement: 2–Bo + Bo–2.
Traction Motors: 4 x Heemaf 145 kW.
Accommodation: 24/40 1T + –/64 (–/80 r).
Weight: 43 + 42 tonnes.
Length over couplings: 26.07 + 26.07 m.
Max. Speed: 140 km/h.

r Post compartment converted to open saloon containing 16 seats in 4+0 layout.

801	r	AM	811	r	AM	821	r	AM	831	r	AM
802	r	AM	812	r	AM	822	r	AM	832	r	AM
803	r	AM	813	r	AM	823	r	AM	833	r	AM
804	r	AM	814	r	AM	824	r	AM	834	r	AM
805	r	AM	815	r	AM	825	r	AM	835	r	AM
806	r	AM	816		AM	826	r	AM	836	r	AM
807	r	AM	817	r	AM	827	r	AM	837	r	AM
808	r	AM	818	r	AM	828	r	AM	838		AM
809	r	AM	819	r	AM	829	r	AM	839		AM
810	r	AM	820	r	AM	830	r	AM	840		AM

PLAN V8–V13   2-CAR UNITS

1964 stock. Talbot version of plan V7.

mAbk + mBPk (DMCso–DMPSO).

Built: 1972–76.
Builder-Mech. Parts: Talbot.
Builder-Elec. Parts: Smit.
Wheel Arrangement: 2–Bo + Bo–2.
Traction Motors: 4 x Heemaf 145 kW.
Accommodation: 24/40 1T + –/64.
Weight: 45 + 43 tonnes.
Length over couplings: 26.07 + 26.07 m.
Max. Speed: 140 km/h.

r Post compartment converted to passenger accommodation with 12 tip-up seats.

841	AM	861	AM	882	AM	902		AM
842	AM	862	AM	883	AM	903		AM
843	AM	863	AM	884	AM	904		AM
844	AM	864	AM	885	AM	905		AM
845	AM	865	AM	886	AM	906		AM
846	AM	866	AM	887	AM	907		AM
847	AM	867	AM	888	AM	908		AM
848	AM	868	AM	889	AM	909		AM
849	AM	869	AM	890	AM	910		AM
850	AM	870	AM	891	AM	911		AM
851	AM	871	AM	892	AM	912		AM
852	AM	872	AM	893	AM	913		AM
853	AM	873	AM	894	AM	914		AM
854	AM	874	AM	895	AM	915		AM
855	AM	875	AM	896	AM	916		AM
856	AM	876	AM	897	AM	917		AM
857	AM	877	AM	898	AM	918		AM
858	AM	879	AM	899	AM	919		AM
859	AM	880	AM	900	AM	920		AM
860	AM	881	AM	901	AM	921	r	AM

922	r	AM	933	r	AM	945	r	AM	955	r	AM
923	r	AM	934	r	AM	946	r	AM	956	r	AM
924	r	AM	935	r	AM	947	r	AM	957	r	AM
925	r	AM	936	r	AM	948	r	AM	958	r	AM
926	r	AM	937	r	AM	949	r	AM	960	r	AM
927	r	AM	939	r	AM	950	r	AM	961	r	AM
928	r	AM	940	r	AM	951	r	AM	962	r	AM
929	r	AM	941	r	AM	952	r	AM	963	r	AM
930	r	AM	942	r	AM	953	r	AM	964	r	AM
931	r	AM	943	r	AM	954	r	AM	965	r	AM
932	r	AM	944	r	AM						

PLAN Y0   SPRINTER SGM0   2-CAR UNITS

The earliest batch of 'Sprinter' units from which BR's new DMUs take their name, these sets work on the Den Haag CS–Rotterdam Hofplein line. The rapid acceleration from a standing start is especially useful on this line which has stations at very close intervals and has been considered for conversion to light rail. All sets have now been modified with first class seating removed, less seats and more room for standees. They are branded "City Pendel".

mABk + mBk (DMCO–DMSO).

Built: 1975–76.
Builder-Mech. Parts: Talbot.
Builder-Elec. Parts: Oerlikon.
Wheel Arrangement: Bo–Bo + Bo–Bo.
Traction Motors: 8 x Oerlikon 160 kW.
Accommodation: –/40 + –/40.
Weight: 52.5 + 52.5 tonnes.
Length over couplings: 26.10 + 26.10 m.
Max. Speed: 125 km/h.

2001	Y	LD	2005	Y	LD	2009	Y	LD	2013	Y	LD
2002	Y	LD	2006	Y	LD	2010	Y	LD	2014	Y	LD
2003	Y	LD	2007	Y	LD	2011	Y	LD	2015	Y	LD
2004	Y	LD	2008	Y	LD	2012	Y	LD			

PLAN Y1   SPRINTER SGM1   2-CAR UNITS

These sets are similar to plan Y0, but were built with a toilet and gangways, although the toilets have now been removed. They work on on the Zoetermeer Stadslijn which is a circular route through the eastern suburbs of Den Haag. The same remarks apply to this route as to the Hofplein line (see above). These sets have also been modified with less seats and more room for standees and branded "City Pendel".

mABk + mBk (DMCO–DMSOL).

Built: 1975–76.
Builder-Mech. Parts: Talbot.
Builder-Elec. Parts: Oerlikon.
Wheel Arrangement: Bo–Bo + Bo–Bo.
Traction Motors: 8 x Oerlikon 160 kW.
Accommodation: –/40 + –/40.
Weight: 54 + 53 tonnes.
Length over couplings: 26.10 + 26.10 m.
Max. Speed: 125 km/h.

2021	Y	LD	2025	Y	LD	2029	Y	LD	2033	Y	LD
2022	Y	LD	2026	Y	LD	2030	Y	LD	2034	Y	LD
2023	Y	LD	2027	Y	LD	2031	Y	LD	2035	Y	LD
2024	Y	LD	2028	Y	LD	2032	Y	LD			

SM'90   RAILHOPPER   2-CAR UNITS

These EMUs for stopping services went into service early in 1994. They feature pressure ventilation, but are somewhat spartan by modern standards. The composite vehicle has a wheelchair lift. They only work between Zwolle and Emmen.

mABk + mBk (DMCO–DMSO).

Built: 1994.
Builder-Mech. Parts: Talbot.
Builder-Elec. Parts: Holec.
Wheel Arrangement: Bo–Bo + Bo–Bo.
Traction Motors: 4 Holec 3 phase per car.
Accommodation: 24/41 1T + –/72.
Weight: 49 + 48 tonnes.
Length over couplings: 26.17 + 26.17 m.
Max. Speed: 160 km/h.

2101	ZL	2104	ZL	2106	ZL	2108	ZL
2102	ZL	2105	ZL	2107	ZL	2109	ZL
2103	ZL						

PLAN Y2/Y3   SPRINTER SGM 1/2   3-CAR UNITS

2836–2880 were built as two-car units but were strengthened with an intermediate trailer and reclassified from Plan Y1 to Plan Y2. 2881–2895 were built as three-car units and are Plan Y3. The units work on stoptreins in the Randstad area such as Amsterdam–Utrecht, Amsterdam–Haarlem–Uitgeest, Amsterdam–Alkmaar and Rotterdam CS–Hoek van Holland.

mBk + AB + mBk (DMSO–TCO–DMSO).

Built: 1978–80/83–84*.
Builder-Mech. Parts: Talbot.
Builder-Elec. Parts: Oerlikon.
Wheel Arrangement: Bo–Bo + 2–2 + Bo–Bo.
Traction Motors: 8 x Oerlikon 160 kW.
Accommodation: –/72 + 40/40 1T + –/72 1T.
Weight: 54 + 36 + 53 tonnes.
Length over couplings: 26.15 + 26.40 + 26.15 m.
Max. Speed: 125 km/h.

2836	(2036)	LD	2856	(2056)	LD	2876	(2076)	LD
2837	(2037)	LD	2857	(2057)	LD	2877	(2077)	LD
2838	(2038)	LD	2858	(2058)	LD	2878	(2078)	LD
2839	(2039)	LD	2859	(2059)	LD	2879	(2079)	LD
2840	(2040)	LD	2860	(2060)	LD	2880	(2080)	LD
2841	(2041)	LD	2861	(2061)	LD	2881		LD
2842	(2042)	LD	2862	(2062)	LD	2882		LD
2843	(2043)	LD	2863	(2063)	LD	2883		LD
2844	(2044)	LD	2864	(2064)	LD	2884		LD
2845	(2045)	LD	2865	(2065)	LD	2885		LD
2846	(2046)	LD	2866	(2066)	LD	2886		LD
2847	(2047)	LD	2867	(2067)	LD	2887		LD
2848	(2048)	LD	2868	(2068)	LD	2888		LD
2849	(2049)	LD	2869	(2069)	LD	2889		LD
2850	(2050)	LD	2870	(2070)	LD	2890		LD
2851	(2051)	LD	2871	(2071)	LD	2891		LD
2852	(2052)	LD	2872	(2072)	LD	2892		LD
2853	(2053)	LD	2873	(2073)	LD	2893		LD
2854	(2054)	LD	2874	(2074)	LD	2894		LD
2855	(2055)	LD	2875	(2075)	LD	2895		LD

mP   SINGLE UNIT POSTAL VANS

The crimson and yellow postal units, formerly painted dark red are unique amongst NS units in having conventional drawgear and buffers to facilitate the taking of a trailing load of up to five special four-wheeled postal vans. The loss of the postal contract to road in 1996 rendered the units redundant and most are now stored although a couple are hired to NedTrain for ferrying stores around. Four units (*) are to be used for signalling trials between Meppel and Leeuwarden and Heerlen and Maastricht.

mP (DMPMV).

Built: 1965–66.
Builder-Mech. Parts: Werkspoor.
Builder-Elec. Parts: Smit.
Wheel Arrangement: Bo–Bo.
Traction Motors: 4 x Heemaf 145 kW.
Weight: 54 tonnes.
Length over couplings: 26.40 m.
Max. Speed: 140 km/h.
Non-Standard Livery: 0 Bright red.

3001	P	(S)	3012	P	(S)	3020	P	(S)	3029	P *	(S)
3004	P	(S)	3013	P	(S)	3022	P	(S)	3030	P	AZ
3005	P	(S)	3014	P	(S)	3023	P	(S)	3033	0 *	(S)
3007	P	(S)	3016	P	(S)	3024	P *	(S)	3034	P *	(S)
3009	P	(S)	3017	P	(S)	3027	P	AZ			

ICM1/2 (PLAN Z0/Z1)   KOPLOPER   3-CAR UNITS

These strikingly modern Intercity units, also known as IC3 units, have raised cabs and through gangways. The coaches in these sets formed the basis for the loco-hauled ICR stock now familiar over many NS routes. The prototype units (4001–7) have been modified to standard as far as the basic layout is concerned, but they still retain different interior decor and differently positioned destination displays. These units and the similar 4-car units can be found on the Intercity services from Amsterdam CS, Schiphol, Den Haag CS and Rotterdam CS to Groningen, Leeuwarden, Enschede Arnhem and Den Helder.

mBDk + AB + sBfk (DMSO (kitchenette/pantry)–TCsoL–DTSOL).

Built: 1977*/83–89.
Builder-Mech. Parts: Talbot.
Builder-Elec. Parts: Oerlikon.
Wheel Arrangement: Bo–Bo + 2–2 + 2–2.
Gangways: Large gangways at both ends with cabs on top.
Traction Motors: 4 x Oerlikon 312 kW.
Accommodation: –/54 + 35/31 2T + –/63 1T + bicycle space.
Weight: 59 + 42 + 42 tonnes.
Length over couplings: 27.05 + 26.50 + 27.05 m.
Max. Speed: 160 km/h.

4001	I	ON	4028	I	ON	4052	I	ON	4075	I	ON
4002	I	ON	4029	I	ON	4053	I	ON	4076	I	ON
4003	I	ON	4030	I	ON	4054	I	ON	4077	I	ON
4004	I	ON	4031	I	ON	4055	I	ON	4078	I	ON
4005	I	ON	4032	I	ON	4056	I	ON	4079	I	ON
4006	I	ON	4033	I	ON	4057	I	ON	4080	I	ON
4007	I	ON	4034	I	ON	4058	I	ON	4081	I	ON
4011	S	ON	4035	I	ON	4059	I	ON	4082	I	ON
4012	S	ON	4036	I	ON	4060	I	ON	4083	I	ON
4013	I	ON	4037	I	ON	4061	I	ON	4084	I	ON
4014	I	ON	4038	I	ON	4062	I	ON	4085	I	ON
4015	I	ON	4039	I	ON	4063	I	ON	4086	I	ON
4016	I	ON	4040	I	ON	4064	I	ON	4087	I	ON
4017	I	ON	4041	I	ON	4065	I	ON	4088	I	ON
4018	I	ON	4042	I	ON	4066	I	ON	4089	I	ON
4019	I	ON	4043	I	ON	4067	I	ON	4090	I	ON
4020	I	ON	4044	I	ON	4068	I	ON	4091	I	ON
4021	I	ON	4045	I	ON	4069	I	ON	4092	I	ON
4022	I	ON	4046	I	ON	4070	I	ON	4093	I	ON
4023	I	ON	4047	I	ON	4071	I	ON	4094	I	ON
4024	S	ON	4048	I	ON	4072	I	ON	4095	I	ON
4025	I	ON	4049	I	ON	4073	I	ON	4096	I	ON
4026	I	ON	4050	I	ON	4074	I	ON	4097	I	ON
4027	I	ON	4051	I	ON						

ICM3 (PLAN Z2)　KOPLOPER　4-CAR UNITS

These units are a four-car version of the IC3s and are used on the same services.

mBDk + B (*A) + A + sBFk (DMSO (kitchenette/pantry)–MSOL–TFsoL–DTSOL).

Built: 1990 onwards.
Builder-Mech. Parts: Talbot.
Builder-Elec. Parts: Oerlikon.
Wheel Arrangement: Bo–Bo + Bo–2 + 2–2 + 2–2.
Gangways: Large gangways at both ends with cabs on top.
Traction Motors: 6 x Oerlikon 312 kW.
Accommodation: –/55 + –/80 1T (*58/– 1T)+ 59/– 2T + –/63 1T.
Weight: 59 + 50 + 42 + 42 tonnes.
Length over couplings: 27.05 + 26.50 + 26.50 + 27.05 m.
Max. Speed: 160 km/h.

* This set was formerly 4231 and has extra first class accommodation for working trains 501/502 (07.14 Groningen–Den Haag CS and 16.36 Den Haag CS–Groningen). The second vehicle has been converted from B to A.

4201	I	ON	4214	I	ON	4227	I	ON	4240	I	ON
4202	I	ON	4215	I	ON	4228	I	ON	4241	I	ON
4203	I	ON	4216	I	ON	4229	I	ON	4242	I	ON
4204	I	ON	4217	I	ON	4230	I	ON	4243	I	ON
4205	I	ON	4218	I	ON	4232	I	ON	4244	I	ON
4206	I	ON	4219	I	ON	4233	I	ON	4245	I	ON
4207	I	ON	4220	I	ON	4234	I	ON	4246	I	ON
4208	I	ON	4221	I	ON	4235	I	ON	4247	I	ON
4209	I	ON	4222	I	ON	4236	I	ON	4248	I	ON
4210	I	ON	4223	I	ON	4237	I	ON	4249	I	ON
4211	I	ON	4224	I	ON	4238	I	ON	4250	I	ON
4212	I	ON	4225	I	ON	4239	I	ON	4444	I *	ON
4213	I	ON	4226	I	ON						

IRM　REGIO RUNNER　3/4-CAR UNITS

These recently-built three and four car double-decker units work various sneltrein and Intercity services over a wide area. Unit numbers are 82xx series for three-car units and 84xx series for four-car units. The set number is determined by the ABv3/4 car. Thus 8203 contains 380 8003.

As we went to press, NS announced that they had ordered another 13 4-car and 12 6-car IRM units plus 128 coaches to upgrade three-car units up to four cars and four-car units up to six cars. All units will be suitable for 25 kV a.c. working as well as 1500 V d.c. The three-car units will have a transformer composite (ABv6) seating 45/34 added between the first and second vehicles, whilst the four-car units will have a motor second (mBv7) seating –/91 1TD plus a transformer composite (ABv6) added between the second and third vehicles. The numbers of these vehicles are not yet known, but space has been left to insert them later.

mBvk + ABv3/4 (+ ABv5*) + mBvk (DMSO–TCO(–TCO*)–DMSO).

Built: 1994–96.
Builder-Mech. Parts: Talbot (De Dietrich*).
Builder-Elec. Parts: Holec.
Wheel Arrangement: 2–Bo + 2–2 (+ 2–2) + Bo–2.
Traction Motors: 2 x Holec-Riddekerk DMKT 60/45 of 302 kW continuous rating per motor car.
Accommodation: –/93 + 47/42 2T 1TD (+ 23/80 1T [47/42 1T§]) + –/93.
Weight: 62.2 + 52.4 (+ 50.4) + 62.2 tonnes.
Length over couplings: 27.28 + 26.50 (+ 26.50) + 27.28 m.
Max. Speed: 160 km/h.

§8498/99 have been renumbered from 8432/33. As the set number is determined by the ABv3/4 car, these have been renumbered 380 8098/99 from 380 8032/33, whilst the ABv5s which have been modified have not been renumbered! The sets can be found on the 16.45 Den Haag CS–Nijmegen and other trains on that route.

8201	I	ON	290 8501		380 8001	290 8502		
8202	I	ON	290 8503		380 8002	290 8504		
8203	I	ON	290 8505		380 8003	290 8506		
8204	I	ON	290 8507		380 8004	290 8509		
8205	I	ON	290 8508		380 8005	290 8510		
8206	I	ON	290 8511		380 8006	290 8512		
8207	I	ON	290 8513		380 8007	290 8514		
8209	I	ON	290 8517		380 8009	290 8518		
8210	I	ON	290 8519		380 8010	290 8520		
8211	I	ON	290 8521		380 8011	290 8522		
8212	I	ON	290 8523		380 8012	290 8525		
8213	I	ON	290 8524		380 8013	290 8526		
8215	I	ON	290 8529		380 8015	290 8530		
8216	I	ON	290 8531		380 8016	290 8532		
8217	I	ON	290 8533		380 8017	290 8534		
8218	I	ON	290 8535		380 8018	290 8536		
8219	I	ON	290 8537		380 8019	290 8538		
8220	I	ON	290 8539		380 8020	290 8540		
8221	I	ON	290 8541		380 8021	290 8542		
8222	I	ON	290 8543		380 8022	290 8544		
8223	I	ON	290 8545		380 8023	290 8546		
8224	I	ON	290 8547		380 8024	290 8548		
8225	I	ON	290 8549		380 8025	290 8550		
8226	I	ON	290 8551		380 8026	290 8552		
8230	I	ON	290 8559		380 8030	290 8560		
8231	I	ON	290 8561		380 8031	290 8562		
8234	I	ON	290 8567		380 8034	290 8568		
8258	I	ON	290 8615		380 8058	290 8616		
8269	I	ON	290 8637		380 8069	290 8638		
8273	I	ON	290 8645		380 8073	290 8646		
8276	I	ON	290 8651		380 8076	290 8652		
8278	I	ON	290 8655		380 8078	290 8656		
8279	I	ON	290 8657		380 8079	290 8658		
8280	I	ON	290 8659		380 8080	290 8660		
8281	I	ON	290 8661		380 8081	290 8662		
8408	I	AZ	290 8515	380 8008			380 8240	290 8516
8414	I	AZ	290 8527	380 8014			380 8246	290 8528
8427	I	AZ	290 8553	380 8027			380 8201	290 8554
8428	I	AZ	290 8555	380 8028			380 8202	290 8556
8429	I	AZ	290 8557	380 8029			380 8203	290 8558
8435	I	AZ	290 8569	380 8035			380 8206	290 8570
8436	I	AZ	290 8571	380 8036			380 8207	290 8572
8437	I	AZ	290 8573	380 8037			380 8208	290 8574
8438	I	AZ	290 8575	380 8038			380 8209	290 8576
8439	I	AZ	290 8577	380 8039			380 8210	290 8578
8440	I	AZ	290 8579	380 8040			380 8211	290 8580
8441	I	AZ	290 8581	380 8041			380 8212	290 8582
8442	I	AZ	290 8583	380 8042			380 8213	290 8584
8443	I	AZ	290 8585	380 8043			380 8214	290 8586
8444	I	AZ	290 8587	380 8044			380 8215	290 8588
8445	I	AZ	290 8589	380 8045			380 8216	290 8590
8446	I	AZ	290 8591	380 8046			380 8217	290 8592
8447	I	AZ	290 8593	380 8047			380 8218	290 8594
8448	I	AZ	290 8595	380 8048			380 8219	290 8596
8449	I	AZ	290 8597	380 8049			380 8220	290 8598
8450	I	AZ	290 8599	380 8050			380 8221	290 8600
8451	I	AZ	290 8601	380 8051			380 8222	290 8602
8452	I	AZ	290 8603	380 8052			380 8223	290 8604
8453	I	AZ	290 8605	380 8053			380 8224	290 8606
8454	I	AZ	290 8607	380 8054			380 8225	290 8608
8455	I	AZ	290 8609	380 8055			380 8226	290 8610
8456	I	AZ	290 8611	380 8056			380 8227	290 8612
8457	I	AZ	290 8613	380 8057			380 8228	290 8614

8459	I		AZ	290 8617	380 8059	380 8230	290 8618
8460	I		AZ	290 8619	380 8060	380 8231	290 8620
8461	I		AZ	290 8621	380 8061	380 8232	290 8622
8462	I		AZ	290 8623	380 8062	380 8233	290 8624
8463	I		AZ	290 8625	380 8063	380 8234	290 8626
8464	I		AZ	290 8627	380 8064	380 8235	290 8628
8465	I		AZ	290 8629	380 8065	380 8236	290 8630
8466	I		AZ	290 8631	380 8066	380 8237	290 8632
8467	I		AZ	290 8633	380 8067	380 8238	290 8634
8468	I		AZ	290 8635	380 8068	380 8239	290 8636
8470	I		AZ	290 8639	380 8070	380 8241	290 8640
8471	I		AZ	290 8641	380 8071	380 8242	290 8642
8472	I		AZ	290 8643	380 8072	380 8243	290 8644
8474	I		AZ	290 8647	380 8074	380 8244	290 8648
8475	I		AZ	290 8649	380 8075	380 8245	290 8650
8477	I		AZ	290 8653	380 8077	380 8247	290 8654
8498	I	§	AZ	290 8563	380 8098	380 8204	290 8564
8499	I	§	AZ	290 8565	380 8099	380 8205	290 8566
Spare	I		AZ			380 8229	

2.6. LOCO-HAULED COACHING STOCK

GENERAL

Early locomotive-hauled coaching stock on the NS was generally referred to by its "plan", which combines the information which in Britain would be provided by the mark and the lot number. The newer Intercity stock is just known as ICR plus a series number. The NS type code consists of the "Plan" plus the type code as described on page 173 of this book.

After A or B comes the number of compartments (or windows in open stock) for each class type, e.g. A4B6–four first class and six second class compartments.

Four categories of stock are in service:

(a) **Internal stock**. As its title suggests, this stock may only work on NS lines. Train heating is 1000 V 50 Hz and 1500 V d.c. only.
(b) **Buurland stock**. This stock may work into neighbouring countries, i.e. West Germany, Belgium and Luxembourg. Folding steps are fitted for low platforms. Train heating – all voltages.
(c) **Benelux Stock**. This is similar to Buurland stock, but is fitted with jumper cables for push-pull working. The name is a misnomer, since the lack of folding steps means it cannot work into Luxembourg (or Germany).
(d) **International stock**. May work anywhere. Train heating – all voltages.

NUMBERING SYSTEM

Intercity loco-hauled coaches and original double-decker stock are numbered according to the UIC system (see appendix A). All internal stock is prefixed "50 84" and therefore these numbers are omitted from the lists below. The new double deckers have a completely new numbering system which is similar to that used on the IRM `Regio Runner' EMUs. The full UIC number is listed for International stock.

2.6.1. INTERCITY STOCK

The standard NS Inter-City stock is known as ICR stock (Intercity Rijtuigen). It comes in three varieties: Internal, Buurland and Benelux. The internal and Benelux stock have fixed steps, whereas the Buurland stock has folding steps. The Benelux stock has jumper cables for push-pull working.

All ICR stock has power-operated doors, pressure ventilation and disc brakes. Maximum speed is 160 km/h. Plan W1 were used in the original Benelux push-pull sets, whereas Plan W2 were for internal use only. All Plan W vehicles are now classified as internal. They have block brakes and a maximum speed of 140 km/h.

PROTOTYPE REFURBISHED IC+ STOCK

Twelve coaches were refurbished as prototypes in 1995. They were renumbered and are listed separately here. They will be the first coaches to be selected for the series refurbishment and thus will shortly be renumbered.

ICR4   BRAKE OPEN SECOND

This vehicles has a second class saloon, a childrens play area with 10 small seats, a luggage compartment, a compartment for a catering trolley and a disabled toilet.

Built: 1988.
Builder: Talbot.   **Accommodation:** –/22 1W 1TD.
Length over Buffers: 26.40 m.   **Weight:** 41 tonnes.

82-70 001-2 (82-70 957-5)   +   LD

ICR1-A10   SEMI-OPEN FIRST

002 has a pair of compartments at each end with an open section in the centre. The arrangement of the 2+1 open seating changes in the centre. 003 has a six-seat and a five-seat compartment at one end, open seating for 29 passengers plus a central lounge with 9 low-backed armchairs grouped in a semi-circle around narrow tables. 004 and 005 have the same layout as standard ICR firsts.

Built: 1981–83.
Builder: Talbot.   **Accommodation:** 59/– 1T (*51/– 1T, §49/– 1T).
Length over Buffers: 26.40 m.   **Weight:** 41 tonnes.

18-70 002-9	(10-70 652-9)	+ *	LD	10-70 004-3	(10-70 655-2)	+	LD
18-70 003-7	(10-70 654-5)	+ §	LD	10-70 005-0	(10-70 661-0)	+	LD

ICR2-B10   OPEN SECOND

006–009 have 2+2 seating at the ends and 3+1 seating in the centre, whilst 010–012 have the conventional layout. 008/009 have less seats and two small luggage areas.

Built: 1982–84.
Builder: Talbot.   **Accommodation:** –/80 1T (*–/78 1T, §–/74 1T).
Length over Buffers: 26.40 m.   **Weight:** 40 tonnes.

20-77 006-9	(20-77 731-2)	+ *	LD	20-77 010-1	(20-77 716-3)	+	LD
20-77 007-7	(20-77 754-4)	+ *	LD	20-77 011-9	(20-77 725-4)	+	LD
29-77 008-6	(20-77 707-2)	+ §	LD	20-77 012-7	(20-77 728-8)	+	LD
29-77 009-4	(20-77 757-7)	+ §	LD				

REFURBISHED ICR STOCK

A major refurbishment programme is just starting for ICR stock. Full details of the interior layouts are not to hand at the time of writing. The details of the new numbering are as follows, but there could be some changes:

ICR1-A10   FIRST

To be rebuilt from 19 coaches from the series 10-70 651–687 plus IC+ coaches 10-70 004–5 and 18-70 002–3.

Built: 1981–83. Buurland stock.
Builder: Talbot.
Length over Buffers: 26.40 m.

Accommodation:
Weight: tonnes.

10-70 351-8 (- -)		10-70 363-3 (- -)
10-70 352-6 (- -)		10-70 364-1 (- -)
10-70 353-4 (- -)		10-70 365-8 (- -)
10-70 354-2 (- -)		10-70 366-6 (- -)
10-70 355-9 (- -)		10-70 367-4 (- -)
10-70 356-7 (- -)		10-70 368-2 (- -)
10-70 357-5 (- -)		10-70 369-0 (- -)
10-70 358-3 (- -)		10-70 370-8 (- -)
10-70 359-1 (- -)		10-70 371-6 (- -)
10-70 360-9 (- -)		10-70 372-4 (- -)
10-70 361-7 (- -)		10-70 373-2 (- -)
10-70 362-5 (- -)		

ICR2-A10   FIRST

To be rebuilt from 10-77 601–637 plus IC+ coaches and five IC+ coaches from the series 20-77 006–12.

Built: 1982–84. Internal Stock.
Builder: Talbot.
Length over Buffers: 26.40 m.

Accommodation:
Weight: tonnes.

10-77 301-6 (- -)		10-77 319-8 (- -)
10-77 302-4 (- -)		10-77 320-6 (- -)
10-77 303-2 (- -)		10-77 321-4 (- -)
10-77 304-0 (- -)		10-77 322-2 (- -)
10-77 305-7 (- -)		10-77 323-0 (- -)
10-77 306-5 (- -)		10-77 324-8 (- -)
10-77 307-3 (- -)		10-77 325-5 (- -)
10-77 308-1 (- -)		10-77 326-3 (- -)
10-77 309-9 (- -)		10-77 327-1 (- -)
10-77 310-7 (- -)		10-77 328-9 (- -)
10-77 311-5 (- -)		10-77 329-7 (- -)
10-77 312-3 (- -)		10-77 330-5 (- -)
10-77 313-1 (- -)		10-77 331-3 (- -)
10-77 314-9 (- -)		10-77 332-1 (- -)
10-77 315-6 (- -)		10-77 333-9 (- -)
10-77 316-4 (- -)		10-77 334-7 (- -)
10-77 317-2 (- -)		10-77 335-4 (- -)
10-77 318-0 (- -)		10-77 336-2 (- -)

ICR2-B10   SECOND

To be rebuilt from 20-77 701–775 plus IC+ coaches and two IC+ coaches from the series 20-77 006–12.

Built: 1982–84. Internal Stock.
Builder: Talbot.
Length over Buffers: 26.40 m.

Accommodation:
Weight: tonnes.

20-77 101-8 (	-	-)
20-77 102-6 (	-	-)
20-77 103-4 (	-	-)
20-77 104-2 (	-	-)
20-77 105-9 (	-	-)
20-77 106-7 (	-	-)
20-77 107-5 (	-	-)
20-77 108-3 (	-	-)
20-77 109-1 (	-	-)
20-77 110-9 (	-	-)
20-77 111-7 (	-	-)
20-77 112-5 (	-	-)
20-77 113-3 (	-	-)
20-77 114-1 (	-	-)
20-77 115-8 (	-	-)
20-77 116-6 (	-	-)
20-77 117-4 (	-	-)
20-77 118-2 (	-	-)
20-77 119-0 (	-	-)
20-77 120-8 (	-	-)
20-77 121-6 (	-	-)
20-77 122-4 (	-	-)
20-77 123-2 (	-	-)
20-77 124-0 (	-	-)
20-77 125-7 (	-	-)
20-77 126-5 (	-	-)
20-77 127-3 (	-	-)
20-77 128-1 (	-	-)
20-77 129-9 (	-	-)
20-77 130-7 (	-	-)
20-77 131-5 (	-	-)
20-77 132-3 (	-	-)
20-77 133-1 (	-	-)
20-77 134-9 (	-	-)
20-77 135-6 (	-	-)
20-77 136-4 (	-	-)
20-77 137-2 (	-	-)
20-77 138-0 (	-	-)
20-77 139-8 (	-	-)
20-77 140-6 (	-	-)
20-77 141-4 (	-	-)
20-77 142-2 (	-	-)
20-77 143-0 (	-	-)
20-77 144-8 (	-	-)
20-77 145-5 (	-	-)
20-77 146-3 (	-	-)
20-77 147-1 (	-	-)
20-77 148-9 (	-	-)
20-77 149-7 (	-	-)
20-77 150-5 (	-	-)
20-77 151-3 (	-	-)
20-77 152-1 (	-	-)
20-77 153-9 (	-	-)
20-77 154-7 (	-	-)
20-77 155-4 (	-	-)
20-77 156-2 (	-	-)

ICR1-B10 SECOND

To be rebuilt from 20-70 801–874, 14 ex-A coaches from the series 10-70 651–687 and 13 ex-BKD.

Built: 1981–82. Buurland Stock.
Builder: Talbot.
Length over Buffers: 26.40 m.

Accommodation:
Weight: tonnes.

20-70 201-3 (	-	-)
20-70 202-1 (	-	-)
20-70 203-9 (	-	-)
20-70 204-7 (	-	-)
20-70 205-4 (	-	-)
20-70 206-2 (	-	-)
20-70 207-0 (	-	-)
20-70 208-8 (	-	-)
20-70 209-6 (	-	-)
20-70 210-4 (	-	-)
20-70 211-2 (	-	-)
20-70 212-0 (	-	-)
20-70 213-8 (	-	-)
20-70 214-6 (	-	-)
20-70 215-3 (	-	-)
20-70 216-1 (	-	-)
20-70 217-9 (	-	-)
20-70 218-7 (	-	-)
20-70 219-5 (	-	-)
20-70 220-3 (	-	-)
20-70 221-1 (	-	-)
20-70 222-9 (	-	-)
20-70 223-7 (	-	-)
20-70 224-5 (	-	-)
20-70 225-2 (	-	-)
20-70 226-0 (	-	-)
20-70 227-8 (	-	-)
20-70 228-6 (	-	-)
20-70 229-4 (	-	-)
20-70 230-2 (	-	-)
20-70 231-0 (	-	-)
20-70 232-8 (	-	-)
20-70 233-6 (	-	-)
20-70 234-4 (	-	-)
20-70 235-1 (	-	-)
20-70 236-9 (	-	-)
20-70 237-7 (	-	-)
20-70 238-5 (	-	-)
20-70 239-3 (	-	-)
20-70 240-1 (	-	-)
20-70 241-9 (	-	-)
20-70 242-7 (	-	-)
20-70 243-5 (	-	-)
20-70 244-3 (	-	-)
20-70 245-0 (	-	-)
20-70 246-8 (	-	-)
20-70 247-6 (	-	-)
20-70 248-4 (	-	-)
20-70 249-2 (	-	-)
20-70 250-0 (	-	-)
20-70 251-8 (	-	-)
20-70 252-6 (	-	-)
20-70 253-4 (	-	-)
20-70 254-2 (	-	-)

20-70 255-9 (- -)		20-70 272-4 (- -)
20-70 256-7 (- -)		20-70 273-2 (- -)
20-70 257-5 (- -)		20-70 274-0 (- -)
20-70 258-3 (- -)		20-70 275-7 (- -)
20-70 259-1 (- -)		20-70 276-5 (- -)
20-70 260-9 (- -)		20-70 277-3 (- -)
20-70 261-7 (- -)		20-70 278-1 (- -)
20-70 262-5 (- -)		20-70 279-9 (- -)
20-70 263-3 (- -)		20-70 280-7 (- -)
20-70 264-1 (- -)		20-70 281-5 (- -)
20-70 265-8 (- -)		20-70 282-3 (- -)
20-70 266-6 (- -)		20-70 283-1 (- -)
20-70 267-4 (- -)		20-70 284-9 (- -)
20-70 268-2 (- -)		20-70 285-6 (- -)
20-70 269-0 (- -)		20-70 286-4 (- -)
20-70 270-8 (- -)		20-70 287-2 (- -)
20-70 271-6 (- -)		

ICR-BDs   DRIVING BRAKE OPEN SECOND

Buurland stock. These vehicles are being rebuilt from BKDs.

Built: 1981–88.
Builder: Talbot.
Length over Buffers: 26.40 m.

Accommodation:
Weight: tonnes.

82-70 001-2 (- -)		82-70 012-9 (- -)
82-70 002-0 (- -)		82-70 013-7 (- -)
82-70 003-8 (- -)		82-70 014-5 (- -)
82-70 004-6 (- -)		82-70 015-2 (- -)
82-70 005-3 (- -)		82-70 016-0 (- -)
82-70 006-1 (- -)		82-70 017-8 (- -)
82-70 007-9 (- -)		82-70 018-6 (- -)
82-70 008-7 (- -)		82-70 019-4 (- -)
82-70 009-5 (- -)		82-70 020-2 (- -)
82-70 010-3 (- -)		82-70 021-0 (- -)
82-70 011-1 (- -)		82-70 022-8 (- -)

ICR-BD   BRAKE OPEN SECOND

Buurland stock. These vehicles are being rebuilt from BKDs.

Built: 1981–88.
Builder: Talbot.
Length over Buffers: 26.40 m.

Accommodation:
Weight: tonnes.

82-70 431-1 (- -)		82-70 438-6 (- -)
82-70 432-9 (- -)		82-70 439-4 (- -)
82-70 433-7 (- -)		82-70 440-2 (- -)
82-70 434-5 (- -)		82-70 441-0 (- -)
82-70 435-2 (- -)		82-70 442-8 (- -)
82-70 436-0 (- -)		82-70 443-6 (- -)
82-70 437-8 (- -)		

STANDARD IC STOCK

ICR3-A10   SEMI-OPEN FIRST

Built: 1986. Benelux push-pull stock.
Builder: Talbot.
Length over Buffers: 26.40 m.
Accommodation: 59/– 1T (24/– in compts, 35/– open).
Weight: 41 tonnes.

10-70 481-3 **B** LD	10-70 484-7 **B** LD	10-70 487-0 **B** LD	10-70 491-2 **B** LD
10-70 482-1 **B** LD	10-70 485-4 **B** LD	10-70 488-8 **B** LD	10-70 492-0 **B** LD
10-70 483-9 **B** LD	10-70 486-2 **B** LD		

ICR4-A10   SEMI-OPEN FIRST

These coaches were originally built as firsts, but were converted to seconds and renumbered 20-70 431–433. They have since been reclassified as firsts but retain 2+2 seating in the open saloon, albeit recovered with moquette.

Built: 1988. Buurland Stock. Through-wired for Benelux service if required.
Builder: Talbot.
Length over Buffers: 26.40 m.
Accommodation: 70/– 1T (24/– in compts, 46/– open).
Weight: 41 tonnes.

10-70 561-2 **I** LD	10-70 562-0 **I** LD	10-70 563-8 **I** LD

ICR4-A10   SEMI-OPEN FIRST

Built: 1988. Buurland Stock. Through-wired for Benelux service if required.
Builder: Talbot.
Length over Buffers: 26.40 m.
Accommodation: 59/– 1T (24/- in compts, 35/– open).
Weight: 41 tonnes.

Note: 565–567 were renumbered from 647/648/691 when they were fitted with through wiring.

10-70 564-6 **I** LD	10-70 565-3 **I** LD	10-70 566-1 **I** LD	10-70 567-9 **I** LD

ICR-A10   SEMI-OPEN FIRST

Built: 1981–88. Buurland Stock.
Builder: Talbot.
Length over Buffers: 26.40 m.
Accommodation: 59/– 1T. (24/– in compts, 35/– open).
Weight: 41 tonnes.

641–646. Plan ICR4. 1988.
651–687. Plan ICR1. 1981–83.

10-70 641-2 **I** LD	10-70 657-8 **I** LD	10-70 668-5 **I** LD	10-70 678-4 **I** LD
10-70 642-0 **I** LD	10-70 658-6 **I** LD	10-70 671-9 **I** LD	10-70 681-8 **I** LD
10-70 643-8 **I** LD	10-70 662-8 **I** LD	10-70 672-7 **I** LD	10-70 682-6 **I** LD
10-70 644-6 **I** LD	10-70 663-6 **I** LD	10-70 673-5 **I** LD	10-70 683-4 **I** LD
10-70 645-3 **I** LD	10-70 664-4 **I** LD	10-70 674-3 **I** LD	10-70 684-2 **I** LD
10-70 646-1 **I** LD	10-70 665-1 **I** LD	10-70 675-0 **I** LD	10-70 685-9 **I** LD
10-70 651-1 **I** LD	10-70 666-9 **I** LD	10-70 676-8 **I** LD	10-70 686-7 **I** LD
10-70 653-7 **I** LD	10-70 667-7 **I** LD	10-70 677-6 **I** LD	10-70 687-5 **I** LD
10-70 656-0 **I** LD			

ICR2-A10   SEMI-OPEN FIRST

Built: 1982–84. Internal Stock.
Builder: Talbot.
Length over Buffers: 26.40 m.
Accommodation: 59/– 1T. (24/– in compts, 35/– open).
Weight: 41 tonnes.

10-77 601-9 **I** LD	10-77 611-8 **I** LD	10-77 621-7 **I** LD	10-77 631-6 **I** LD
10-77 602-7 **I** LD	10-77 612-6 **I** LD	10-77 622-5 **I** LD	10-77 632-4 **I** LD
10-77 603-5 **I** LD	10-77 613-4 **I** LD	10-77 623-3 **I** LD	10-77 633-2 **I** LD
10-77 604-3 **I** LD	10-77 614-2 **I** LD	10-77 624-1 **I** LD	10-77 634-0 **I** LD
10-77 605-0 **I** LD	10-77 615-9 **I** LD	10-77 625-8 **I** LD	10-77 635-7 **I** LD
10-77 606-8 **I** LD	10-77 616-7 **I** LD	10-77 626-6 **I** LD	10-77 636-5 **I** LD
10-77 607-6 **I** LD	10-77 617-5 **I** LD	10-77 627-4 **I** LD	10-77 637-3 **I** LD
10-77 608-4 **I** LD	10-77 618-3 **I** LD	10-77 628-2 **I** LD	

ICR3-B10 OPEN SECOND

Built: 1986–87. Benelux push-pull stock.
Builder: Talbot.
Length over Buffers: 26.40 m.
Accommodation: –/80 1T.
Weight: 40 tonnes.

20-70 401-9 **B** AZ	20-70 406-8 **B** AZ	20-70 413-4 **B** AZ	20-70 417-5 **B** AZ
20-70 402-7 **B** AZ	20-70 407-6 **B** AZ	20-70 414-2 **B** AZ	20-70 418-3 **B** AZ
20-70 403-5 **B** AZ	20-70 408-4 **B** AZ	20-70 415-9 **B** AZ	20-70 421-7 **B** AZ
20-70 404-3 **B** AZ	20-70 411-8 **B** AZ	20-70 416-7 **B** AZ	20-70 422-5 **B** AZ
20-70 405-0 **B** AZ	20-70 412-6 **B** AZ		

ICR4-B10 OPEN SECOND

Built: 1988. Buurland Stock. Through-wired for Benelux service if required.
Builder: Talbot.
Length over Buffers: 26.40 m.
Accommodation: –/80 1T.
Weight: 40 tonnes.

20-70 571-9 **I** LD	20-70 573-5 **I** LD	20-70 574-3 **I** LD	20-70 575-0 **I** LD
20-70 572-7 **I** LD			

ICR4-B10 OPEN SECOND

Built: 1988. Buurland Stock. Through-wired for Benelux service if required.
Builder: Talbot.
Length over Buffers: 26.40 m.
Accommodation: –/80 1T.
Weight: 40 tonnes.

Note: These coaches were renumbered 423–427 for a time when in Benelux service.

20-70 581-8 **I** LD	20-70 583-4 **I** LD	20-70 584-2 **I** LD	20-70 585-9 **I** LD
20-70 582-6 **I** LD			

ICR1-B10 OPEN SECOND

Built: 1981–82. Buurland Stock.
Builder: Talbot.
Length over Buffers: 26.40 m.
Accommodation: –/80 1T.
Weight: 40 tonnes.

20-70 801-0 **I** LD	20-70 818-4 **I** LD	20-70 837-4 **I** LD	20-70 856-4 **I** LD
20-70 802-8 **I** LD	20-70 821-8 **I** LD	20-70 838-2 **I** LD	20-70 857-2 **I** LD
20-70 803-6 **I** LD	20-70 822-6 **I** LD	20-70 841-6 **I** LD	20-70 858-0 **I** LD
20-70 804-4 **I** LD	20-70 823-4 **I** LD	20-70 842-4 **I** LD	20-70 861-4 **I** LD
20-70 805-1 **I** LD	20-70 824-2 **I** LD	20-70 843-2 **I** LD	20-70 862-2 **I** LD
20-70 806-9 **I** LD	20-70 825-9 **I** LD	20-70 844-0 **I** LD	20-70 863-0 **I** LD
20-70 807-7 **I** LD	20-70 826-7 **I** LD	20-70 845-7 **I** LD	20-70 864-8 **I** LD
20-70 808-5 **I** LD	20-70 827-5 **I** LD	20-70 846-5 **I** LD	20-70 865-5 **I** LD
20-70 811-9 **I** LD	20-70 828-3 **I** LD	20-70 847-3 **I** LD	20-70 866-3 **I** LD
20-70 812-7 **I** LD	20-70 831-7 **I** LD	20-70 848-1 **I** LD	20-70 867-1 **I** LD
20-70 813-5 **I** LD	20-70 832-5 **I** LD	20-70 851-5 **I** LD	20-70 868-9 **I** LD
20-70 814-3 **I** LD	20-70 833-3 **I** LD	20-70 852-3 **I** LD	20-70 871-3 **I** LD
20-70 815-0 **I** LD	20-70 834-1 **I** LD	20-70 853-1 **I** LD	20-70 872-1 **I** LD
20-70 816-8 **I** LD	20-70 835-8 **I** LD	20-70 854-9 **I** LD	20-70 873-9 **I** LD
20-70 817-6 **I** LD	20-70 836-6 **I** LD	20-70 855-6 **I** LD	20-70 874-7 **I** LD

ICR2-B10 OPEN SECOND

Built: 1982–84. Internal Stock.
Builder: Talbot.
Length over Buffers: 26.40 m.
Accommodation: –/80 1T.
Weight: 40 tonnes.

20-77 701-5 **I** LD	20-77 708-0 **I** LD	20-77 717-1 **I** LD	20-77 726-2 **I** LD
20-77 702-3 **I** LD	20-77 711-4 **I** LD	20-77 718-9 **I** LD	20-77 727-0 **I** LD
20-77 703-1 **I** LD	20-77 712-2 **I** LD	20-77 721-3 **I** LD	20-77 732-0 **I** LD
20-77 704-9 **I** LD	20-77 713-0 **I** LD	20-77 722-1 **I** LD	20-77 733-8 **I** LD
20-77 705-6 **I** LD	20-77 714-8 **I** LD	20-77 723-9 **I** LD	20-77 734-6 **I** LD
20-77 706-4 **I** LD	20-77 715-5 **I** LD	20-77 724-7 **I** LD	20-77 735-3 **I** LD

20-77 736-1 I	LD	20-77 746-0 I	LD	20-77 756-9 I	LD	20-77 766-8 I	LD
20-77 737-9 I	LD	20-77 747-8 I	LD	20-77 758-5 I	LD	20-77 767-6 I	LD
20-77 738-7 I	LD	20-77 748-6 I	LD	20-77 761-9 I	LD	20-77 768-4 I	LD
20-77 741-1 I	LD	20-77 751-0 I	LD	20-77 762-7 I	LD	20-77 771-8 I	LD
20-77 742-9 I	LD	20-77 752-8 I	LD	20-77 763-5 I	LD	20-77 772-6 I	LD
20-77 743-7 I	LD	20-77 753-6 I	LD	20-77 764-3 I	LD	20-77 773-4 I	LD
20-77 744-5 I	LD	20-77 755-1 I	LD	20-77 765-0 I	LD	20-77 774-2 I	LD
20-77 745-2 I	LD						

ICR1-B10   SEMI-OPEN SECOND

Built: 1981–84. Internal Stock. Rebuilt from Buurland semi-open first 648.
Builder: Talbot. **Accommodation:** –/70 1T (24/– in compts, 46/– open).
Length over Buffers: 26.40 m. **Weight:** 40 tonnes.

20-77 775-9 I   LD |

PLAN W1-B11   OPEN SECOND

Original Benelux push & pull stock. Swivel doors. Renumbered from 21-30 series. All were stored out of use, but all have now either been reinstated or scrapped.

Built: 1966–67.
Builder: Werkspoor. **Accommodation:** –/88 1T.
Length over Buffers: 26.40 m. **Weight:** 35 tonnes.

21-37 451-2 I	LD	21-37 456-1 I	LD	21-37 464-5 I	LD	21-37 471-0 I	LD
21-37 452-0 I	LD	21-37 457-9 I	LD	21-37 465-2 I	SLD	21-37 473-6 I	LD
21-37 453-8 I	LD	21-37 458-7 I	SLD	21-37 466-0 I	LD	21-37 475-1 I	LD
21-37 454-6 I	LD	21-37 461-1 I	LD	21-37 467-8 I	LD	21-37 476-9 I	S LD
21-37 455-3 I	LD	21-37 463-7 I	LD	21-37 468-6 I	LD		

PLAN W2-B11   OPEN SECOND

Internal stock. Swivel doors. All were stored out of use, but all have now either been reinstated or scrapped.

Built: 1968.
Builder: Werkspoor. **Accommodation:** –/88 1T.
Length over Buffers: 26.40 m. **Weight:** 35 tonnes.

21-37 501-7 I	LD	21-37 513-2 I	LD	21-37 521-5 I	LD	21-37 525-6 I	LD
21-37 502-5 I	LD	21-37 514-0 I	LD	21-37 522-3 I	LD	21-37 527-2 I	LD
21-37 503-3 I	LD	21-37 515-7 I	LD	21-37 523-1 I	LD	21-37 528-0 I	LD
21-37 505-8 I	LD	21-37 516-5 I	LD	21-37 524-9 I	LD	21-37 531-4 I	LD
21-37 511-6 I	LD	21-37 517-3 I	LD				

ICR3-Bvs   DRIVING OPEN SECOND

Built: 1986. Benelux push-pull stock.
Builder: Talbot. **Accommodation:** –/64 1T.
Length over Buffers: 26.40 m. **Weight:** 41 tonnes.

28-70 101-7 **B** AZ	28-70 104-1 **B** AZ	28-70 107-4 **B** AZ	28-70 112-4 **B** AZ
28-70 102-5 **B** AZ	28-70 105-8 **B** AZ	28-70 108-2 **B** AZ	28-70 113-2 **B** AZ
28-70 103-3 **B** AZ	28-70 106-6 **B** AZ	28-70 111-6 **B** AZ	

ICR3-A4B6   OPEN COMPOSITE

Built: 1986. Benelux push-pull stock.
Builder: Talbot. **Accommodation:** 23/48 2T.
Length over Buffers: 26.40 m. **Weight:** 40 tonnes.

30-70 061-9 **B** AZ	30-70 064-3 **B** AZ	30-70 067-6 **B** AZ	30-70 071-8 **B** AZ
30-70 062-7 **B** AZ	30-70 065-0 **B** AZ	30-70 068-4 **B** AZ	30-70 072-6 **B** AZ
30-70 063-5 **B** AZ	30-70 066-8 **B** AZ		

ICR4-BKD KITCHEN BRAKE OPEN SECOND

These vehicles consist of a brake open second plus a kitchenette from which a trolley refreshment service operates.

Built: 1988. Buurland Stock. Through-wired for Benelux service if required.
Builder: Talbot. **Accommodation:** –/49 1T.
Length over Buffers: 26.40 m. **Weight:** 41 tonnes.

82-70 591-2 **I** LD | 82-70 592-0 **I** LD | 82-70 593-8 **I** LD |

ICR-BKD KITCHEN BRAKE OPEN SECOND

Buurland stock. These vehicles consist of a brake open second plus a kitchenette from which a trolley refreshment service operates.

Built: 1981–88.
Builder: Talbot. **Accommodation:** –/53 1T (–/49 1T ICR4).
Length over Buffers: 26.40 m. **Weight:** 41 tonnes.

901–953. Plan ICR1. 1981–82.
954–958. Plan ICR4. 1988.

82-70 901-3 I LD	82-70 915-3 I LD	82-70 931-0 I LD	82-70 945-0 I LD
82-70 902-1 I LD	82-70 916-1 I LD	82-70 932-8 I LD	82-70 946-8 I LD
82-70 903-9 I LD	82-70 917-9 I LD	82-70 933-6 I LD	82-70 947-6 I LD
82-70 904-7 I LD	82-70 918-7 I LD	82-70 934-4 I LD	82-70 948-4 I LD
82-70 905-4 I LD	82-70 921-1 I LD	82-70 935-1 I LD	82-70 951-8 I LD
82-70 906-2 I LD	82-70 922-9 I LD	82-70 936-9 I LD	82-70 952-6 I LD
82-70 907-0 I LD	82-70 923-7 I LD	82-70 937-7 I LD	82-70 953-4 I LD
82-70 908-8 I LD	82-70 924-5 I LD	82-70 938-5 I LD	82-70 954-2 I LD
82-70 911-2 I LD	82-70 925-2 I LD	82-70 941-9 I LD	82-70 955-9 I LD
82-70 912-0 I LD	82-70 926-0 I LD	82-70 942-7 I LD	82-70 956-7 I LD
82-70 913-8 I LD	82-70 927-8 I LD	82-70 943-5 I LD	82-70 958-3 I LD
82-70 914-6 I LD	82-70 928-6 I LD	82-70 944-3 I LD	

ICR-BKD KITCHEN BRAKE OPEN SECOND

These vehicles consist of a brake open second plus a kitchenette from which a trolley refreshment service operates.

Built: 1986/8. Benelux push-pull stock.
Builder: Talbot. **Accommodation:** –/45 1T.
Length over Buffers: 26.40 m. **Weight:** 41 tonnes.

971–981. Plan ICR3. 1986.
982. Plan ICR4. 1988. Renumbered from 594.

82-70 971-6 **B** AZ	82-70 974-0 **B** AZ	82-70 977-3 **B** AZ	82-70 981-5 **B** AZ
82-70 972-4 **B** AZ	82-70 975-7 **B** AZ	82-70 978-1 **B** AZ	82-70 982-3 **B** AZ
82-70 973-2 **B** AZ	82-70 976-5 **B** AZ		

PLAN E-Df BICYCLE BRAKE

Built: 1958 as post office vehicles. Converted 1989–93 to carry cycles. Used in summer on Haarlem–Maastricht service.
Builder: Werkspoor.
Length over Buffers: 23.05 m.
Accommodation: –/4.
Weight: 45 tonnes.

92-37 001-2 (87-37 202-3) I LE	92-37 005-9 (87-37 216-3) I LE
92-37 002-0 (87-37 213-0) I LE	92-37 006-7 (87-37 222-1) I LE
92-37 003-8 (87-37 225-4) I LE	92-37 007-5 (87-37 212-2) I LE
92-37 004-6 (87-37 226-2) I LE	92-37 008-3 (87-37 206-4) I LE

2.6.2. ORIGINAL DOUBLE-DECKER STOCK (DDM1)

The double-decker stock operates on outer suburban trains on the Amsterdam–Hoorn and Amsterdam–Lelystad routes. The driving coaches are named after endangered species. Certain coaches have been modified to work in loco-hauled Intercity trains on the Haarlem–Maastricht service and certain Bvs have been modified with ICR and Class 1700 on Roosendaal–Zwolle.

DOUBLE DECKER DRIVING OPEN SECOND (Bvs)

Built: 1985–86.   **Builder**: Talbot.
Length over Buffers: 26.89 m.
Accommodation: –/108 1T (64 upper deck, 44 lower deck).
Weight: tonnes.

26-37 101-1	LD	Kondor	26-37 108-6	LD	Olifant
26-37 102-9	LD	Ooieveer	26-37 111-0	LD	Tijger
26-37 103-7	LD	Bison	26-37 112-8	LD	Cheeta
26-37 104-5	LD	Walvis	26-37 113-6	LD	Dolfijn
26-37 105-2	LD	Neushoorn	26-37 114-4	LD	Otter
26-37 106-0	LD	Arend	26-37 115-1	LD	Panda
26-37 107-8	LD	Zeehond			

DOUBLE DECKER SECOND (Bv)

Built: 1985–86.   **Builder**: Talbot.
Length over Buffers: 26.40 m.
Accommodation: –/140 1T (64 upper deck, 76 lower deck).
Weight: tonnes.

* Converted from ABv 26-37 603–606 respectively.

26-37 417-1	LD	26-37 425-4	AZ	26-37 433-8	AZ	26-37 441-1	AZ
26-37 418-9	LD	26-37 426-2	AZ	26-37 434-6	AZ	26-37 470-0	AZ
26-37 421-3	LD	26-37 427-0	AZ	26-37 435-3	AZ	26-37 471-8	AZ
26-37 422-1	AZ	26-37 428-8	AZ	26-37 436-1	AZ	26-37 472-6	AZ
26-37 423-9	AZ	26-37 431-2	AZ	26-37 437-9	AZ	26-37 473-4	AZ
26-37 424-7	AZ	26-37 432-0	AZ	26-37 438-7	AZ		

DOUBLE DECKER COMPOSITE (ABv)

Built: 1985–86.   **Builder**: Talbot.
Length over Buffers: 26.40 m.
Accommodation: 64/60 1T (32/24 upper deck, 32/36 lower deck).
Weight: tonnes.

26-37 607-7	AZ	26-37 615-0	AZ	26-37 623-4	AZ	26-37 631-7	AZ
26-37 608-5	AZ	26-37 616-8	AZ	26-37 624-2	AZ	26-37 632-5	AZ
26-37 611-9	AZ	26-37 617-6	AZ	26-37 625-9	AZ	26-37 633-3	AZ
26-37 612-7	AZ	26-37 618-4	AZ	26-37 626-7	AZ	26-37 634-1	AZ
26-37 613-5	AZ	26-37 621-8	AZ	26-37 627-5	AZ	26-37 635-8	AZ
26-37 614-3	AZ	26-37 622-6	AZ	26-37 628-3	AZ		

DOUBLE DECKER SECOND (Bv)

Details as for 417–441, but fitted with static inverters for use in Intercity trains as loose coaches.

Built: 1985–86.   **Builder**: Talbot.
Length over Buffers: 26.40 m.
Accommodation: –/140 1T. (64 upper deck, 76 lower deck).
Weight: tonnes.

These vehicles were converted Bv 26-37 801–816 and ABv 26-37 601/602 respectively.

26-37 801-6	MT	26-37 805-7	MT	26-37 811-5	MT	26-37 815-6	MT
26-37 802-4	MT	26-37 806-5	MT	26-37 812-3	MT	26-37 816-4	MT
26-37 803-2	MT	26-37 807-3	MT	26-37 813-1	MT	26-37 850-2	MT
26-37 804-0	MT	26-37 808-1	MT	26-37 814-9	MT	26-37 851-0	MT

2.6.3. NEW DOUBLE-DECKER STOCK TYPE DD–AR

This double-deck stock works in suburban trains all around the Randstad area. The numbering system strays away from the normally mandatory UIC system. The coaches work as "virtual EMUs", i.e. in sets of fixed formation originally consisting of a Class 1700 locomotive, a composite, one or two seconds and a driving second. For this purpose the locomotive is fitted with an auto-coupler at one end. However fifty "mDDM" power cars have now been delivered and these have released 50 Class 1700s for Intercity use. Set numbers consist of a `7', a digit denoting the formation and the last two digits of the driving trailer. Thus 7345 would be a three car set with the driving trailer 7045, 7445 would be a four-car set with the driving trailer 7045 and 7845 would be a loco-powered four-car set with the driving trailer 7045. Formations are changed from time to time.

DOUBLE DECKER DRIVING OPEN SECOND (Bvs)

Built: 1992–94.
Builder: Talbot.
Length over Buffers: 26.89 m.
Accommodation: –/120 1T. (64 upper deck, 52 lower deck and 4 in ends).
Weight: 53 tonnes.

270 7001	LD	270 7021	LD	270 7041	LD	270 7061	LD
270 7002	LD	270 7022	LD	270 7042	LD	270 7062	LD
270 7003	LD	270 7023	LD	270 7043	LD	270 7063	LD
270 7004	LD	270 7024	LD	270 7044	LD	270 7064	LD
270 7005	LD	270 7025	LD	270 7045	LD	270 7065	LD
270 7006	LD	270 7026	LD	270 7046	LD	270 7066	LD
270 7007	LD	270 7027	LD	270 7047	LD	270 7067	LD
270 7008	LD	270 7028	LD	270 7048	LD	270 7068	LD
270 7009	LD	270 7029	LD	270 7049	LD	270 7069	LD
270 7010	LD	270 7030	LD	270 7050	LD	270 7070	LD
270 7011	LD	270 7031	LD	270 7051	LD	270 7071	LD
270 7012	LD	270 7032	LD	270 7052	LD	270 7072	LD
270 7013	LD	270 7033	LD	270 7053	LD	270 7073	LD
270 7014	LD	270 7034	LD	270 7054	LD	270 7074	LD
270 7015	LD	270 7035	LD	270 7055	LD	270 7075	LD
270 7016	LD	270 7036	LD	270 7056	LD	270 7076	LD
270 7017	LD	270 7037	LD	270 7057	LD	270 7077	LD
270 7018	LD	270 7038	LD	270 7058	LD	270 7078	LD
270 7019	LD	270 7039	LD	270 7059	LD	270 7079	LD
270 7020	LD	270 7040	LD	270 7060	LD		

DOUBLE DECKER SECOND (Bv)

Built: 1992–94.
Builder: Talbot.
Length over Buffers: 26.40 m.
Accommodation: –/140 1T. (64 upper deck, 64 lower deck and 12 in ends).
Weight: 46 tonnes.

280 7201	LD	280 7214	LD	280 7227	LD	280 7240	LD
280 7202	LD	280 7215	LD	280 7228	LD	280 7241	LD
280 7203	LD	280 7216	LD	280 7229	LD	280 7242	LD
280 7204	LD	280 7217	LD	280 7230	LD	280 7243	LD
280 7205	LD	280 7218	LD	280 7231	LD	280 7244	LD
280 7206	LD	280 7219	LD	280 7232	LD	280 7245	LD
280 7207	LD	280 7220	LD	280 7233	LD	280 7246	LD
280 7208	LD	280 7221	LD	280 7234	LD	280 7247	LD
280 7209	LD	280 7222	LD	280 7235	LD	280 7248	LD
280 7210	LD	280 7223	LD	280 7236	LD	280 7249	LD
280 7211	LD	280 7224	LD	280 7237	LD	280 7250	LD
280 7212	LD	280 7225	LD	280 7238	LD	280 7251	LD
280 7213	LD	280 7226	LD	280 7239	LD	280 7252	LD

280 7253	LD	280 7266	LD	280 7279	LD	280 7292	LD
280 7254	LD	280 7267	LD	280 7280	LD	280 7293	LD
280 7255	LD	280 7268	LD	280 7281	LD	280 7294	LD
280 7256	LD	280 7269	LD	280 7282	LD	280 7295	LD
280 7257	LD	280 7270	LD	280 7283	LD	280 7296	LD
280 7258	LD	280 7271	LD	280 7284	LD	280 7297	LD
280 7259	LD	280 7272	LD	280 7285	LD	280 7298	LD
280 7260	LD	280 7273	LD	280 7286	LD	280 7299	LD
280 7261	LD	280 7274	LD	280 7287	LD	280 7300	LD
280 7262	LD	280 7275	LD	280 7288	LD	280 7301	LD
280 7263	LD	280 7276	LD	280 7289	LD	280 7302	LD
280 7264	LD	280 7277	LD	280 7290	LD	280 7508	LD
280 7265	LD	280 7278	LD	280 7291	LD		

DOUBLE DECKER COMPOSITE (ABv)

Built: 1992–94.
Builder: Talbot.
Length over Buffers: 26.40 m.
Accommodation: 64/60 1T. (32/24 upper deck, 32/24 lower deck and 12 in ends).
Weight: 46 tonnes.

380 7501	LD	380 7521	LD	380 7540	LD	380 7559	LD
380 7502	LD	380 7522	LD	380 7541	LD	380 7560	LD
380 7503	LD	380 7523	LD	380 7542	LD	380 7561	LD
380 7504	LD	380 7524	LD	380 7543	LD	380 7562	LD
380 7505	LD	380 7525	LD	380 7544	LD	380 7563	LD
380 7506	LD	380 7526	LD	380 7545	LD	380 7564	LD
380 7507	LD	380 7527	LD	380 7546	LD	380 7565	LD
380 7509	LD	380 7528	LD	380 7547	LD	380 7566	LD
380 7510	LD	380 7529	LD	380 7548	LD	380 7567	LD
380 7511	LD	380 7530	LD	380 7549	LD	380 7568	LD
380 7512	LD	380 7531	LD	380 7550	LD	380 7569	LD
380 7513	LD	380 7532	LD	380 7551	LD	380 7570	LD
380 7514	LD	380 7533	LD	380 7552	LD	380 7571	LD
380 7515	LD	380 7534	LD	380 7553	LD	380 7572	LD
380 7516	LD	380 7535	LD	380 7554	LD	380 7573	LD
380 7517	LD	380 7536	LD	380 7555	LD	380 7574	LD
380 7518	LD	380 7537	LD	380 7556	LD	380 7575	LD
380 7519	LD	380 7538	LD	380 7557	LD	380 7576	LD
380 7520	LD	380 7539	LD	380 7558	LD	380 7577	LD

DOUBLE DECKER MOTOR SECOND (mABk)

Built: 199 .
Builder: Talbot.
Length over Buffers: 26.40 m.
Accommodation: .
Weight: tonnes.

390 7701	LD	390 7714	LD	390 7727	LD	390 7739	LD
390 7702	LD	390 7715	LD	390 7728	LD	390 7740	LD
390 7703	LD	390 7716	LD	390 7729	LD	390 7741	LD
390 7704	LD	390 7717	LD	390 7730	LD	390 7742	LD
390 7705	LD	390 7718	LD	390 7731	LD	390 7743	LD
390 7706	LD	390 7719	LD	390 7732	LD	390 7744	LD
390 7707	LD	390 7720	LD	390 7733	LD	390 7745	LD
390 7708	LD	390 7721	LD	390 7734	LD	390 7746	LD
390 7709	LD	390 7722	LD	390 7735	LD	390 7747	LD
390 7710	LD	390 7723	LD	390 7736	LD	390 7748	LD
390 7711	LD	390 7724	LD	390 7737	LD	390 7749	LD
390 7712	LD	390 7725	LD	390 7738	LD	390 7750	LD
390 7713	LD	390 7726	LD				

2.6.4. INTERNATIONAL STOCK

PARCELS VANS   Dm

Ex Deutsche Post. Owned by NS Internationaal and hired to Railion for the carriage of air freight between Amsterdam and Milano on the new Overnight Express.

Built: **Builder:**
Length over Buffers: 26.40 m.   **Weight:**   tonnes.
Max. Speed: 200 km/h.

51 84 92-99 060-2	(51 80 00-95 004-9)	D	LD
51 84 92-99 061-0	(51 80 00-95 122-9)	D	LD
51 84 92-99 062-8	(51 80 00-95 091-6)	D	LD
51 84 92-99 063-6	(51 80 00-95 054-4)	D	LD
51 84 92-99 070-0	(51 80 00-95 050-2)	D	LD
51 84 92-99 071-8	(51 80 00-95 100-5)	D	LD

Note 070 and 071 also carried 51 84 91-95 052-1 and 053-9 when in service with NS Internationaal as bicycle coaches.

COUCHETTES

Ex DB type Bcm. These coaches have six berths per compartment.

Built: 1963–68.   **Builder:**
Length over Buffers: 26.40 m.
Accommodation: 10 compartments with six berths in each.
Weight: 39 tonnes.   **Max. Speed:** 160 (140*) km/h.

51 84 50-70 001-9	(51 80 50-30 012-9)	D		LD
51 84 50-70 002-7	(51 80 50-30 017-8)	D		LD
51 84 50-70 004-3	(51 80 50-30 023-6)	D		LD
51 84 50-70 005-0	(51 80 50-30 025-1)	D		LD
51 84 50-30 006-7	(51 80 50-30 026-9)	D	*	LD
51 84 50-70 007-6	(51 80 50-30 031-9)	D		LD
51 84 50-70 008-4	(51 80 50-30 035-0)	D		LD
51 84 50-70 009-2	(51 80 50-30 036-8)	D		LD
51 84 50-70 010-0	(51 80 50-30 038-4)	D		LD
51 84 50-70 011-8	(51 80 50-30 048-3)	D		LD
51 84 50-70 012-6	(51 80 50-30 049-1)	D		LD
51 84 50-70 013-4	(51 80 50-30 051-7)	D		LD
51 84 50-70 014-2	(51 80 50-30 054-1)	D		LD
51 84 50-30 015-8	(51 80 50-30 056-6)	D		LD
51 84 50-70 016-6	(51 80 50-30 065-7)	D		LD
51 84 50-70 017-4	(51 80 50-30 071-5)	D		LD
51 84 50-70 018-2	(51 80 50-30 079-8)	D		LD
51 84 50-30 019-0	(51 80 50-30 084-8)	D	*	LD
51 84 50-30 020-8	(51 80 50-30 020-2)	D	*	LD

COMPARTMENT FIRST   A9

Ex DB type Avmz. For use on the new Amsterdam–Milano Overnight Express.

Built: 1974–75.   **Builders:** Orenstein & Koppel (250), Wegmann (others).
Length over Buffers: 26.40 m.
Accommodation: 54/– 2T.   **Bogies:** Minden-Deutz MD36.
Weight: 44 tonnes.   **Max. Speed:** 200 km/h.
Non-standard livery: 0 NS plain Intercity royal blue.

61 84 19-90 250-6	(61 80 19-90 155-1)	0	LD
61 84 19-90 251-4	(61 80 19-90 164-3)	0	LD
61 84 19-90 252-2	(61 80 19-90 207-0)	0	LD
61 84 19-90 253-0	(61 80 19-90 180-9)	0	LD

COUCHETTES

Ex German Touristik Union International (TUI). These coaches have four berths per compartment. They have been refurbished for use on international night services, holiday and Motorail services to the south of France and Austria.

Built: 1981.   **Builder:**
Length over Buffers: 26.40 m.
Accommodation: 11 compartments with four berths in each.
Weight: 53 tonnes.   **Max. Speed:** 160 (200*) km/h.

61 84 50-90 101-1	(61 80 50-90 101-5)	D	*	LD
61 84 50-90 102-9	(61 80 50-90 102-3)	D	*	LD
61 84 50-90 103-7	(61 80 50-90 103-1)	D	*	LD
61 84 50-90 104-5	(61 80 50-90 104-9)	D	*	LD
61 84 50-90 105-2	(61 80 50-90 105-6)	D	*	LD
61 84 50-90 106-0	(61 80 50-90 106-4)	D	*	LD
61 84 50-90 107-8	(61 80 50-90 107-2)	D	*	LD
61 84 50-90 108-6	(61 80 50-90 108-0)	D	*	LD
61 84 50-90 109-4	(61 80 50-90 109-8)	D	*	LD
61 84 50-90 110-2	(61 80 50-90 110-6)	D	*	LD
61 84 50-70 111-4	(61 80 50-70 111-8)	D		LD
61 84 50-70 112-2	(61 80 50-70 112-6)	D		LD
61 84 50-70 113-0	(61 80 50-70 113-4)	D		LD
61 84 50-70 115-5	(61 80 50-70 115-9)	D		LD
61 84 50-70 116-3	(61 80 50-70 116-7)	D		LD
61 84 50-70 117-1	(61 80 50-70 117-5)	D		LD
61 84 50-70 118-9	(61 80 50-70 118-3)	D		LD
61 84 50-70 119-7	(61 80 50-70 119-1)	D		LD
61 84 50-70 120-5	(61 80 50-70 120-9)	D		LD
61 84 50-70 121-3	(61 80 50-70 121-7)	D		LD
61 84 50-70 122-1	(61 80 50-70 122-5)	D		LD
61 84 50-70 123-9	(61 80 50-70 123-3)	D		LD
61 84 50-70 124-7	(61 80 50-70 124-1)	D		LD
61 84 50-70 125-4	(61 80 50-70 125-8)	D		LD
61 84 50-70 126-2	(61 80 50-70 126-6)	D		LD
61 84 50-70 127-0	(61 80 50-70 127-4)	D		LD
61 84 50-70 128-8	(61 80 50-70 128-2)	D		LD
61 84 50-70 129-6	(61 80 50-70 129-0)	D		LD

SLEEPING CAR TYPE AB30

Originally CIWLT type P, these coaches have stainless steel bodies. They were rebuilt for 160 km/h in 1992 and refurbished. Note: Numbers in parentheses are CIWL numbers.

Built: 1955.   **Builder:**
Length over Buffers: 24.00 m.
Accommodation: 10 three-berth compartments.
Weight: 44 tonnes.   **Max. Speed:** 160 km/h.

61 84 70-70 016-1	(4558)	D	LD		61 84 70-70 019-5	(4529)	D	LD
61 84 70-70 017-9	(4552)	D	LD		61 84 70-70 020-3	(4535)	D	LD
61 84 70-70 018-7	(4536)	D	LD					

SLEEPING CAR TYPE MU

New coaches rented from Wagons-Lits for the new Overnight Express from Amsterdam to Milano.

Built: 2000.   **Builder:**
Length over Buffers: 26.40 m.   **Accommodation:** 12 three-berth compartments
Weight: tonnes.   **Max. Speed:** 200 km/h.
Non-standard livery: 0 NS plain Intercity royal blue.

61 84 70-90 201-5	0	LD		61 84 70-90 203-1	0	LD
61 84 70-90 202-3	0	LD		61 84 70-90 204-9	0	LD

SLEEPING CAR TYPE MU

These coaches have been Modernised and fitted with air conditioning by Wagons-Lits at Oostende. They are used on holiday trains and Motorail services to the South of France and Austria. Note: Numbers in parentheses are CIWL numbers.

Built: 1973.
Length over Buffers: 28.40 m.
Weight: 55 tonnes.

Builder: Fiat.
Accommodation: 12 three-berth compartments.
Max. Speed: 160 km/h.

61 84 72-70 622-4	(4832)	D	LD	61 84 75-70 321-0	(4751)	D	LD
61 84 75-70 311-1	(4741)	D	LD	61 84 75-70 324-4	(4754)	D	LD
61 84 75-70 312-9	(4742)	D	LD	61 84 75-70 327-7	(4757)	D	LD
61 84 75-70 313-7	(4743)	D	LD	61 84 75-70 328-5	(4758)	D	LD
61 84 75-70 317-8	(4747)	D	LD	61 84 75-70 329-3	(4759)	D	LD
61 84 75-70 318-6	(4748)	D	LD	61 84 75-70 330-1	(4760)	D	LD
61 84 75-70 320-2	(4750)	D	LD				

SLEEPING CAR TYPE T2

Built: 1975. Note: Numbers in parentheses are CIWL numbers.
Builder:
Length over Buffers: 26.40 m.
Accommodation: 18 compartments with two berths in each.
Weight: 55 tonnes.
Max. Speed: 160 km/h.

61 84 75-70 458-0	(6458)	D	LD	61 84 75-70 459-8	(6459)	D	LD

RESTAURANT CAR

Built: 1971–72. Bought from DB 1989.
Length over Buffers: .
Weight: tonnes.

Builder:
Accommodation: .
Max. Speed: 140 km/h.

61 84 88-70 015-3	D	LD	ADAGIO	61 84 88-70 017-9	D	LD	ALLEGRO
61 84 88-70 016-1	D	LD	ANDANTE	61 84 88-70 018-7	D	LD	ALLEGRETTO

BUFFET/RESTAURANT CAR

Rebuilt from SNCF Gril-Express coaches. Used on Den Haag–Alps overnight services in winter and on holiday trains and Motorail services to the South of France and Austria in summer.

Built: 1970–71.
Length over Buffers: 24.50 m.
Weight: 54 tonnes.

Builder: CIMT or B&L.
Accommodation: 22 .
Max. Speed: 160 km/h.

61 84 88-70 020-3	(61 87 88 90 145-1)	I	LD
61 84 88-70 021-1	(61 87 88 90 134-5)	I	LD
61 84 88-70 022-9	(61 87 88 90 114-7)	I	LD
61 84 88-70 023-7	(61 84 88 70 131-5)	I	LD
61 84 88-70 024-5	(61 84 88 70 143-0)	I	LD
61 84 88-70 025-2	(61 84 88 70 148-9)	I	LD
61 84 88-70 026-0	(61 84 88 70 127-3)	I	LD

ROYAL SALOON

Converted: 1994 from plan ICR4-A10 semi-open first built 1988.
Builder: Talbot.
Length over Buffers: 26.40 m.
Weight: 41 tonnes.
Non-standard livery: 0 NS plain Intercity royal blue.

61 84 89-70 003-8	(50 84 10-70 647-9)	0	LD

2.7. DEPARTMENTAL STOCK

This section contains departmental vehicles which are either self-propelled or perform a special-ised technical function.

MOSI PW VEHICLES   B

In 1996 NS ordered three vehicles from Tilburg Works. They consist of a cabin and a small load space with a crane. They are called "MOSIs" which is an abbreviation of "moderne sik".

Built: 1996
Builder: NS, Tilburg Works.   **Engine:**
Transmission: Mechanical   **Max. Speed:** 40 km/h.
* Still carries former number (which is the works number).

300096	(27)	S	Inge
300097*	(28)	V	Nano
300098	(29)	S	Ingrid

RAVOT PW VEHICLES   B

In 1996 NS ordered three vehicles from various suppliers. They consist of a cabin and a small load space with a crane. They are called "MOSIs" which is an abbreviation of "moderne sik".

Built: 1996
Builder: Windhoff, Plasser, Unilok.   **Engine:**
Transmission: Mechanical   **Max. Speed:** 40/90 km/h.

RAVOT 1	V
RAVOT 2	S
RAVOT 3	V

EURAILSCOUT MEASURING CAR   2-CAR UNIT

B-B + 2-2

Built: 1999   **Builder:** Plasser & Theurer.
Engine: Caterpillar.   **Transmission:** Hydraulic.
Continuous Rating: 745 kW   **Weight:** 74 tonnes
Max. Speed: 120 km/h.

UFM 120

NS-TO TEST CAR

This is a loco-hauled coach which was converted from a Plan D postal coach. It performs meas-urements on overhead line equipment, track, rolling stock etc. To be replaced by UFM 20.

Converted: 1981.   **Max. Speed:** 140 km/h.

60 84 978 1 005-1	(7918)	Utrecht

ULTRASONIC TEST CAR USO-1   2-B

This vehicle is similar in appearance to metre-gauge railcars in service on the Chemins de Fer de Provence and the Chemins de Fer Corses in France. It is often hired out to other European countries.

Built: 1975   **Builder:** CFD Montmirail.
Engine: **Transmission:** Hydraulic. Voith
Weight: **Max. Speed:**

80 84 978 1 002-4	Zutphen

ULTRASONIC TEST CAR USO-2   2-B

This vehicle is similar in appearance to the rebuilt 3100 Class DMUs, but was actually converted from an SNCF Gril-Express restaurant car! It is likely that it will also be hired out to other Euro-pean countries in future.

Converted: 1997
Builder:
Engine:
Transmission: Hydraulic. Voith
Weight:
Max. Speed: 100 km/h.

80 84 978 1 003-2   Zutphen

ATB TEST CAR "JULES 2"   Bo-Bo

This is a test car for the Dutch form of ATP which is known as ATB. It was converted from a mP postal unit. It has been fitted with a diesel engine for operating on non-eletrified lines.

Converted: 1997
Builder:
Engine:
Traction Motors: 4 x Heemaf 145 kW.
Weight: 52 tonnes
Max. Speed: 140 km/h.

Length over couplings: 26.40 m.

80 84 978 1 003-2   (3032)   Amersfoort

3. DUTCH PRIVATE OPERATORS

Two new train operating companies – Syntus and NoordNed – recently started to run regional services on the Dutch rail network. Both have taken over services on lines which Dutch National Railways (NS) considered as loss making. In the near future more loss-making lines or regional networks are to be put out to tender on a regional basis with the aim of lowering costs and improving performance. There are also two private freight operators running services over the network, ACTS and Short Lines.

3.1. ACTS

A new open access freight operator which operates block trains. Lines worked at present are Kijfhoek–Amsterdam Westhaven (via Gouda), Kijfhoek–Onnen/Leeuwarden (via Gouda, Duivendrecht and Amersfoort).

Livery Codes

A   ACTS. Dark blue with yellow stripe. Black underframe and running gear.
V   Vos Logistics. Black with orange stripe. Black underframe and running gear.

3.1.1. ELECTRIC LOCOMOTIVES
CLASS 1200   Co-Co

The striking 1200s were constructed as 'kit-form' locomotives with the bogies being supplied by Baldwin and electrical components by Westinghouse, the clasic American styling clearly showing their design origin. Until refurbishment by the NS, the mixed parentage was displayed on elaborate worksplates carried on the nose ends. After withdrawal by the NS, four of them have been bought by ACTS for use on freight trains and painted in the new dark blue livery.

Built: 1951–53.
Builder-Mech. Parts: Werkspoor.
Builder-Elec. Parts: Heemaf.
Traction Motors: 6 x Heemaf TM94 axle-hung.
One Hour Rating: 2360 kW.   **Weight:** 108 tonnes.
Maximum Tractive Effort: 194 kN.   **Length over Buffers:** 18.085 m.
Driving Wheel Dia.: 1100 mm.   **Max. Speed:** 130 km/h.

Multiple working fitted. Can be worked in mulltiple with Class 6700.

| 1251 (1215) | A TB | 1253 (1218) | A TB | 1255 (1221) | V TB |
| 1252 (1225) | A TB | 1254 (1214) | A TB | | |

3.1.2. DIESEL LOCOMOTIVES
CLASS 6000   B-B

This class is ex CD (Czech Railways) Class V 60D. They shunt at Amsterdam Westhaven and in the Rotterdam area. 6001 is stored for spares.

Built: for CSD
Builder: LEW.
Engine: 12KVD21VW of 478 kW
Transmission: Hydraulic.
Weight in Full Working Order: 55 tonnes.
Maximum Tractive Effort: 175 kN.   **Length over Buffers:** 10.88 m.
Driving Wheel Dia: 1100 mm.   **Max. Speed:** 60 km/h.

| 6001 | A TB (S) | 6002 | A TB | 6003 | A TB |

CLASS 6700   Bo-Bo

These locomotives have been purchased from SNCB/NMBS and have been renumbered.

Built: 1961–66.
Builder-Mech. Parts: BN.
Builder-Elec. Parts: ACEC.
Engine: GM 12-567C of 1050 kW at 835 rpm.
Transmission: Electric. Four axle-hung traction motors.
Weight in Full Working Order: 78.6 tonnes.
Maximum Tractive Effort: 212 kN.   **Length over Buffers:** 16.79 m.
Driving Wheel Dia.: 1010 mm.   **Max. Speed:** 120 km/h.
Train Heating: Steam. Vapor OK4616 (except 6701).

Multiple working fitted. Can be worked in mulltiple with Class 1200.

6701	(6321)	**V**	TB		6703	(6391)	**A**	TB		6705	(6393)	**A**	TB
6702	(6325)	**A**	TB		6704	(6392)	**A**	TB				

Note: 6290 is also available for spares.

▲ ACTS class 1200 loco No. 1253, obtained from NS Cargo after the withdrawal from NS services, on the turntable at Tilburg works on 31/03/1999.   **Quintus Vosman**

3.2. SHORTLINES

Shortlines is an open access freight operator based in Rotterdam which uses locos hired from Köln (Hafen und Guterverkehr Köln (HGK) for traffic between the Netherlands and Germany, also between Rotterdam and Born. Details of the locos will be found in a forthcoming book in this series covering Germany. Short Lines have also ordered a 7-car Cargo Sprinter from Windhoff and this should be ready by the end of 2000.

▲ HGK DE 13 works a ShortLines container train at Born on 11/09/1999. **Quintus Vosman**

3.3. SYNTUS

Oostnet, the regional bus operator won the tender to operate the Almelo–Mariënberg line from May 1997. For this it obtained three Type DEII DMUs from the NS. At this time, Oostnet was owned by VSN, the holding organisation for Dutch regional bus operators. Since then VSN has been split up and Oostnet, together with bus companies Midnet, ZWN and NZH, has become part of a company initially called VSN 1 but now been renamed ConneXXion. The concession finishes in 2001 but there is an option for two one-year extensions.

On 31st May 1999 a company called Syntus started to operate regional train services on the single track Winterswijk–Doetinchem and Winterswijk–Zutphen lines. This concession lasts until 2004 with the possibility of extending its length by a further five years. Syntus is owned by NS Reizigers, ConneXXion and Cariane Multimodal International (a joint venture by SNCF 90%-owned subsidiary Cariane and SNCF International), with each company owning one third of the shares. Unusually for the Netherlands, Syntus operational staff are able to drive both buses and trains as well as checking tickets and giving information. Oostnet services are now operated by Syntus, although the Oostnet branding is retained on the DE-II DMUs which operate the service. ConneXXion still owns these DMUs but these will soon be transferred to Syntus.

Maintenance is carried out by NedTrain at Arnhem and Zutphen or at Zwolle depot. A small depot for light maintenance of the new DMUs and a fuelling point is to be constructed on the site of the former Winterswijk yard. This will also be used by Syntus buses.

At present Syntus operates services with hired stock from NS Financial Services (3450–53). On the Doetinchem–Winterswijk line services are operated by four DM'90 two-car DMUs hired from NS. Due to the introduction of ATB-NG (new generation automatic train protection) DM'90 is the only type of train allowed on this line. The four sets are still in NS yellow livery but are distinguished by Syntus stickers on the sides. Syntus operates Zutphen–Winterswijk services with four Plan U three-car DMUs (113–5/125) as there is no ATP on this line present.

3.3.1. DIESEL MULTIPLE UNITS

CLASS DEII (PLAN X-v)   2-SECTION UNITS

These articulated units (ex 61–106 series) were originally liveried in light blue with wings on the front and were nicknamed "blue angels". They have been extensively rebuilt and modernised and have large pods on the roof for pressure ventilation equipment. 164 is used for spares.

mABk+mBk (DMCO–DMSO).

Built: 1953–54. Rebuilt 1975/77–82.
Builder: Allan. Rebuilt NS Haarlem.
Wheel Arrangement: Bo-2-Bo.
Engine: Two Cummins NT895R2 of 180 kW at 1740 r.p.m.
Transmission: Electric. 4 Smit traction motors.
Accommodation: 16/56 + –/76.   **Weight**: 45 + 45 tonnes.
Length over couplings: 45.40 m.   **Max. Speed**: 100 km/h.

| 164 | (106) | ZW | | 180 | (73) | ZW | | 186 | (87) | ZW |

LINT 41   2-SECTION UNITS

11 new 2-car low-floor units on order from Alstom, Salzgitter, Germany. Numbers not yet known.

mABk+mBk (DMCO–DMSO).

To be Built: December 2000–June 2001.
Builder: Alstom, Salzgitter (Formerly LHB).
Wheel Arrangement: B-2-B.
Engine: Two Cummins of 315 kW.
Transmission: Electric.
Accommodation: –/143 (total).   **Weight**:   tonnes.
Length over couplings: 41 m (approx.).   **Max. Speed**: 140 km/h.

3.4. NOORDNED

At the same time as Syntus started operations, the new operator NoordNed took over regional train services on the Leeuwarden–Harlingen and Leeuwarden–Stavoren lines in the far north of the country. NoordNed (meaning Network North), whose shares are held by NS Reizigers (49%) and Britain's third largest bus operator Arriva (49%) plus a third party (2%), made the best bid when these two lines were opened to tender. NoordNed has won a licence to operate these lines until 2004.

Besides these two lines, NoordNed operates the train services between Leeuwarden and Groningen on behalf of NS Reizigers. The Leeuwarden–Groningen line does not belong to the list of loss-making services, but NS Reizigers considered it better to leave operation to NoordNed. The service is expected to have been transferred before this book appears. This is a major advantage for NoordNed, as the company has now also won the tender to operate regional train services from Groningen to Roodeschool, Delfzijl and Nieuweschans. Initially the international train service Groningen–Leer (Germany) was also included, but ultimately the German authorities pulled out of the tendering procedure.

NoordNed has no rolling stock of its own, but hires DMUs from NS Financial Services. These are Class 3200 "Wadloper" two-car diesel-hydraulic MUs and their single car equivalents of Class 3100 plus DM'90 two-car DMUs. In fact – as far as rolling stock is concerned – nothing has changed compared to the NS era. The NoordNed DM'90 sets mainly operate the service between Leeuwarden and Groningen, especially the express services during peak hours. "Wadloper" sets are used for certain stopping trains on this line. It is possible that the complete fleet of Wadlopers – 30 two-car sets and 19 single cars – will be transferred from NS Reizigers to NoordNed when the latter takes over full operation of the Groningen lines this year (2000), but at the moment some sets are still operated by NS Reizigers.

FURTHER OPERATING CONCESSIONS

Tendering for local lines in the Netherlands is continuing and the following is the list of concessions to be let in the next three years:

2000
• Groningen–Nieuweschans (–Leer)
• Groningen–Roodeschool
• Groningen–Delfzijl

2001
• Zutphen–Apeldoorn
• Zutphen–Hengelo–Oldenzaal
• Hoorn–Alkmaar
• Alkmaar–Schagen–Den Helder
• Zaandam–Hoorn–Enkhuizen
• Haarlem–Uitgeest
• Haarlem–Zandvoort
• Amsterdam–Uitgeest–Alkmaar (?)
• Rotterdam–Hoek van Holland
• Gouda–Alphen a/d Rijn
• Dordrecht–Geldermalsen

2002
• Utrecht–Rhenen (?)
• Utrecht–Baarn (?)
• Amersfoort–Ede-Wageningen
• Zwolle–Emmen
• Zwolle–Kampen

2003
• Roermond–Nijmegen
• Maastricht–Kerkrade
• Den Haag CS–Rotterdam Hofplein
• Den Haag CS–Zoetermeer
• Lelystad–Weesp
• Zwolle–Almelo
• Tiel–Arnhem Velperpoort
• Arnhem–Doetinchem

128

3.5. STRUKTON

The private infrastructure company "Strukton" operates a number of ex-NS locomotives. Their numbers are the former NS numbers with 300000 added. For details see the relevant NS pages.

Livery: All yellow.

CLASS 600   0-6-0

300609 Riek
300640

CLASS 2200   Bo-Bo

302270 Berta
302282 Anneke
302328 José

▲ Class 200 "Sik" shunter No. 252, now owned by NS infrastructure subsidiary NBM Rail, at Kijfhoek on 31/08/1998. **Adrian Norton**

▼ The NS Class 600s are basically the same as the British Class 08. Radio remote-control fitted 683, owned by NS Reizigers, is seen at Den Haag CS on 09/12/1998. **W.J. Freebury**

Class 1700 No. 1754 'DIEMEN' with the 09.54 Schiphol–Berlin service at Amersfoort on 03/05/2000. The train is formed of DB IR stock. **Peter Fox**

▲ Class 1300 No. 1305 'ALPHEN AAN DER RIJN' arrives at Nijmegen with the 10.54 freight from Arnhem on 23/03/1995. This class is stored by Railion Benelux at the time of writing, but may be sold or leased to NS Reizigers in future. **David Haydock**

▼ Class 1600 No. 1602 'Schiphol' passes through Zwijndrecht on 29/08/1999 with a train of empty flat wagons heading for Kijfhoek yard. **Brian Garvin**

▲ Class 2200 No. 2384 in NS Cargo livery at Terneuzen.   **David Haydock**

▼ Class 6400 No. 6475 stabled at Roosendaal on 01/05/1999.   **Colin Boocock**

▲ DE3 DEMU 119 runs into Kesteren on 28/05/1998 with the 13.17 to Tiel.   **W.J. Freebury**

▼ Class 3100 No. 3104 (coupled to Class 3200 No. 3217) at Roodeschool on 24/03/2000 with the 12.47 service for Groningen.   **Peter Fox**

▲ DMUs 3429 and 3401 stabled at Arnhem on 29/08/1999. **Brian Garvin**

▼ Plan V 2-car EMUs 465 & 897 arrive at Amersfoort with the 10.21 Utrecht CS–Ede-Wageningen on 22/03/2000. **Peter Fox**

▲ Plan T EMU No. 523 approaching Den Haag CS with the 16.04 from Hoorn.　**Peter Fox**

▼ SM'90 Railhopper EMU No. 2108 at Zwolle forming the 11.55 for Emmen on 30/03/1996.
Chris Wilson

▲ Plan Y1 2-car Sprinter EMUs 2035 + 2029 (branded "City Pendel") leave Den Haag CS with the 17.56 Zoetemeer Stadslijn service on 24/03/2000. **Peter Fox**

▼ Plan Y2 3-car Sprinter EMU No. 2846 at Utrecht with a Hoorn service on 01/06/1997. **Colin J. Marsden**

▲ Koploper EMU No. 4028 at Rotterdam CS on 01/06/1997.   **Colin J. Marsden**
▼ A pair of IRM RegioRunner EMUs (8453 leading) approoach Utrecht CS on 01/06/1997.
Colin J. Marsden

▲ A four car DD-AR set stabled at Arnhem on 29/08/1999 with mDDM double-decker power car 390 7710 at the front.   **Brian Garvin**

▼ A Benelux Push-Pull set seen at Dordrecht en route from Amsterdam to Brussels on 09/07/1999. The set is being pushed by a Belgian Class 11 loco.   **Quintus Vosman**

▲ 2-car EMU set 253 arrives in Luxembourg during February 1994. **David Haydock**

▼ EMU 2001 at Ettelbruck on 01/08/1998 forming the 10.15 Wiltz–Petange. **W.J. Freebury**

▲ GM Class 800 loco 801 on station pilot duties at Luxembourg on 12/09/1999. **Brian Garvin**

▼ GM Class 850 loco 852 at Petange. **W.J. Freebury**

▲ Class 1800 Co-Co diesel electric No. 1815 at Arlon with the 12.15 from Luxembourg on 07/12/1998.
W.J. Freebury

▼ Class 3600 No. 3604 leaves Luxembourg on 11/09/1997 with the 17.39 to Esch-sur-Alzette.
Colin J. Marsden

▲ Thalys TGV-unit 4539 at Zevenbergen en route from Amsterdam to Paris on 13/03/1999.
Quintus Vosman

▼ ICE-3M set (406 001/501) on trial, seen at Amsterdam CS on 05/11/1999. Although sporting the NS logo, this set is one of the sets to be owned by DB after delivery. NS has ordered four of these sets. At the time the photo was taken the set still was property of the manufacturer, Siemens.
Quintus Vosman

▲ Ex-British Railways Class EM2 No. 27003 (NS 1501) owned by Werkgroep 1501 at Onnen Yard on 28/09/1996 on the occasion of the "Dark side of the Moon" railtour. **Chris Booth**

▼ Ex-PKP Kriegslok Ty2.3554 restored as "26.101" at Eeklo after working a shuttle service to Maldegem during the Stoomcentrum Maldegem's steam festival on 03/05/1998. **Colin Boocock**

Colin Boocock

SNCB/NMBS Class 1 4-6-2 No. 1.002 with a special for Eeklo at Leuven on 03/05/1998.

4. LUXEMBOURG RAILWAYS (CFL)

Luxembourg Railways are known by the abbreviation CFL (Societé Nationale des Chemins de Fer Luxembourgeois). The total length of the system is only 270 km, but this does not mean that the network is uninteresting. The CFL operates locomotives and multiple units of types that are also found in neighbouring countries, and the city of Luxembourg also sees through workings of locomotives from the DB, SNCB and SNCF. Electrification is at 25 kV a.c. 50 Hz and all CFL electric locomotives and multiple units operate on this system. SNCB/NMBS 3000 V d.c. electircs can also run into Luxembourg station.

NUMBERING SYSTEM

The CFL loco numbering system was based on the horse power of the locomotives. 1801 is an 1800 h.p locomotive, whilst 3620 is one of 3600 h.p. However, departmental vehicles are numbered 10XX and new locomotives and multiple units are not numbered in accordance with this practice.

DEPOTS AND WORKSHOPS

With such a compact system there is no need for many depots. All locomotives are allocated to Luxembourg shed. There are stabling points at Ettelbruck, Wasserbillig, Troisvierges, Bettembourg Yard, Pétange and Esch sur Alzette. Locomotives also stable overnight at the various branch termini as required. Because of the small fleet only one workshop is required and this is located opposite the station at Luxembourg.

DEVELOPMENTS

In 1993, CFL completed electirification of its network at 25 kV a.c. 50 Hz, except for the line to Arlon (B), electrified at 3000 V d.c. and short freight branches Kleinbettingen–Steinfort and Schieren–Bissen, which remain diesel worked. For international services, CFL owns two Class AM80/82/83 three-car EMUs 325 and 326 which are maintained by Belgian Railways and shown in the Belgian section of this book, two Class 628.4 two-car DMUs 628 505 and 506 which are maintained by DB and shown in the Platform 5 book "German Railways" and 16 Corail coaches which are maintained by SNCF but are shown in this section.

By the end of 2000, CFL should have received all 20 Class 3000 dual-voltage (3000 V d.c./25 kV a.c.) electric locomotives. Once these are performing properly, they will be managed in a pool with SNCB/NMBS Class 13 and should take over the majority of work from Classes 1800 and 3600 most of which will be withdrawn. CFL has recently ordered six diesel railcars of Class 2100 based on the SNCF Class X 73500 for delivery in 2000. These will operate branch shuttles, freeing EMUs for more heavily-loaded services. CFL also has hired six heavy diesel locos from Siemens for freight services to Germany.

In 1998 a revised, more frequent passenger timetable was introduced which entails more intensive use of traction and rolling stock.

LIVERIES

CFL locos are generally painted in a red livery, whilst EMUs are yellow and red. Loco-hauled coaches are green and white, except for the International Corail stock which is painted in SNCF livery. The new Class 3000 locos are painted white with blue stripes.

4.1. ELECTRIC MULTIPLE UNITS

CLASS 250   2-CAR UNITS

These are based on similar units supplied to the SNCF and feature monomotor bogies and thyristor control. Up to three units may work in multiple within the class and with Class 260. Despite only four units being diagrammed, they managed to cover all electrified lines except the Wiltz branch in 1999.

AB + BD (DMCO–DMBSO).

Built: 1975.
Builder-Mech. Parts: CF.
Builder-Elec. Parts: MTE, CEM.
Wheel Arrangement: 2-B + 2-2.
Traction Motors: 1 x GRLM 792 B of 615 kW.
Accommodation: 14/80 1T + –/74.
Total Weight: 79.5 tonnes.
Length over couplings: 25.325 + 25.325 m.
Max. Speed: 120 km/h.

251	252	253	254	255	256

CLASS 260   3-CAR UNITS

These units were acquired second-hand from the SNCF and were previously SNCF Z6169/68 respectively, acquired in 1982 and 1985. The centre cars can operate in Class 250. The class supplements Class 250 and operate certain shuttles to Dudelange and Audun-le-Tiche.

BD + B + AB (DMBSO–TSO–DTCO).

Built: 1970.
Builder-Mech. Parts: CF/Alsthom.
Builder-Elec. Parts: CEM.
Wheel Arrangement: 2-B + 2-2 + 2-2.
Traction Motors: 1 x GRLM 792 B of 615 kW.
Accommodation: –/79 + –/107 + 16/71 1T.
Weight: 52 + 27 + 29 tonnes.
Length over couplings: 25.325 + 23.8 + 25.325 m.
Max. Speed: 120 km/h.

261	262

CLASS 2000   2-CAR UNITS

These EMUs are similar to SNCF Class Z11500 and they inter-work with SNCF Z11500 units based just across the frontier at Thionville reaching Longwy and even Nancy. 2003 and 2012 were severely damaged in separate head-on crashes and are being rebuilt. At the end of 1999 odd coaches were operating together. Units operate on all lines in Luxembourg.

ABD + B (DMBCO-DTSO).

Built: 1990–92.
Builders: De Dietrich/ANF/Alsthom.
Wheel Arrangement: Bo-Bo + 2-2.
Traction Motors: 4 x TAB 676 B1 of 305 kW each.
Accommodation: 24/60 1T + –/80 1T.
Weight: 64 + 40 tonnes.
Length over couplings: 25.10 + 25.10 m.
Max. Speed: 160 km/h.

* Equipped with SNCF's KVB automatic train control system.

2001	2005	2009	2013	2017	2020	
2002	2006	2010	2014	2018	2021	*
2003	2007	2011	2015	2019	2022	*
2004	2008	2012	2016			

2018 is named TROISVIERGES.

4.2. DIESEL LOCOMOTIVES

Note: Self-propelled departmental vehicles are also numbered in this series.

CLASS 800   Bo-Bo

These locos are unique to the CFL and are typical American switchers of the early 1950s. They are used for shunting and trip working at Bettembourg Yard (4) and Luxembourg Triage (1). One loco works a trip to Esch on Sundays.

Built: 1954.
Builder: AFB.
Engine: GM 8-567B of 600 kW at 835 rpm.
Transmission: Electric. Four GM 4-EMD-D27B axle-hung traction motors.
Train Heating: None   **Weight**: 74 tonnes.
Maximum Tractive Effort: 179 kN.   **Length over Buffers**: 13.795 m.
Driving Wheel Dia.: 1050 mm.   **Max. Speed**: 80 km/h.

| 801 | 802 | 803 | 804 | 805 | 806 |

CLASSES 850/900   Bo-Bo

These are from the same family as SNCF Class BB 63500. Used on station pilot and trip freight duties. These locos operate station pilot, shunting and trip freight duties at Luxembourg (5), Pétange (3), Ettelbruck (2), Wasserbillig (2) and Esch (2).

Built: 1956–58.
Builder: BL.
Engine: SACM MGO V12SH of 615 kW at 1500 r.p.m. (* MGO V12SHR of 690 kW at 1500 r.p.m.).
Transmission: Electric. Four BL 453-29B (* BL 453-29D) axle-hung traction motors.
Train Heating: None.   **Weight**: 72 tonnes.
Maximum Tractive Effort: 174 kN.   **Length over Buffers**: 14.75 m.
Driving Wheel Dia.: 1100 mm.   **Max. Speed**: 105 km/h.

851	855	901 *	905 *	908 *	911 *
852	856	902 *	906 *	909 *	912 *
853	857	903 *	907 *	910 *	913 *
854	858	904 *			

902 is named STEINFORT.

CLASS 1000   B

Used for light shunting duties and usually found at Bettembourg p.w. Depot, Luxembourg and Ettelbruck. In October 1999, 1003 was based at Luxembourg Works and the other three at Bettembourg.

Built: 1972.
Builder: Jung.
Engine: Deutz F12 L413 of 186 kW at 2150 rpm.
Transmission: Hydraulic. Voith L2r4SU2.
Train Heating: None   **Weight**: 32 tonnes.
Maximum Tractive Effort: 94 kN.   **Length over Buffers**: 7.20 m.
Driving Wheel Dia.: 950 mm.   **Max. Speed**: 60 km/h.

| 1001 | 1002 | 1003 | 1004 | |

CLASS 1010   B

This shunter has an auto-coupler. It is usually found at Luxembourg depot.

Built: 1964.
Builder: Henschel.
Engine: Henschel 6R 1215A of 160 kW at 1800 rpm.
Transmission: Hydraulic. Voith DIWABUS 200S/355.
Train Heating: None   **Weight**: 22 tonnes.
Maximum Tractive Effort: 64 kN.   **Length over Buffers**: 7.10 m.
Driving Wheel Dia.: 850 mm.   **Max. Speed**: 24 km/h.

1011 (2011)

CLASS 1020   B

Used for light shunting duties. 1021 is usually at Luxembourg shed. 1024 is fitted with auto-couplers and are used at Pétange Wagon Works.

Built: 1952–57.
Builder: Deutz.
Engine: Deutz A8 L614 of 100 kW at 1800 rpm.
Transmission: Hydraulic. Voith L33Y.
Train Heating: None   **Weight**: 22 tonnes.
Maximum Tractive Effort: 64 kN.   **Length over Buffers**: 7.57 m.
Driving Wheel Dia.: 850 mm.   **Max. Speed**: 53 km/h.

1022 | 1024

CLASS 1030   B

1031 is fitted with remote control. It is used by the track department. In October 1999, 1031 was allocated to Ettelbruck, the others at Bettembourg.

Built: 1988.
Builder: Jenbacher Werke, Austria.
Engine: MTU 8V 183 TA12 of 267 kW at 2200 rpm.
Transmission: Hydraulic. Voith L2r4SV2.
Train Heating: None   **Weight**: 36 tonnes.
Maximum Tractive Effort: 117 kN.   **Length over Buffers**: 8.55 m.
Driving Wheel Dia.: 950 mm.   **Max. Speed**: 60 km/h.

1031 | 1032 | 1033

CLASS 1050   P.W. TROLLEYS

These permanent way trolleys have a large cabin at one end for the driver and staff and a hydraulic arm at the other. They are allocated to Bettembourg infrastructure depot.1051 was formerly numbered departmental 10.

Built: 1980–82.
Builder: Donelli/Geismar.
Engine: Deutz F8 L413F of 173.5 kW. at 1500 rpm.
Transmission: Hydraulic. Clark R 28624-9.
Length over Buffers: 9.90 m.   **Weigh**: 36 tonnes.
Driving Wheel Dia.: 850 mm.   **Max. Speed**: 80 km/h.

1051 | 1052 | 1053 | 1054

CLASS 1060   O.H.L. TROLLEYS

This is another departmental vehicle numbered in the capital stock series. It features a dummy pantograph and a working area above the crew accommodation. It is used for overhead line maintenance. Based at Luxembourg depot.

Built: 1985.
Builder: Donelli/Geismar.
Engine: Deutz F8 L413F of 173.5 kW at 1500 rpm.
Transmission: Hydromechanical. MHR 28628-2.
Length over Buffers: 12.14 m.   **Weight**: 24 tonnes.
Driving Wheel Dia.: 850 mm.   **Max. Speed**: 80 km/h.

1061 | 1062

CLASS 1070   P.W. TROLLEY

A "motorised wagon". Can operate on its own at 5 km/h but is usually coupled to 1062. No details available. Based at Luxembourg depot.

1071

CLASS 1800 Co-Co

Identical to SNCB Class 55 except for the coupling of traction motors. 12 of the class are dia-grammed, mainly on freights between Stockem yard in Belgium and Bettembourg yard or through to Thionville or Metz in France. The class no longer takes freight to Ronet in Belgium. Boilered locos passenger trains to Kleinbettingen and Arlon plus odd trips to Wasserbillig and Troisvierges. In principal, Class 3000 is to take over Stockem-Metz freights in 2000 and some Class 1800 will be equipped with Indusi to operate freight through to Ehrang near Trier in Germany.

Built: 1963–64.
Builder-Mech. Parts: BN.
Builder-Elec. Parts: ACEC/SEM.
Engine: GM 16-567C of 1435 kW at 835 r.p.m.
Transmission: Electric. Six ACEC DS7 axle-hung traction motors.
Train Heating: Steam. Vapor OK 4616. **Weight**: 110 (114 s) tonnes.
Maximum Tractive Effort: 272 kN. **Length over Buffers**: 19.55 m.
Driving Wheel Dia.: 1010 mm. **Max. Speed**: 120 km/h.
Rheostatic braking.

s-Steam heating fitted.

1801	s	STADT GÖPPINGEN	1812		
1802	s	Blankenberge	1813		Schieren
1803	s		1814		
1804	s		1815		KAUTENBACH 1881-1981
1805	s	MONDORF-LES-BAINS	1816	s	LAROCHETTE
1806		COMMUNE DE WALFERDANGE	1817	s	
1807		COMMUNE DE PÉTANGE	1818	s	
1808			1819	s	PRINCE HENRI
1809			1820	s	Bettembourg
1810					

CLASS ME26 Co-Co

These locos were originally built for Norwegian Railways (NSB) as Class Di6 but returned to the builders after continued unreliability and one loco fire. Siemens, who took over MaK during construction, had the locos overhauled by Danish State Railways (DSB), the work including generator replacement, change of headlights to German standards and the addition of Indusi signalling equipment. Six locos have been hired by CFL for three years starting summer 2000. They will be used on freight over the Luxembourg–Wasserbillig line, hopefully through to Ehrang Yard (Trier), Germany and on the line to Gouvy. Although CFL have hired six specific locos, they will be changed by Siemens if any major problem occurs. Note: "ME26" indicates Motor, Electric transmission and 2650 kW).

ME26-01–12 were formerly Di 6 661–672 respectively.

Built: 1995–96.
Builder: MaK.
Engine: MaK 12M282 of 2650 kW at 1000 r.p.m.
Transmission: Electric. Six type 1TB2324-0AG02 asynchronous traction motors.
Train Heating: None. **Weight**: 119 tonnes.
Maximum Tractive Effort: 405 kN. **Length over Buffers**: 20.96 m.
Driving Wheel Dia.: 1060 mm. **Max. Speed**: 160 km/h.

ME26-02 | ME26-05 | ME26-09 | ME26-xx | ME26-xx | ME26-xx

4.3. DIESEL RAILCARS
CLASS 2100   SINGLE UNITS
These are based on similar units supplied to the SNCF (Class X 73500). The centre section has a low floor (550 mm).

Built: 2000.
Builders: De Dietrich.
Wheel Arrangement: 1A-A1.
Engines: Two MAN D2866 LUE 602 6-cylinder in line (258 kW) per car.
Transmission: Hydraulic. Voith T211 rzz.
Accommodation: 16/45 1T.
Weight: 49 tonnes.
Length: 28.90 m.
Maximum Speed: 140 km/h.

2101 | 2102 | 2103 | 2104 | 2105 | 2106

▲ CFL shunter No. 1032 at Petange 0n 01/08/1998.   **W.J. Freebury**

CFL

4.4. ELECTRIC LOCOMOTIVES
CLASS 3000   Bo-Bo

These dual-voltage locos are designed to operate in a pool with SNCB/NMBS Class 13 which are identical. They are used on Luxembourg–Liège passenger trains and will be employed on freight over the Namur–Bertrix–Rodange "Athus-Meuse" line when electrified in 2001. Initially, locos are operating most Luxembourg–Troisvierges passenger trains. Severe problems occurred in mid 1999 with locos causing current surges which damaged SNCF and DB locos in Luxembourg station. Two of the four traction motors were isolated while the problem was sorted out. This problem has delayed introduction on Stockem (Belgium)–Thionville–Woippy–Metz (France) freights.

Built: 1998–2000
Systems: 3000 V d.c./25 kV a.c. 50 Hz (1500 V d.c. at reduced power)
Builder-Mech. Parts: Alstom, Bombardier Eurorail.
Builder-Elec. Parts: Alstom (ACEC)
Traction Motors: Four PXA 4339B
One Hour Rating: 5200 kW
Maximum Tractive Effort: 288 kN
Driving Wheel Dia.: 1160 mm
Train Protection: KVB, TBL, MEMOR.

Weight: 90 tonnes
Length over Buffers: 19.11 m.
Maximum Speed: 200 km/h

Push-pull and multiple working fitted. Equipped with rheostatic and regenerative braking.

3001	3011
3002	3012
3003	3013
3004	3014
3005	3015
3006	3016
3007	3017
3008	3018
3009	3019
3010	3020

CLASS 3600   Bo-Bo

These 25 kV a.c. electric locos are similar to SNCF Class BB 12000. 14 locos are diagrammed, mainly on freight over the Bettembourg–Esch–Rodange line, generated by the steelworks at Belval. Four locos haul passenger in each peak on weekdays. Locos also take Netherlands–Southern France trains from Gouvy to Metz during the night.

Built: 1958-59.
Builder-Mech. Parts: MTE.
Builder-Elec. Parts: MTE.
Traction Motors: Four SW 435.
One Hour Rating: 2650 kW.
Maximum Tractive Effort: 186 kN.
Driving Wheel Dia.: 1250 mm.

Weight: 84 tonnes.
Length over Buffers: 15.20 m.
Max. Speed: 120 km/h.

3601		3610	
3602		3611	
3603		3612	
3604		3613	GUILLAUME LUXEMBOURG
3605		3617	
3606		3618	WILTZ
3607	ESCH/ALZETTE	3619	WASSERBILLIG
3608	LORENTZWEILER	3620	REISERBANN
3609			

4.5. LOCO-HAULED COACHING STOCK
WEGMANN COACHES

These coaches are 26.1 m. in length. All have asbestos removed and have been refurbished. There were originally four types of coaching stock vehicles in use on the CFL, types B, AB and BD and ABD. The ABD vehicles were identical to the BD vehicles and the AB vehicles were identical to the B vehicles, except for the upholstery on the first class seats.

Since these vehicles were built, many have been renumbered more than once and some have been modified. In order to sort out the renumbering, it helps to use the pre-UIC number as a reference. The build details of these were as follows: 2101-36 type B12, 2137-38 A3B9, 2161-69 A3B9, 2181-93 B9D. The serial number of the vehicle is digits 10 to 12 of the UIC number. The first of these digits changes from a '3' to a '4' and vice-versa when the coaches are shopped, depending on whether 120 or 140 km/h bogies are fitted and these are changed during overhauls. Thus the list is in the order of the last two digits of the serial number. In the list which follows, three numbers are quoted:

1. The present UIC number.
2. The UIC number shown in 'Benelux Locomotives and Coaching Stock 3rd edition'.
3. The original number.

The livery of all coaches was dark green, but this has now been changed to cream and green. Vehicles upgraded to 140 km/h are also allowed to work into Belgium, the Netherlands and Germany.

D
BICYCLE CARRYING CAR

Converted from collision-damaged coaches in April 1993. Used on demand, mainly on the scenic Troisvierges line and occasionally on hire trains as improvised disco or buffet cars.

Max Speed: 140 km/h.
Livery: Blue with yellow stripes.

* Formerly open second (B12) and originally open composite (A3B9).
§ Formerly brake composite (A3B9D) and originally brake second (B9D).

50 82 92-40 001-9	50 82 22-10 359-2	2129	*
50 82 92-40 002-7	50 82 81-10 393-9	2182	§

A6B6
OPEN COMPOSITE

Accommodation: 48/48 2T.
Max Speed: 120 or 140 km/h.

* Formerly open second (B12).
§ Formerly A3B9.

50 82 32-40 422-0	50 82 22-10 353-5	2123	*
50 82 32-40 423-8	50 82 32-40 418-8	2168	§

B12 (BR§)
OPEN SECOND

Accommodation: –/96 2T.
Max Speed: 120 or 140 km/h.

* Converted from A3B9 (CO).
§ Classified BR and known as the "Rendezvous" coach. Equipped with a kitchen at the expense of Luxembourg railway enthusiasts group Groupement des Amis du Rail (GAR). Still CFL property and only used on special trains and in the summer-only Blankenberge Express to Blankenberge on the Belgian coast.
w One compartment stripped of seats to accommodate wheelchairs. Accommodation -/88 2T.

50 82 22-40 431-3	50 82 22-10 331-1	2101	
50 82 22-10 332-9	50 82 22-10 332-9	2102	
50 82 22-40 433-9	50 82 22-40 433-9	2103	
50 82 22-40 434-7	50 82 22-10 334-5	2104	w
50 82 22-40 435-4	50 82 22-40 435-4	2105	
50 82 22-40 436-2	50 82 22-40 436-2	2106	

50 82 22-40 437-0	50 82 22-10 337-8	2107
50 82 22-40 438-8	50 82 22-40 438-8	2108
50 82 22-40 439-6	50 82 22-10 339-4	2109
50 82 22-10 340-2	50 82 22-40 440-4	2110
50 82 22-40 441-2	50 82 22-10 341-0	2111
50 82 22-40 442-0	50 82 22-10 342-8	2112
50 82 22-40 443-8	50 82 22-10 343-6	2113
50 82 22-10 344-4	50 82 22-10 344-4	2114
50 82 22-10 345-1	50 82 22-40 445-3	2115
50 82 22-40 446-1	50 82 22-10 346-9	2116
50 82 22-40 447-9	50 82 22-40 447-9	2117
50 82 22-40 448-7	50 82 22-10 348-5	2118
50 82 22-10 449-5	50 82 22-10 349-3	2119
50 82 22-40 450-3	50 82 22-40 450-3	2120
50 82 22-40 451-1	50 82 22-10 351-9	2121
50 82 22-40 452-9	50 82 22-10 352-7	2122
50 82 22-10 354-3	50 82 22-10 354-3	2124
50 82 22-40 455-2	50 82 22-10 355-0	2125
50 82 22-10 356-8	50 82 22-40 456-0	2126
50 82 22-40 457-8	50 82 22-40 457-8	2127 §
50 82 22-10 358-6	50 82 22-40 458-6	2128
50 82 22-40 460-2	50 82 22-40 460-2	2130
50 82 22-10 361-8	50 82 22-40 461-0	2131
50 82 22-10 362-6	50 82 22-10 362-6	2132
50 82 22-10 363-4	50 82 22-10 363-4	2133
50 82 22-10 364-2	50 82 22-10 364-2	2134
50 82 22-10 365-9	50 82 22-40 465-1	2135
50 82 22-40 466-9	50 82 22-40 466-9	2136
50 82 22-10 367-5	50 82 22-40 467-7	2161 *
50 82 22-10 368-3	50 82 22-10 368-3	2162 *
50 82 22-10 369-1	50 82 22-40 469-3	2163 *
50 82 22-40 470-1	50 82 22-40 470-1	2166 *
50 82 22-10 371-7	50 82 22-40 471-9	2169 *
50 82 22-40 472-7	50 82 22-40 472-7	2137 *
50 82 22-10 373-3	50 82 22-40 373-3	2138 *
50 82 22-40 474-3	50 82 22-40 474-3	2164 *
50 82 22-40 475-0	50 82 22-40 475-0	2165 *
50 82 22-40 477-6	50 82 32-40 417-0	2167 *

A3B6D (A6B3D§)   BRAKE OPEN COMPOSITE

All converted from B9D (BSO).

Accommodation: 24/48 1T (48/24 1T*).
Max Speed: 120 or 140 km/h.

§ Centre compartment is first instead of end compartment.

50 82 81-40 480-8	50 82 81-40 480-8	2189 §
50 82 81-40 481-6	50 82 81-10 381-4	2191
50 82 81-10 382-2	50 82 81-40 482-4	2193
50 82 81-10 383-2	50 82 81-40 483-2	2183
50 82 81-10 384-8	50 82 81-40 484-0	2184
50 82 81-40 485-7	50 82 81-40 485-7	2186 §
50 82 81-40 486-5	50 82 81-40 486-5	2187 §
50 82 81-40 487-3	50 82 81-40 487-3	2188 §
50 82 81-10 388-9	50 82 81-10 388-9	2190
50 82 81-10 389-7	50 82 81-10 389-7	2192
50 82 81-10 391-3	50 82 81-40 491-5	2181
50 82 81-40 494-9	50 82 81-10 394-6	2185

CORAIL STOCK

This air conditioned stock operates in a pool with the SNCF fleet but is owned by CFL despite the UIC numbering with the 87 indicating SNCF ownership.

TYPE B10tu   OPEN SECOND

Built: 1980–1983.
Builder: Alsthom/Franco-Belge.
Bogies: SNCF Y32A.
Length: 26.40 m.
Weight: 41 tonnes.
Accommodation: –/80 2T.
Maximum speed: 160 km/h.

61 87 20 71 334-5	61 87 20 71 377-4	61 87 20 71 392-3
61 87 20 71 341-0	61 87 20 71 383-2	61 87 20 71 393-1
61 87 20 71 347-7	61 87 20 71 384-0	61 87 20 71 394-9
61 87 20 71 367-5	61 87 20 71 386-5	61 87 20 71 395-6
61 87 20 71 370-9		

TYPE A4B6u   COMPOSITE

Built: 1974.
Builder: De Dietrich/ANF.
Bogies: SNCF Y32A.
Length: 26.40 m.
Weight: 39 tonnes
Accommodation: 24/36 2T.
Maximum speed: 160 km/h.

61 87 30 70 073-8	61 87 30 70 074-6	61 87 30 70 075-3.

5. INTERNATIONAL HIGH SPEED TRAINS

This section contains details of international high speed trains which may be seen in the Benelux countries. The following livery codes are used:

E   Eurostar livery. White with dark blue window band roof and yellow lower bodysides.
I   ICE livery. White with red stripe under windows.
0   Non standard livery (refer to text).
T   Thalys livery. Metallic grey with red front ends and roof.
V   TGV livery. Metallic grey with blue window band.

Depot codes from outside the Benelux countries are:

LL   Le Landy (Paris)
NP   North Pole (London)

Note: Owner code EU denotes Eurostar (UK) Ltd.

5.1. TRAINS À GRAND VITESSE (Tgvs)

EUROSTAR   9-CAR "THREE CAPITALS" SETS

Eurostar sets work services through the Channel Tunnel between London and Paris and Brussels. The four-voltage sets also work London–Bourg St. Maurice ski trains in winter. 3203–04 and 3225–28 are not used on Channel Tunnel services. They have been used on the Brussels–Nice service. Eurostars are based on the French TGV design concept, and the individual cars are numbered like French TGVs. Each train consists of two 9-coach sets back-to-back with a power car at the outer end. All sets are articulated with an extra motor bogie on the coach next to the power car. Coaches are also referred to by their position in the set viz. R1–R9 (and in traffic R10–R18 in the second set). Coaches R18–R10 are identical to R1–R9.

TGV + TGVZBD + 4 TGVRB + TGVRr + 2TGVRA + TGVRAD.

Systems: 750 V (3rd rail)/3000 V d.c./25 kV a.c 50 Hz/(v 1500 V d.c.).
Built: 1992–93.
Builders: GEC-Alsthom/Brush/ANF/De Dietrich/BN Construction/ACEC.
Axle Arrangement: Bo-Bo + Bo-2-2-2-2-2-2-2-2-2.
Accommodation: 0 + –/48 1T + –/58 1T + –/58 2T + –/58 1T + –/58 2T + bar/kitchen + 39/– 1T + 39/– 1T + 25/– 1T.
Length: 22.15 + 21.845 + (7 x 18.70) + 21.845 m.
Max. Speed: 300 km/h.
Cab Signalling: TVM 430.
Non-standard Livery: 0 As E but Eurostar branding removed.

Trailer cars are numbered in the following sequence.

Set nnnn: 37nnnn1/37nnnn2/37nnnn3/37nnnn4/37nnnn5/37nnnn6/37nnnn7/37nnnn8/37nnnn9.

Set	Owner	Power Car			Set	Owner	Power Car		
3001	EU	3730010	E	NP	3020	EU	3730200	E	NP
3002	EU	3730020	E	NP	3021	EU	3730210	E	NP
3003	EU	3730030	E	NP	3022	EU	3730220	E	NP
3004	EU	3730040	E	NP	3101	SNCB	3731010	E	FF
3005	EU	3730050	E	NP	3102	SNCB	3731020	E	FF
3006	EU	3730060	E	NP	3103	SNCB	3731030	E	FF
3007	EU	3730070	E	NP	3104	SNCB	3731040	E	FF
3008	EU	3730080	E	NP	3105	SNCB	3731050	E	FF
3009	EU	3730090	E	NP	3106	SNCB	3731060	E	FF
3010	EU	3730100	E	NP	3107	SNCB	3731070	E	FF
3011	EU	3730110	E	NP	3108	SNCB	3731080	E	FF
3012	EU	3730120	E	NP	3201	SNCF	3732010	E	v	LY
3013	EU	3730130	E	NP	3202	SNCF	3732020	E	v	LY
3014	EU	3730140	E	NP	3203	SNCF	3732030	0	v	LY
3015	EU	3730150	E	NP	3204	SNCF	3732040	0	v	LY
3016	EU	3730160	E	NP	3205	SNCF	3732050	E		LY
3017	EU	3730170	E	NP	3210	SNCF	3732100	E		LY
3018	EU	3730180	E	NP	3211	SNCF	3732110	E		LY
3019	EU	3730190	E	NP	3212	SNCF	3732120	E		LY

3213	SNCF	3732130	E		LY		3223	SNCF	3732230	E	v	LY
3214	SNCF	3732140	E		LY		3224	SNCF	3732240	E	v	LY
3215	SNCF	3732150	E	v	LY		3225	SNCF	3732250	0	v	LY
3216	SNCF	3732160	E	v	LY		3226	SNCF	3732260	0	v	LY
3217	SNCF	3732170	E		LY		3227	SNCF	3732270	0	v	LY
3218	SNCF	3732180	E		LY		3228	SNCF	3732280	0	v	LY
3219	SNCF	3732190	E		LY		3229	SNCF	3732290	E	v	LY
3220	SNCF	3732200	E		LY		3230	SNCF	3732300	E		LY
3221	SNCF	3732210	E	v	LY		3231	SNCF	3732310	E		LY
3222	SNCF	3732220	E	v	LY		3232	SNCF	3732320	E		LY

Spare Power Car

3999	EU	3739990	E	NP		

THALYS   8-CAR FOUR-VOLTAGE SETS

This is basically a four-voltage version of TGV-Réseau but with the new generation of power car with a central driving position as first seen with TGV Duplex. Trailer cars are exactly the same as TGV Réseau PBA sets 4531–4540 (see below). The power car includes all equipment necessary for operation in France, Belgium, the Netherlands and Germany including German Indusi and LZB cab signalling. With all this extra equipment, it was necessary to design a lighter transformer in order to keep the power car weight to 68 tonnes because of the 17 tonne axle load limit on French high-speed lines.

These sets entered service on Paris–Brussels–Liège services in 1997 then on Paris–Brussels–Köln/Amsterdam when the Belgian high-speed line opened in December 1997. Sets can operate in multiple with TGV-Réseau sets. The sets belong to the four railways concerned but will be based and maintained at Paris Le Landy or Brussels Forest.

TGV + TGVRAD + 2TGVRA + TGVRr + 2TGVRB + TGVRBD + TGV.

Systems: 1500 V d.c./ 25 kV a.c. 50 Hz/3000 V d.c./15 kV a.c. 16.7 Hz.
Built : 1996–98.
Builder-Mech. Parts: GEC-Alsthom/De Dietrich/Bombardier Eurorail.
Builder-Elec. Parts: GEC-Alsthom/ACEC/Holec.
Continuous Rating: 25 kV 8800 kW; 3000 V d.c. 5120 kW; 1500 V d.c. and 15 kV a.c. 3680 kW.
Axle arrangement: Bo-Bo + 2-2-2-2-2-2-2-2-2 + Bo-Bo.
Accommodation: 0 + 42/– 1T + 39/– 1T + 39/– 1T + –/16 bar + –/56 2T + –/56 2T + –/56 1T + –/73 2T + 0.
Weight: 67 + 43 + 28 + 28 + 28 + 28 + 28 + 43 + 67 tonnes.
Length: 22.15 + 21.845 + 18.7 + 18.7 + 18.7 + 18.7 + 18.7 + 18.7 + 21.845 + 22.15 m.
Maximum Speed: 300 km/h.
Cab Signalling: TVM 430.

Trailer cars are numbered in the following sequence, prefixed TGVR:

Set nnnn: nnnn1 + nnnn2 + nnnn3 + nnnn4 + nnnn5 + nnnn6 + nnnn7 + nnnn8

Set	Owner	Power Car 1	Power Car 2	Liv	Depot
4301	SNCB	TGV 43010	TGV 43019	T	FF
4302	SNCB	TGV 43020	TGV 43029	T	FF
4303	SNCB	TGV 43030	TGV 43039	T	FF
4304	SNCB	TGV 43040	TGV 43049	T	FF
4305	SNCB	TGV 43050	TGV 43059	T	FF
4306	SNCB	TGV 43060	TGV 43069	T	FF
4307	SNCB	TGV 43070	TGV 43079	T	FF
4321	DB	TGV 43210	TGV 43219	T	FF
4322	DB	TGV 43220	TGV 43229	T	FF
4331	NS	TGV 43310	TGV 43319	T	FF
4332	NS	TGV 43320	TGV 43329	T	FF
4341	SNCF	TGV 43410	TGV 43419	T	LY
4342	SNCF	TGV 43420	TGV 43429	T	LY
4343	SNCF	TGV 43430	TGV 43439	T	LY
4344	SNCF	TGV 43440	TGV 43449	T	LY
4345	SNCF	TGV 43450	TGV 43459	T	LY
4346	SNCF	TGV 43460	TGV 43469	T	LY

TGV RESEAU (TGV-R)   8-CAR THREE-VOLTAGE SETS

Apart from three-voltage capabilities, these sets are otherwise identical to TGV-Réseau two-voltage sets and are designed to operate Belgium–south of France services. They were first infiltrated onto TGV Nord Europe services which they still work. From January 1995, they replaced certain Paris–Brussels services then in June 1995, operated a Brussels–Nice service via Lille. From 1996, there were more Brussels–south of France services and the sets also started operation on Paris–Brussels services in common with Thalys PBA sets. They no longer operate these.

The final 10 three-voltage sets have been equipped with a special pantograph and Dutch ATB automatic train protection in order to operate Paris–Brussels–Amsterdam services. Because of this they are known as PBA sets. These units also have a completely different "Thalys" livery and improved interiors with red moquette seats throughout. Initially, they interworked with sets 4501–4530 but the latter were replaced by the "real" Thalys sets from 1997.

4501–06 are equipped to work into Italy and do not operate in the Benelux countries.

TGV + TGVRAD + 2TGVRA + TGVRr + 2TGVRB + TGVRBD + TGV.

Systems: 1500 V d.c./25 kV a.c. 50 Hz/3000 V d.c.
Built: 1994–96.
Builder-Mech. Parts: GEC-Alsthom/De Dietrich.
Builder-Elec. Parts: Francorail-MTE.
Traction Motors: 8 x FM 47 synchronous of 1100 kW each.
Continuous Rating: 25 kV a.c. 8800 kW; 3000 V d.c. and 1500 V d.c. 3680 kW.
Axle Arrangement: Bo-Bo + 2-2-2-2-2-2-2-2 + Bo-Bo.
Accommodation: 0 + 42/– 1T + 39/– 1T + 39/– 1T + –/16 bar + –/56 2T + –/56 2T + –/56 1T + –/73 2T + 0.
Weight: 65 + 43 + 28 + 28 + 28 + 28 + 28 + 43 + 65 tonnes.
Length: 22.15 + 21.845 + 18.7 + 18.7 + 18.7 + 18.7 + 18.7 + 18.7 + 21.845 + 22.15 m.
Maximum Speed: 300 km/h.
Cab Signalling: TVM 430.

Trailers are numbered in the following sequence, prefixed TGVR:

Set nnnn: 38nnnn1 + 38nnnn2 + 38nnnn3 + 38nnnn4 + 38nnnn5 + 38nnnn6 + 38nnnn7 + 38nnnn8

4507	TGV 380013	TGV 380014	V	LY	
4508	TGV 380015	TGV 380016	V	LY	
4509	TGV 380017	TGV 380018	V	LY	
4510	TGV 380019	TGV 380020	V	LY	
4511	TGV 380021	TGV 380022	V	LY	Villeneuve d'Ascq
4512	TGV 380022	TGV 380023	V	LY	
4513	TGV 380024	TGV 380025	V	LY	
4514	TGV 380027	TGV 380028	V	LY	
4515	TGV 380029	TGV 380030	V	LY	
4516	TGV 380031	TGV 380032	V	LY	
4517	TGV 380033	TGV 380034	V	LY	
4518	TGV 380035	TGV 380036	V	LY	
4519	TGV 380037	TGV 380038	V	LY	
4520	TGV 380039	TGV 380040	V	LY	
4521	TGV 380041	TGV 380042	V	LY	
4522	TGV 380043	TGV 380044	V	LY	
4523	TGV 380045	TGV 380046	V	LY	
4524	TGV 380047	TGV 380048	V	LY	
4525	TGV 380049	TGV 380050	V	LY	
4526	TGV 380051	TGV 380052	V	LY	
4527	TGV 380053	TGV 380054	V	LY	
4528	TGV 380055	TGV 380056	V	LY	
4529	TGV 380057	TGV 380058	V	LY	
4530	TGV 380059	TGV 380060	V	LY	
4531	TGV 380061	TGV 380062	T	LY	
4532	TGV 380063	TGV 380064	T	LY	
4533	TGV 380065	TGV 380066	T	LY	
4534	TGV 380067	TGV 380068	T	LY	
4535	TGV 380069	TGV 380070	T	LY	

4536	TGV 380071	TGV 380072	**T**	LY
4537	TGV 380073	TGV 380074	**T**	LY
4538	TGV 380075	TGV 380076	**T**	LY
4539	TGV 380077	TGV 380078	**T**	LY
4540	TGV 380079	TGV 380080	**T**	LY
Spare		TGV 380081	**V**	LY

5.2. INTERCITY EXPRESS (ICEs)

ICE-3M   8-CAR MULTI-VOLTAGE UNITS

These units have been under construction since 1998. They are expected to come into service from late 2000 on the Köln–Amsterdam route. Later some trains will start back from Basel. When the new high speed line between Frankfurt-am-Main and Köln is opened the units will work Frankfurt–Köln–Amsterdam and Frankfurt–Köln–Brussels–Paris.

DMFO–TFO–MFO–TRB–TSO–MSO–TSO–DMSO.

Systems: 1500 V d.c./25 kV a.c. 50 Hz/3000 V d.c./15 kV a.c. 16.7 Hz.
Built: 1998–
Builders: Siemens/Adtranz/Alstom/Bombardier.
Continuous Rating: 8000 kW (a.c.), 4300 kW (d.c.).
Axle arrangement: Bo-Bo + 2-2 + Bo-Bo +2-2 +2-2 + Bo-Bo +2-2 + Bo-Bo.
Accommodation: 46/– + 43/– 2T + 45/– 2T + 24 dining + –/44 1T 1TD + –/68 2T + –/66 2T + –/60.
Total Weight: 465 tonnes.
Length: 25.675 + (6 x 24.775) + 25.675 m.
Maximum Speed: 330 km/h (a.c.), 220 km/h (d.c.).

These units use the DB numbering system where each vehicle is separately numbered.

406 001-8	406 101-6	406 201-4	406 301-2	406 801-1	406 701-3	406 601-5	406 501-7	DB	I
406 002-6	406 102-4	406 202-2	406 302-0	406 802-9	406 702-1	406 602-3	406 502-5	DB	I
406 003-4	406 103-2	406 203-0	406 303-8	406 803-7	406 703-9	406 603-1	406 503-3	DB	I
406 004-2	406 104-0	406 204-8	406 304-6	406 804-5	406 704-7	406 604-9	406 504-1	DB	I
406 005-9	406 105-7	406 205-5	406 305-3	406 805-2	406 705-4	406 605-6	406 505-8	DB	I
406 006-7	406 106-5	406 206-3	406 306-1	406 806-0	406 706-2	406 606-4	406 506-6	DB	I
406 007-5	406 107-3	406 207-1	406 307-9	406 807-8	406 707-0	406 607-2	406 507-4	DB	I
406 008-3	406 108-1	406 208-9	406 308-7	406 808-6	406 708-8	406 608-0	406 508-2	DB	I
406 009-1	406 109-9	406 209-7	406 309-5	406 809-4	406 709-6	406 609-8	406 509-0	DB	I
406 010-9	406 110-7	406 210-5	406 310-3	406 810-2	406 710-4	406 610-6	406 510-8	DB	I
406 011-7	406 111-5	406 211-3	406 311-1	406 811-0	406 711-2	406 611-4	406 511-6	DB	I
406 012-5	406 112-3	406 212-1	406 312-9	406 812-8	406 712-0	406 612-2	406 512-4	DB	I
406 013-3	406 113-1	406 213-9	406 313-7	406 813-6	406 713-8	406 613-0	406 513-2	DB	I
406 051-3	406 151-1	406 251-9	406 351-7	406 851-6	406 751-8	406 651-0	406 551-2	NS	I
406 052-1	406 152-9	406 252-7	406 352-5	406 852-4	406 752-6	406 652-8	406 552-0	NS	I
406 053-9	406 153-7	406 253-5	406 353-3	406 853-2	406 753-4	406 653-6	406 553-8	NS	I
406 054-7	406 154-5	406 254-3	406 354-1	406 854-0	406 754-2	406 654-4	406 554-6	NS	I

6. PRESERVED LOCOMOTIVES & RAILCARS

STATUS CODES

A   Active (location could vary).
P   Plinthed.
K   Retained for special excursions.
M   Museum or Museum line loco.
R   Under restoration (perhaps at another place).
S   Stored or for spares..

For society and railway abbreviations see the "Museums and Museum Lines" section.

6.1. BELGIUM

6.1.1. Steam Locomotives

Number	Type	Built	Status	Location
1.002	4-6-2	1923	MA	FLV
7.039	4-6-0	1921	MS	FLV
10.018	4-6-2	1911	MA	FLV
12.004	4-4-2	1939	MS	CFV3V, Treignes
16.042	4-4-2T	1907	MS	FLV
18.051	4-4-0	1905	MS	CFV3V, Treignes
29.013	2-8-0	1945	MA	FLV
41.195	0-6-0	1910	MS	Haine St. Pierre
44.021	0-6-0	1906	MS	FLV (as A621.11)
44.225	0-6-0	1907	MS	FLV
53.320	0-8-0T	1906	MS	FLV (as 5620)
64.045	4-6-0	1918	MS	FLV
2	2-2-2ST	1842	M	Brussels Nord
615	0-8-0T	1859	MS	FLV (as MF72)
1152	0-6-0PT	1879	MS	FLV
336A	0-4-0VB	1877	MP	Starruga House, Susquehanna, PA, USA

6.1.2. Diesel & Electric Locomotives

Number	Type	Built	Status	Location
1804	C-C e	1974	MA	NK
2912	Bo-Bo e	1949	MS	Haine St. Pierre (as 101.012)
2913	Bo-Bo e	1949	P	FM
5204	Co-Co de	1955	MS	FEO (stored for PFT)
5404	Co-Co de	1957	MA	NK
5910	Bo-Bo de	1955	MA	FNDM (as 201.010)
5922	Bo-Bo de	1955	MA	Vennbahn, Raeren
5927	Bo-Bo de	1955	MS	FSR (stored for PFT)
5930	Bo-Bo de	1955	MA	Vennbahn, Raeren
6003	Bo-Bo de	1960	MS	FEO (stored for PFT)
6019	Bo-Bo de	196?	MA	CFV3V, Momignies
6041	Bo-Bo de	1965	MA	NK
6052	Bo-Bo de	1965	MS	PFT
6077	Bo-Bo de	1965	MA	PFT, St. Ghislain (as 210.077)
6086	Bo-Bo de	1965	MA	CFV3V, Momignies
6106	Bo-Bo de	1965	MA	PFT, St. Ghislain
6406	BB dh	1962	MS	FLV (as 211.006)
7103	D dh	1957	MA	FLV
7209	D dh	1956	MS	FNDM
8309	C dh	1956	M	CFV3V
8319	C dh	1956	MA	Haine St. Pierre
8320	C dh	1956	MS	LNC

6.1.3. Diesel & Electric Railcars

Number	Type	Built	Status	Location
4001	3-car DHMU	1957	MA	CFV3V
4006	3-car DHMU	1957	MS	LK
4302	2-B DHMU	1954	MA	SDP, Basrode
4309	2-B DHMU	1954	MS	SDP, Basrode
4333	2-B DHMU	1955	MA	PFT, St. Ghislain
4601	1A-A1 DHMU	1952	MR	NK
4602	1A-A1 DHMU	1952	MA	PFT, St. Ghislain
4603	1A-A1 DHMU	1952	P	Charleroi
4604	1A-A1 DHMU	1952	P	ULM, Isières
4605	1A-A1 DHMU	1952	MA	PFT, St. Ghislain
4608	1A-A1 DHMU	1952	M	CFV3V, Treignes
4610	1A-A1 DHMU	1952	MS	Maubeuge, France
4611	1A-A1 DHMU	1952	MA	CFV3V, Mariembourg
4612	1A-A1 DHMU	1952	MA	PFT, St. Ghislain (operates from Chimay in season)
4614	1A-A1 DHMU	1952	MA	LSV, As
4616	1A-A1 DHMU	1952	MA	CFV3V, Mariembourg
4618	1A-A1 DHMU	1952	MA	FSR, PFT (as 554.18)
4620	1A-A1 DHMU	1952	MA	SCM, Maldegem
4903	1A-A1 DMMU	1942	MA	FNDM
4906	1A-A1 DMMU	1942	MA	CFV3V, Treignes (as 553.29)
551.26	A-A DMMU	1939	MS	PFT
551.34	A-A DMMU	1939	MS	FLV (ex-ES 301)
551.48	A-A DMMU	1939	MS	PFT, St. Ghislain
608.05	1A-A1 DMMU	1939	MS	FNDM
654.02	1/3 DEMU ·	1936	MS	FLV
ES 106		19	MS	SCM, Maldegem
ES 308	A-A DMMU	1939	MA	FSR, PFT (as 551.26)
002	2-car EMU	1939	MS	Haine St. Pierre
002	2-car EMU	1935	MS	Haine St. Pierre
027	A1-1A EMU	1950	MS	GT
039	A1-1A EMU	1953	MS	GT
082	2-car EMU	1954	MR	FSR, PFT
901	2-car EMU	1957	MR	CWFM
7.312/7.724	4-car EMU	1935	MA	FSR
ES102	Departmental		MS	LSV, Winterslag
ES202	Departmental		MS	SCM
ES206	Departmental		MS	LSV, Winterslag
ES208	Departmental		MS	LSV, Winterslag

6.1.4. Foreign Locomotives & Railcars

Railway	Number	Type	Built	Status	Location
DR	50 3666	2-10-0	1943	MA	Vennbahn, Raeren
DR	50 3696	2-10-0	1939	MA	CFV3V
ÖBB	52 3314	2-10-0	1944	MR	CFV3V, Mariembourg (at GT)
DR	52 8200	2-10-0	1943	MR	CFV3V, Mariembourg
PMP	Ty2-3554	2-10-0	1943	MA	FSR, PFT (as "26.101")
DB	64.250	2-6-2T	1930	MR	CFV3V, Mariembourg
PKP	OI49.12	2-6-2	1952	MA	SLM, Maldegem
PKP	TKt-48.87	2-8-2T	1952	MS	CFV3V, Treignes
DB	310 778	B dm	1939	MA	Vennbahn, Raeren (as Kö 4878)
DB	323 149	B dh	1959	MA	Vennbahn, Raeren (as Köf 6436)
DB	795 662	A1 DMMU	1955	MA	CFV3V (as 551.662)
SNCF	X 3998	B-2 DMMU	1957	MA	CFV3V
SNCF	X 4345	2-car DMMU	1965	MR	CFV3V
SNCF	X 4367	2-car DMMU	1965	MR	CFV3V
SNCF	Y 5130	B de	1961	M	CFV3V
SNCF	Y 6502	B de	1956	MA	CFV3V
SNCF	Y 6563	B de	1957	MA	CFV3V

6.2. NETHERLANDS
6.2.1. Steam Locomotives

Number	Type	Built	Status	Location
13	2-4-0	1865	M	NSM, Utrecht
89	2-4-0	1880	M	NSM, Utrecht
107	4-4-0	1889	M	NSM, Utrecht
326	2-4-0	1881	M	NSM, Utrecht
2104	4-4-0	1914	M	NSM, Utrecht
3737	4-6-0	1911	M	NSM, Utrecht
5085	2-10-0	1945	M	NSM, Utrecht (ex-WD 73755)
6317	4-8-4T	1931	M	NSM, Utrecht
7742	0-6-0T	1914	MA	SHM
8811	0-6-0ST	1943	M	SSN
8815	0-6-0ST	1943	MR	UK
8817	0-6-0ST	1943	P	Autotron, Rosmalen
8826	0-6-0ST	1943	MR	Tilburg
657	0-4-0T	1901	MA	MBS

6.2.2. Diesel & Electric Locomotives

Number	Type	Built	Status	Location
103	B pm	1931	M	NSM, Utrecht
116	B pm	1931	MA	VSM, Beekbergen
137	B pm	1929	M	NSM, Utrecht
162	B dm	1941	MR	STIBANS, Watergraafsmeer (ex-WD 70033)
197	B pm	1932	M	MBS
204	B dm	1934	MA	STAR (on loan from Volker Stevin)
218	B dm	1935	MA	VSM (on loan from Volker Stevin)
225	B dm	1935	MA	VSM
228	B dm	1935	MA	SSN (on loan from NBM Rail)
231	B dm	1935	MA	GSS (on loan from Volker Stevin)
244	B dm	1935	MR	STAR
249	B dm	1935	MR	STAR (on loan from Volker Stevin)
251	Bo de	1935	MR	SGB, Goes
259	B dm	1936	MA	MBS (on loan from Volker Stevin)
262	B dm	1936	MA	SGB (on loan from Volker Stevin)
264	B dm	1936	MA	SGB (on loan from Volker Stevin)
289	B dm	1938	MA	VSM (on loan from Volker Stevin)
293	Bo de	1938	MA	MBS, Haaksbergen
306	D dm	1938	MA	VSM (on loan from Volker Stevin)
311	B de	1940	MA	NSM, Utrecht
316	B dm	1940	MA	SH (on loan from Volker Stevin)
321	B dm	1940	MA	VSM
353	B dm	1950	MA	STAR (on loan from Volker Stevin)
451	C de	1956	MA	MBS
508	C de	1944	MS	NSM, Utrecht (stored at WG)
512	C de	1944	M	Leuvehaven, Rotterdam
532	C de	1954	MA	VSM
636	C de	1956	MA	VSM, Beekbergen
654	C de	1956	MA	Corus, Beverwijk (as 48)
1010	1A-Bo-A1 e	1949	M	STIBANS, Utrecht
1125	Bo-Bo e	1951	M	Utrecht (as 1122)
1201	Co-Co e	1951	MS	NSM, Utrecht
1202	Co-Co e	1951	MA	NSM, Utrecht
1211	Co-Co e	1952	MR	BSSO
1501	Co-Co e	1954	MA	BSSO
1502	Co-Co e	1954	MA	Midland Railway Trust, Butterley, UK (as BR 27000)
1505	Co-Co e	1954	M	Greater Manchester, UK
2208	Bo-Bo de	1955	MA	VSM (as 2233)
2299	Bo-Bo de	1958	MA	VSM

2459	Bo-Bo de	1955	MS	VSM
2498	Bo-Bo de	1955	M	NSM, Utrecht (stored at WG)
2530	Bo-Bo de	1957	MA	VSM

6.2.3. Diesel & Electric Railcars

Number	Type	Built	Status	Location
20	Bo-Bo DEMU	1954	M	NSM, Utrecht
27	3-car DEMU	1934	M	NSM, Utrecht
41	Bo-Bo DMU	1935	MS	NSM, Utrecht (stored at WG)
179	Bo-2-Bo DEMU	1953	MS	ZLSM, Simpleveld
252	2-car EMU	1950	MS	STIBANS (stored at WG)
273	2-car EMU	1952	MS	NSM, Utrecht (stored at WG)
375	Bo-2 + 2-Bo EMU	1962	M	Verkeerspark, Assen
386	Bo-2 + 2-Bo EMU	1962	MS	NSM, Utrecht (stored at Blerick)
766	4-car EMU	1960	MA	Stichting Hondekop Vier (kept at WG)
3031	Bo-Bo mP	1966	MS	NSM, Utrecht (stored at WG)
9107	Bo-Bo EMU	1924	MA	NSM, Utrecht ('De Blokkendoos' [box of bricks])
8104	EMU dt	1924	MA	NSM, Utrecht (Driving Trailer for above)
9002	Bo-Bo EMU	19	MR	Haarlem Works (ex-'Jaap')
9952	EMU		MR	NSM, Utrecht (to arrive ex-Germany)

6.2.4. Foreign Locomotives & Railcars

Railway	Number	Type	Built	Status	Location
DB	01 1075	4-6-2	1937	MA	SSN
DB	23 023	2-6-2	1952	MR	SSN
DB	23 071	2-6-2	1956	MA	VSM
DB	23 076	2-6-2	1956	MR	VSM
DB	41 105	2-8-2	1939	MR	SSN
DR	44 1593	2-10-0	1943	MA	VSM
DB	50 1255	2-10-0	1941	MR	SSN
DR	50 3520	2-10-0	1943	MS	VSM
DR	50 3564	2-10-0	1940	MA	VSM
DR	50 3654	2-10-0	1942	MR	VSM
DR	50 3681	2-10-0	1940	MS	VSM
ÖBB	52 3879	2-10-0	1944	MA	SSN
DR	52 8010	2-10-0	1943	MS	VSM
DR	52 8053	2-10-0	1943	MA	VSM
DR	52 8082	2-10-0	1943	MA	STAR, Veendam
DR	52 8091	2-10-0	1943	P	Medical University, Amsterdam Zuidoost
DR	52 8139	2-10-0	1944	MA	VSM
DR	52 8160	2-10-0	1943	MA	VSM (as 52 532)
DB	64 415	2-6-2T	1936	MA	SSN
DB	65 018	2-8-4T	1956	MA	SSN
DB	80 036	0-6-0T	1929	MR	VSM
DB	94 1640	0-10-0T	1923	P	Gennep
DB	201 093	B-B dh	1968	MA	VSM (as V 100 093)
DB	323 036	B dh	1941	MA	STAR, Stadskanaal (as BE 010)
DB	332 187	B dh	1964	MA	ZLSM, Simpleveld
DB	798 647	AA DMU	1956	MA	ZLSM
SJ	E2 1040	2-8-0	1910	MR	ZLSM
SJ	E 1090	0-8-0	1911	MA	ZLSM
SJ	B 1220	4-6-0	1914	MR	ZLSM
SJ	B 1289	4-6-0	1916	MA	ZLSM

6.3. LUXEMBOURG

6.3.1 Locomtives & Railcars

Number	Type	Built	Status	Location
Z 105	1A-A1 DMMU	1949	MA	Luxembourg
151	A-1 DMMU	1951	MA	Fond de Gras
201 + 211	2-car DMMU	1956	MA	CFV3V
206 + 216	2-car DMMU	1956	MA	Vennbahn
208 + 218 *	2-car DMMU	1956	MA	Luxembourg
455	C dh	1955	MS	Luxembourg
1602	Co-Co de	1955	MA	PFT, St. Ghislain (B) (as "202.020")
1603	Co-Co de	1955	MA	Vennbahn, Raeren (B)
1604 *§	Co-Co de	1955	MA	Luxembourg
2001	B dh	1957	MS	Luxembourg
5519	2-10-0	1947	MA	Luxembourg

* Preserved by CFL as a "listed national monument".
§ Named 'FOND-DE-GRAS'.

6.3.2 Foreign Locomotives & Railcars

Railway	Number	Type	Built	Status	Location
ÖBB	52 3504	2-10-0	1943	MR	GAR, Luxembourg (as CFL 5621)
DB	795 669	A-1 DMMU	1955	MA	AMTF, Rodange (as "551 669")

7. MUSEUMS & MUSEUM LINES

Preservation in the three Benelux countries for many years was only represented by the offical collections in Belgium and the Netherlands. Then came the preservation boom of the late 1960s and it has really taken off since then. Unfortunately the Benelux countries were some of the first in Europe to eliminate main line steam so that steam preservation has been mostly of Industrial types or of locos obtained from other countries – notably Germany. Like other countries on the European mainland, museum line operations tend to be at weekends only but there are notable exceptions with some lines having daily trains in the peak summer months. All railways/tramways are standard gauge (1435 mm) unless otherwise shown. Two museum lines have closed down in recent years and another has relocated. Those that have closed are the MSTB at Vilvoorde and Li Tremleu at Trembleur. The Zolder line has relocated.

7.1. BELGIUM

Antwerps Tram en Autobus Museum　　　　　AMUTRA

Edegem. This is part of the AMUTRA organisation. Access by bus 32 from Antwerpen or Berchem stations or trams 7 and 15 from Antwerpen. The museum is located in the Fort V recreational park and is open weekends and holidays Easter to end of October. 14.00–18.00.

1 steam tram, 1 diesel tram, 17 trams and trailers (1000 mm)

Association pour le Musée du Tramway　　　　AMUTRA

Schepdaal. 600, 1000. 1435 mm.

A large collection of tramway equipment which includes 3 steam locos. Located 13 km from Brussels, access is by bus N Brussels–Ninove. Open Sundays and holidays Easter–October and also Saturdays in July and August, 14.00–18.00.

2 steam trams, 1 diesel tram, 25 trams and trailers.

Association pour la Sauvegarde du Vicinal　　　ASVi

Lobbes–Thuin. 5 km. 1000 mm.

A tramway operation over a scenic cross country SNCV route. Operates Sunday and holiday afternoons May to mid-October. Tram from Charleroi Sud to Anderlues. First departure is 13.25 from Lobbes. This departure only starts from Anderlues Junction at 13.00 and the last return trip leaves Thuin at 18.00 and runs through to Anderlues arr. 18.40. The trams are kept at TEC's Anderlues depot.

1 diesel tram, 5 Trams & trailers.

ATF Kinkempois

This is a regional railway museum located at the SNCB depot where the staff have restored diesel 6041 and have now obtained railcar 4601.

Buurtspoorwegmuseum Schepdaal

Ninoofsesteenweg 955, Schepdaal. 1000 mm.

This tram museum is open Sundays and holidays May–Mid-October and on Saturdays in July and August. 14.00–18.00. Bus N (Brussels–Ninove).

Chemin de Fer de Sprimont　　　　　　　　　CFS

Sprimont. 600 mm.

This line is built on the trackbed of a former SNCV line and uses old mining diesel locos. Operates first and third Sundays of the month May_September from 14.00. Festival on the last weekend of August. Public transport access is believed to be by bus from Poulseur–Trooz. Nearest main towns are Liège and Spa.

6 diesels.

Chemin de Fer à Vapeur des Trois Vallées   CFV3V

Mariembourg–Chimay–Momignies. 29 km.
Mariembourg–Treignes. 14 km.
Dinant–Heer Agimont–Givet. 22 km.

The CFV3V has expanded considerably in the last few years. Its main base remains Mariembourg from where operations now reach Momignies and even sometimes Anor in France. At the other end of the system at Treignes a new locomotive and rolling stock museum has been erected and opened its doors in May 1994. Locos are kept at Treignes, Mariembourg, Haine St. Pierre and Heer Agimont. This last outpost is for working along the scenic valley line to Givet in France. Operating days are Saturdays, Sundays and holidays 2nd April–30th October and daily Mariembourg–Treignes in July and August and on Saturdays and Sundays May–Mid-September between Dinant and Givet.

26 steam, 11 diesel, 9 diesel railcars.

De Bakkersmolen

Essen Wildert. ("the Baker's Mill"). Historic windmill and bakery with 600 mm railway circuit which operates Sundays May–September.

3 steam, 1 diesel.

De Mijlpaal

Regional railway museum believed to be located in part of the NMBS workshops at Mechelen.

1 electric, 1 EMU.

Haine St. Pierre Depot

The old SNCB depot here (adjacent to La Louvière Sud station) is now closed and being used to store and restore SNCB and private museum line stock. SNCB has many carriages and wagons here but the locos present are mostly from the Mariembourg collection. Not normally open to the public.

5–7 steam, 4 EMU.

Limburgse Stoomvereniging   LSV

As–Eisden 6 km.

This is the former Zolder operation relocated. Besides the 'main line' operation there is also a short narrow gauge mining line. Operates Sundays June–August with steam usually operating in July and August. Santa trains run in November.

5 steam and other stock.

Musée Nationale des Chemins de Fer/Museum van de Spoorwegen

The National Railway Museum is located in Brussels Nord station, the entrance being off the booking hall. Only one loco is present, the others in the collection being stored at Leuven until suitable premises can be found. There are many models and photos etc. explaining the development of railways in Belgium. Open Monday–Friday and first Saturday of the month if it is not a holiday. 09.00–16.30.

Leuven Works (SNCB/NMBS)

Former NMBS depot and workshop. Most of the locomotives and rolling stock belonging to the National Collection are housed here. The premises are classed as a workshop and are not open to the public. Restoration work is carried out here. However, recognising the public interest in the collection, there are usually open days several times a year especially in early September.

19 steam, 2 diesel, 2 EMUs, 3 DMUs.

Musée des Transports en Commun du Pays de Liège

An excellent collection of trams and buses in the former Natalis tram depot. The museum is located at Rue Richard Heintz, 9 and is on bus routes 4, 26. 28 and 31. The layout is very spacious and excellent for photography. Open daily March–November. 10.00–12.00 and 14.00–17.00 Mondays to Fridays, 14.00–18.00 Weekends and holidays.

22 trams.

Musée du Transport Urbain Bruxellois   MTUB

This tram and bus museum is located in the Brussels suburb of Woluwe St. Pierre at the old depot there. Open weekends and holidays April–mid October 13.30–19.00. Access is by trams 39 or 44 and buses 36 or 42. Tourist services operate over part of route 44. A preserved tram service is operated to Tervuren and Cinquantenaire-Jubelpark.

More than 45 trams/trailers.

Patrimoine Ferroviaire Touristique   PFT

PFT have taken over the old wagon shop at St. Ghislain where most of their stock will eventually be located. Some stock is still kept at Schaerbeek as many members live in the Brussels area and work on the locos there. A very active society finishing off their restored items in first class condition. The St. Ghislain site is likely to be a workshop and a museum.

The society has preserved many SNCB diesel locos and railcars and imported a working "Kriegslok" from Poland now renumbered '26.101'.

The organisation also operates an occasional service using DMUs on the 9 km line between Cinay and Spontin.

1 steam, 9 diesel, 1 EMU, 6 DMU.

Rail Rebecq–Rognon   RRR

Rebecq–Rognon. 3 km. 600 mm.

Located near Tubize from where there is an infrequent bus service or a 45 minute walk. The line serves a pleasant area along the River Senne. Operates Sundays and holidays May–September.

3 steam, 3 diesel.

Stoom Centrum Maldegem   SCM

600 mm and 1435 mm.

A museum has been established alongside the old station at Maldegem and a 2 km narrow gauge line constructed. The society now also operates over the SNCB line to Eeklo (10 km). The museum is open daily July and August and Sundays and holidays 1st May–30th September, 10.00–17.00. Trains operate Sundays and holidays 1st May–30th September. Traction engines and agricultural equipment are also present.

4 steam, 3 diesel, 1 battery electric (600 mm): 7 steam, 1 diesel railcar (1435 mm).

Stoomspoorlijn Dendermonde–Puurs   SDP

Dendermonde–Puurs. 14 km.

Operates over closed NMBS line. Operates on Sundays in July and August with some extra operating days on certain Saturdays and holidays. Mixed steam and diesel operation. The stock is kept at Basrode Noord.

6 steam, 2 diesel, 1 diesel railcar.

Tramway Touristique de l'Aisne   TTA
Erezee–Dochamps. 12 km. 1000 mm.

An interesting preserved tramway deep in the Ardennes and rather inaccessible. The operating base is Blier, rue du TTA, 5461 Amonines, which is not on the railway network. Public transport details are not known. Operates weekends and holidays mid-April–mid-October and daily in July and August.

1 steam, 4 diesel trams.

TTO Nordzee
Oostende.

Excursions operate from time to time over the coastal tramway system using vintage stock.

Vennbahn   VB
Eupen–Raeren–Bullingen/Trois Ponts. 65 km!

This line straddles the German border area and was of strategic importance until quite recently. Operates on Sundays and Belgian/German holidays 30th April–30th October. Steam loco used on first weekend of each month operating the first Saturday from Eupen to Trois Ponts and the first Sunday to Bütgenbach. Belgian and DR diesel locos used at other times. A German offshoot provided a connecting shuttle from Stolberg using ex-ÖBB DMUs but this is temporarily suspended.

▲ SNCB/NMBS 4-4-0 18.051 on display at Treignes, CFV3V.   **Colin Boocock**

7.2. NETHERLANDS

Amsterdams Openbaar-vervoer Museum   AOM

This organisation operates musem trams on the GVB network in Amsterdam from 12.00 to 16.00 mid-June–Mid-September from Amsterdam Centraal Station. The trams are based at museum depots at Tollenstraat and Oranje Vrijstaatkade.

Bond van Spoorweg, Sport en Ontspanningsverenigingen BSSO

Leidschendamm depot, Den Haag. This organisation includes Werkgroep 1501 and now owns 1211 as well as 1501 (ex BR 27003 DIANA) plus 1208 for spares.

2 electric.

Corus Excursietrein

Beverwijk. 9 km.

This is a steam hauled excursion train around the vast steelworks covering 18 km return journey which takes some around 1½ hours. Photo stops are made on the journey. Departure is from Beverwijk station at 10.45 and 13.00 on the last Sunday of the month May to September. Note: Corus is the new name for Hoogovens which has now merged with British Steel.

2 steam, 3 diesel.

Eerste Drentse Vereniging van Stoomliefhebbers   EDS

Barger Compascuum. 1 km. 700 mm.

This operation is in the National Veenpark and a short train journey is made through the old village. This Moorland Park is open every day from April to October. The train rides are included in the entrance fee.

2 steam, 9 diesel.

Efteling Stoomtrein Maatschaapij

Kaatsheuvel. 1.5 km. 600 mm.

This is a steam operation in a vast amusement park close to Tilburg. The park is open and trains run each day April to October between 10.00–18.00.

4 steam.

Electrische Museumtramlijn Amsterdam   EMA

Amsterdam Haarlemmermeer–Bovenkerk

This organisation operates museum trams on Sundays and holidays (11.00–17.00) and Wednesdays (13.45, 15.15) April–October. Reached by tram lines 6/16. The EMA operates a large collection of museum trams and trailers, not only from the Netherlands but also from Berlin, Bonn, Lisboa, Praha and Wien. Most of the stock is at the Karperweg depot but some may also be found at Havenstraat depot.

61 trams, 20 trailers, 2 electric locomotives, 5 diesel locomotives and numerous other tramway type equipment.

Haagse Openbaar Vervoer Museum   HOVM

Parallelweg 224, Den Haag. Museum trams operate on Sundays April–October around Den Haag. from this museum and depot. Entrance to the museum is free but a charge is made for rides. Trams 8, 9,11, 12 from Den Haag HS or 9, 12 from Den Haag CS.

25 trams.

Industrieel Smalspoormuseum ISM

Erica. 700 mm.

A rather new museum, it has a tourist line on a railway used for transporting turf.

69 diesels, 1 electric.

Museum Buurt Spoorweg MBS

Haaksbergen–Boekelo. 7 km.

The depot is located at Haaksbergen which is 9 km from Enschede and can be accessed by TET buses 53, 57 from Hengelo and buses 20, 21 from Enschede. Operates Sundays May–September and Wednesdays and Thursday in July and August plus other odd days. Three round trips normally operate departing Haaksbergen at 11.30, 13.30 and 15.30.

7 steam, 8 diesel, 2 DMU.

Musemstoomtram Hoorn–Medemblik MHM

Hoorn–Medemblik. 20 km.

This line is well established and a visit is recommended. The depot is adjacent to Hoorn NS station. NS day trip tickets can be purchased if a railrover is not being used. It is possible to do a train-boat-train circular journey. During July/August operation is daily whilst at other times between May and September there are no trains on Mondays. This line has also moved into the wine and dine market and runs the 'Candle Light Express' on Friday and Saturday evenings.

9 steam, 5 diesel, 2 DMU.

NZH Bedrijfsmuseum

Haarlem. Leidsevaart 396.

This small museum is dedicated to the former Den Haag "blue trams" (NZH) undertaking. Open Saturdays 11.00–16.00. Free. Reached by Connexxion bus 90 from Haarlem station.

trams.

Nederlands Openlucht Museum, Arnhem

This well-established museum has now built a tramway and has acquired stock from various cities.

1 steam, 7 trams.

Nederlands Spoorweg Museum NSM

Maliebaanstation, Johan van Oldenbarneveldtlaan 6, Utrecht.

The NS museum was considerably enlarged for the 1989 NS celebrations and work has continued since then to further improve the site. Open Tuesday–Friday 10.00–17.00 , Saturdays and Sundays 11.30–17.00. Bus 3 from Utrecht CS to Maliebaan.

11 steam, 4 electric, 7 diesel, 6 EMU, 3 DMU and trams.

Stichting RTM Ouddorp

RTM De Punt Remise–Port Zélande te Ouddorp. 1067 mm. ca 7 km.

Steam and diesel trains run on this line in the dune area of Ouddorp in Summer with steam on Wednesdays and diesel on Saturdays. There is a museum and depot at RTM De Punt-West. It can be reached by Connexxion bus 104 (Spijkenisse MetroCentrum–Vlissingen).

3 steam, 3 diesel, 2 diesel railcars.

Stichting Stadskanaal Rail STAR

A relative newcomer to the Dutch preservation scene, this line started up when stock was acquired from a closed line in Germany. Operating days are believed to be Sundays June to early September.

3 steam, 6 diesel.

Stoomtrein Goes–Borsele SGB
Goes–Oudelande. 16 km.

This line uses a former NS passenger line. The depot is located at Goes station and is in fact the old NS depot. In July and August the line operates daily except Saturdays. Early and late operations are normally Sundays only but in September there is usually an 'Historic Weekend' when extra attractions are laid on. On some evenings in July and August there is a wine and dine train departing Goes at 19.00 with a return arrival at 22.00.

4 steam, 3 diesel.

Stoomtrein Valkenburgse Meer SVM
Valkenburg. Zuid Holland. ca 3 km.

This is the new location for the Nederlandse Smalspoorweg Stichting, formally at Katwijk. A completely new depot and workshop has been built to house their ever increasing stock. Operates each Saturday and Sunday mid-May to end September. Bus route ZWN 43 Leiden–Wassenaar–Den Haag.

15 steam, 66 dieses, 1 electric (700, 900 mm gauges).

Stoom Stichting Nederland SSN
Rotterdam. This progressive organisation has now moved to a purpose-built loco depot near the NS yard at Rotterdam Noord Goederen. The depot also houses a museum. The SSN does not have a museum line but is able to run its locos several times each year on excursion trains over the NS. Most of the locos are former DB ones. The depot is open each Wednesday 10.0–15.00 and Saturday 10.00–17.00. Ten minutes walk from the end of bus route 38 (Crooswijk).

8 steam, 2 diesel.

Tramweg Stichting (Rotterdamsch Trammuseum) TS
Tramweg Stichting has preserved several Rotterdam trams and their museum is at Nieuwe Binnenweg 362. It is open on Saturdays April–September 11.00–16.00. Tram 4 from Rotterdam Centraal to Heemraadsplein, or Metro Oost–westlijn station Delfshaven. The organisation also has a depot in Den Haag at Harstenhoekplein Scheveningen which is open on Wednesday evenings 19.30–22.30.

trams.

Veluwsche Stoomtrein Maatschappij VSM
Apeldoorn–Dieren. 22 km.

Uses mostly former DB/DR locos. Operates over a closed NS branch line on which the depot is located at Beekbergen. Main operating days are Mondays–Fridays and Sundays in July and August. Uses mostly former DB locos.

15 steam, 13 diesel, 1 diesel railcar.

Zuid Limburgsche Stoomtrein Maatschappi ZLSM
Schin op Geul–Simpelveld–Kerkrade. 16 km.

This new society operates over a closed NS line using mostly Swedish steam locomotives, but also has an ex-DB railbus and trailer and in 1999 obtained NS railcar 179 which is very apt as operations were expected to start in 1999 along the closed line towards Aachen where these units used to work at one time. Operates Wednesdays and Sundays April–October, also Thursdays in July and August. Good NS connections. A winter service may also operate from November.

5 steam, 3 diesel, 1 DMU.

7.3. LUXEMBOURG.

Association des Musée et Tourisme Ferroviaires AMTF

Rodange. 7 km. The depot for this line is at Fond de Gras. Access to the line is Rodange station and a mile walk southwards to Bois de Rodange where the museum line station is located. Operations are on Sundays and holidays May to September. Usually two trips during the afternoon are made by the steam train and a DMU is also used for the second train. There is also a 700 mm gauge line at Fond-de-Gras.

7 steam, 2 diesel, 1 DMU.

CFL Luxembourg Depot   CFL

Staff here have restored CFL 5519 (2-10-0) and it is used on excursions from time to time. Two diesel locos are also preserved here.

1 steam, 2 diesel.

Groupement des Amis du Rail   GAR

This society is also based at the CFL Depot and has a former ÖBB Class 52 2-10-0 and a CFL diesel railcar.

▲ Set 766, a four car 'Hondekop' (dog head) EMU, has been preserved by "Stichting Hondekop Vier"and is seen at Amsterdam CS on 08/05/1999. The current livery is not historically correct, but it is expected to be repainted in original green livery in the near future.   **Quintus Vosman**

APPENDIX 1. BUILDERS

The following builder codes are used in this publication:

ABR	Ateliers Belges Réunis SA.
ACEC	SA Ateliers de Constructions Electriques de Charleroi.
AFB	Société Anglo-Franco-Belge des Ateliers de la Croyère.
Allan	N.V. Allan & Co., Rotterdam.
Alsthom	Société Générale de Constructions Electriques et Mechaniques Alsthom.
Alstom	Alstom Transport SA France (new multinational).
Alkmaar	Nederlandse Maschinenfabriek Alkmaar.
ANF	Ateliers Construction du Nord de la France.
Ansaldo	Ansaldo Trasporti SA, Napoli, Italy.
B&L	Brissonneau & Lotz.
BLC	Usines de Braine le Comte. Belgium
BM	Baume et Marpent SA, Morlanwelz, Belgium
BN	La Brugeoise et Nivelles SA.
BND	La Brugeoise, Nicaise & Delcuve SA.
Bombardier	Bombardier Eurorail, Brugge
BRCW	The Birmingham Railway Carriage & Wagon Co. Ltd., Smethwick, England.
Breda	Società Italiana Ernesto Breda per Construzzione Meccaniche, Milano, Italy.
CEM	Companie Electro Mecanique, Le Havre, France.
CFC	Établissements Carel Fouché & Cie., Le Mans, France.
CFCF	Constructions Ferroviaires du Centre (Familleureux).
CIMT	Compagnie Industrielle de Matériel de Transport, Marly, Valenciennes, France.
Cockerill	SA Cockerill-Ougrée (Seraing).
CWFM	SNCB Central Workshops, Mechelen.
De Dietrich	De Dietrich et Cie, SA Reichshoffen, France.
Deutz	Klöckner, Humboldt, Deutz AG, Köln.
Donauwörth	Waggon und Maschinenbau GmbH, Donauwörth, Germany
Donelli	Donelli SpA, Poviglio, Reggio, Emilia, Italy.
Duewag	Duewag Uerdingen.
EE	English Electric (Dick Kerr Works, Preston).
EIC	Entreprises Industrielles Charentaises, Aytré, La Rochelle, France (now B&L).
Fam.	Ateliers de Contruction de Familleureux, SA.
Fiat	Fiat, Torino,Italy.
FUF	Forges, Usines et Fonderies, Haine St. Pierre.
GM	General Motors, USA.
Geismar	Société des Anciens Établissements L. Geismar, Colmar, France.
Germain	Ateliers Germain, Monceau.
Hansa	Hansa Waggon, Bremen, Germany.
Heemaf	Heemaf NV., Hengelo .
Henschel	Henschel und Sohn GmbH, Kassel.
Holec	Holec-Riddekerk
Jenbach	Jenbacher Werke, Jenbach, Austria.
Jung	Arnold Jung Lokomotivfabrik GmbH, Kirchen an der Sieg, Germany.
Krupp	Fried. Krupp, Essen, Germany
LEW	Lokomotivbau-Elektronische Werke "Hans Beimler", Hennigsdorf, East Germany.
MaK	Maschinenbau Kïel GmbH, Kiel, Germany.
MTE	Société de Matériel de Traction Électrique, France.
Niv.	Les Ateliers de Construction Metallurgiques S.A., Nivelles, Belgium.
Oerlikon	Oerlikon, Switzerland.
Ragheno	SA Usines Ragheno, Malines, Mechelen, Belgium.
Reggio	Officine Meccaniche Itialiane, Reggio d'Emilia, Italy.
St. Eloi	Société Metallurgique d'Enghien-St Eloi, Enghien, Belgium.
SEM	Société d'Électricité et de Mécanique, Charleroi.
SEMG	Société d'Électricité et de Mécanique, Gent.
Seneffe	Ateliers de Seneffe
Schneider	Société des Forges et Ateliers du Creusot, Usines Schneider, Le Creusot, France.
Smit	Smit, Slikkerveer.
Talbot	Waggonfabrik Talbot, Aachen.
Vollert	Hermann Vollert, KG, Maschinenfabrik Weinsberg, Germany.
Vossloh	Vossloh Kiel, former Siemens Schienenfahrzeug Technik, GmbH, previously MaK.
Wegmann	Wegmann & Co., Kassel, Germany.

Werkspoor Werkspoor NV, Utrecht.
Westwaggon Vereinigte Westdeutsche Waggonfabriken AG, Köln, Germany.
Windhoff Windhoff AG, Rheine, Germany.

APPENDIX 2. VEHICLE TYPE CODES FOR MULTIPLE UNITS AND HAULED STOCK

These are given in the continental system with the British codes in parentheses.

(1) CONTINENTAL SYSTEM:

f* Bicycle Van (Dutch – bicycles=fietsen)
k* Vehicle with with driving cab(s)
m* Motor
s* Driving Trailer
A 1st Class
B 2nd Class
D Luggage, i.e., vehicle with luggage space and guard's compartment
R Restaurant
K Buffet Kitchen
P Post, i.e., vehicle with compartment(s) for mail (and guard)

* NS only.

Examples:

BD Second Class with luggage/guard's compartment.
AB Composite

Note-The continental system does not differentiate between open and compartment stock.

(2) BRITISH SYSTEM:

Coaching Stock codes are as used in our British Railways books e.g., F=first, S=second, C=composite, B=brake, O=open, K=side corridor with lavatory, so=semi-open. However note that the use of the word "brake" to denote a vehicle with a guard's compartment is a misnomer on the continent.

The number of seats, toilet compartments and wheelchair spaces are shown as nF/nS nT nTD nW, e.g.: 24/36 1T 1TD 1W has 24 first class seats, 36 second class seats, two toilet compartments (1 suitable for a disabled person) and 1 wheelchair space

APPENDIX 3. UIC HAULED STOCK NUMBERING SYSTEM

Loco-hauled coaches are numbered according to the UIC standard system as follows:

The number consists of four pairs of digits, which describe owner, speed, heating type etc., a three digit serial number and a check digit. The system is as follows:

(a) Digits 1 and 2. These indicate the exchange condition.

50 Passenger coach. Internal use only
51 Passenger coach. International use
60 Departmental passenger coach
61 Special service hauled stock
71 Sleeping cars. International use

(b) Digits 3 and 4. These give the railway of origin, e.g.

80 DB (German Federal Railways)
82 CFL (Chemins de Fer Luxembourgios)
84 NS (Netherlands Railways)
87 SNCF (French Railways)
88 SNCB (Belgian Railways)

(c) Digit 5. The fifth digit gives the class or type of vehicle.

1   First class
2   Second class
3   Composite
4   Couchette-first class
5   Couchette-second class or composite
6   Sleeping car-first class
7   Sleeping car-second class or composite
8   Special purpose vehicle
9   Postal or luggage van

(d) Digit 6. The sixth digit gives the number of compartments (or windows/seating bays in the case of open stock).

0   10 compartments or bays
1   11 compartments or bays
2   12 compartments or bays
3   six-wheeled carriage
4   four-wheeled carriage
5   Reserved
6   6 compartments or bays or double decker
7   7 compartments or bays
8   8 compartments or bays
9   9 compartments or bays

(d) Digits 7 and 8. These give the maximum speed and type of operation.

Digit 7:

0   120 km/h, electric heating
1   120 km/h, dual heating
2   120 km/h, steam heating (except for 29-no heating)
3   121-140 km/h, electric heating
4/5 121-140 km/h, dual heating
6   121-140 km/h, steam heating (except for 69-no heating)
7   141-160 km/h, electric heating
8   141-160 km/h, dual heating (except for 84-steam, 89-no heating)
9   Above 160 km/h

Digit 8 sometimes depends on digit 7, but in general:

0   All voltages
6   All voltages except 3000 V dc
7   1500 V d.c. or 50 Hz a.c.
8   3000 V dc
9   If digit 7 is 0,1,7 – 3000 V d.c. If digit 7 is 3,4,5 – 3000 V d.c. + 1000 V $16^2/_3$ Hz a.c.

Digits 9, 10 and 11. These give the serial number of the individual vehicle.

Digit 12. This gives the check digit. Multiply as follows:

Digit	1	2	3	4	5	6	7	8	9	10	11
x	2	1	2	1	2	1	2	1	2	1	2

Add all resultant digits and subtract the last number of the result from 10. This gives the check digit, example:

	5	0	8	4	2	9	3	7	2	4	8
x	2	1	2	1	2	1	2	1	2	1	2

1+0   +0   +1+6   +4   +4   +9   +6   +7   +4   +4   +1+6 = 53

Subtract 3 from 10 – check digit is 7.

APPENDIX 4. COMMON TERMS IN ENGLISH, FRENCH & DUTCH

English	French	Dutch
railway	le chemin de fer	de spoorweg
train	le train	de trein
locomotive	la locomotive	de locomotief (de loc)
passenger coach	la voiture	het rijtuig
freight wagon	le wagon (de marchandise)	de goederenwagen
sleeping car	la voiture-lits	het slaaprijtuig
stock	le materiel	materieel
passenger	le voyageur	de reiziger
station	la gare	het station
platform	le quai	het perron
ticket	le billet	het kaartje
single	aller simple	de enkele reis
return	aller-retour	het dagretour (day return)
first class	la première classe	de eerste klas
second class	la deuxième classe	de tweede klas
to change (trains)	changer	overstappen
rail	le rail	de rail
track	la ligne/la voie	het spoor
steam	la vapeur	de stoom
wheel	la roue	het wiel
class (of vehicles)	série	de serie
marshalling yard	(la gare de) triage	het rangeerterrein
late	en retard	de vertraging
driver	le conducteur	de machinist
guard, conductor	le chef de train	de conducteur

Front Cover: CFL has taken delivery of their new dual-voltage Class 3000. These are the same as the SNCB/NMBS Class 1300 No. 3009 is seen hauling a set of CFL Wegmann coaches near Bovigny between Trois-Ponts and Gouvy in June 1999. **Max Delie**

Back Cover Top: Class 3200 DMU No. 3222 has been painted in NoordNed livery and is seen at Dronrijp, working a Leeuwarden to Harlingen regional service on 09/06/1999. **Quintus Vosman**

Back Cover Bottom: The new Belgian Class 77 shunting/trip freight locomotives are in the process of delivery. The first of these, No. 7701 is seen at Antwerpen Dam depot. **Carlo Hertogs**